A BHOY CALLED
BERTIE

A BHOY CALLED
BERTIE

Bertie Auld
with Alex Gordon

BLACK & WHITE PUBLISHING

First published 2008
by Black & White Publishing Ltd
29 Ocean Drive, Edinburgh EH6 6JL

1 3 5 7 9 10 8 6 4 2   08 09 10 11 12

ISBN: 978 1 84502 219 8

A CIP catalogue record for this book is available from the British Library.

Typeset by Ellipsis Books Limited, Glasgow
Printed and bound by MPG Books Ltd, Bodmin

CONTENTS

This is for my wife Liz who has been a constant source of inspiration to me. She has been my rock and I wouldn't have made it in the game if it hadn't been for her.

FOREWORD
BY TOMMY GEMMELL

The word 'character' is much overused and misused these days. Not in Bertie Auld's case, I can assure you of that. The word could have been invented for my old Celtic team-mate.

Originally, we missed each other by just five months when I joined Celtic from Coltness United in October 1961 and Bertie had already left for Birmingham City. I will be forever thankful, though, to the person at Celtic who decided to bring him back to the club in 1965. We have had so much fun together – on and off the field.

When we were playing he was the first team-mate I looked for when I had the ball. You could be sure he wouldn't be too far away, thirty yards or so, and, like all superior footballers, had found a pocket of space in which to work. His touch was instantaneous. He could kill the ball immediately and know exactly where it was about to be launched with radar accuracy. He had an instinctive feel for the game. He must have possessed peripheral vision, too. Bertie wouldn't have to look round when he was hitting the ball wide for me to run on to; he just knew I would be there.

He was a marvellous team man, too, and a guy who could get you out of a tight spot if you felt hemmed in. 'I'm here,

TG,' I would hear and I knew the cavalry had arrived and all was well.

He was frightened of nothing and no-one. The bigger the occasion, the more he revelled in the atmosphere. It was like oxygen to Bertie. I recall the European Cup semi-finals against Leeds United in 1970. The Elland Road side had just about written us off as no-hopers. If my wee pal had ever needed anything to galvanise him – and I am sure he never did – then that was the very spur.

Leeds were about to prove to everyone they were the best Europe had to offer and they had the finest midfield pairing in Billy Bremner and Johnny Giles. Allegedly. They were known as the Untouchables in England where they ruled the roost. Bertie was having none of that.

His performances against Leeds, whose side contained eleven international players, were awesome, especially at Hampden Park in the second leg. There was little our opponents could do as Bertie and his fellow midfield partner Bobby Murdoch dominated proceedings in a 3-1 aggregate triumph.

If anyone wanted to see how football should be played they should have been there that night. Bertie was world class and, remember, my Scottish international pal Bremner and Giles were no pushovers. That evening they had no answer to Bertie and Bobby. That, by the way, was not the only occasion where Bertie turned in a world class display. Far from it. To my mind, he was one of the finest exponents of passing the ball on the planet. I truly mean that. His precision was extraordinary. It didn't matter if it was six yards or sixty yards – most of Bertie's passes arrowed in on the target with breathtaking accuracy. He had one of the sweetest left pegs I have ever witnessed. A lot of that, he told me, was down to his dad. He made Bertie play football as a youngster with only one boot – his left. He made Bertie practice more and more with what he considered his weaker foot. By the time Bertie was ready to step up to the Juniors that left foot was fairly well honed and it just got better and better after he joined Celtic.

He was a supreme professional, but he could be a joker away from the action. We were in a nightclub on one of Celtic's tours of the States in the Sixties. I got up on stage to take the microphone and probably strangle the life out of a Sinatra number. There were a few tables at the front of the stage that had been empty when I took the stage. They started to fill up. People were coming down to the front to see me. 'I must be doing OK,' I thought. I kept on singing and they kept turning up. There was rapturous applause after every number. They wouldn't let me off the stage.

I smelled a rat. It was only afterwards I discovered that Bertie had been going round members of the audience and telling them the true identity of the bloke up on stage. 'Do you know that great American comedian and singer, Danny Kaye?' he would ask them. Well, of course, they did because he was one of the biggest names around at the time. 'That's him up there!'

Yes, I have to admit I did have a passing resemblance to Danny Kaye. He was one of the biggest heart-throbs in Hollywood, wasn't he?

Bertie was an excellent colleague, a great friend to this very day and, yes, he was the real deal – a genuine character.

INTRODUCTION

This is my first – and last – book. I have been approached many times over the years, but until now I have never felt the need to put my life story into print. Let's face it, I was never exactly a shrinking violet when it came to courting publicity over the years. I had many friends in the media, I received my fair share of the headlines in newspapers and I wasn't slow to do a television or radio interview, either. You want me to pose for a photograph? I'm your man!

So, why have I had a change of mind? Simple, really – I realised there was an awful lot that was still left unsaid. There were subjects I wouldn't have discussed, say forty-odd years ago, that I will happily delve into today. When Celtic won the European Cup in 1967 it seemed every scribe in the country wanted the players to write autobiographies. Some took up the offer, but I wasn't even tempted. Until now.

I've gone through my life and times as thoroughly as possible and I have found myself laughing out loud at some of the memories. There are other recollections that I must admit have brought a tear to the eye. I have received so much help from so many people in so many walks of life that I want to say thank you to them.

It's been a white-knuckle ride since the days of knocking the ball around the streets of Maryhill. There have been highs and there have been lows, but one thing is absolutely certain – it's not been boring.

I have had my fair share of rows with Jock Stein. I have had my brushes with authority. I have had players threatening me with all sorts of violence. I have been bought and sold and, as a manager, I have had some memorable sorties into the transfer market. There's one guy who wouldn't sign for me because I swore too much!

I'm the guy, though, who signed the player who would cause absolute uproar in Scottish football.

There has been the magical memory of Lisbon and there has been the gut-wrenching misery of Milan in two European Cup Finals three years apart. There were some astonishing times with the Scottish international team – all three games!

What goes on during the heat of the battle of Old Firm games? Did I enjoy them? You bet I did. These were the encounters where you had to stand up to be counted; no quarter asked or given. Those were bone-shuddering confrontations played against the backdrop of bedlam on the terracings.

European nights at a packed and rocking Celtic Park were simply breathtaking. Every player believes that they can go on for ever, but there is a limit to what the human body can endure and you have to know when to get out.

My trip through the managerial maze has been more than just a shade interesting. I made some real friends and, I have to admit, an enemy or two. There are certain chairmen and directors who never received a Christmas card from yours truly. To some, it seemed lies were obligatory.

Anyway, let's go for a journey through my life and times. I promise you it won't be dull. Bertie Auld doesn't do dull.

1

IN THE BEGINNING

There was this wonderful lady who would steer a horse and cart through the streets of the Ayrshire holiday resort of Girvan and the nearby villages as she sold fish and fruit to the locals. This was back in the late 1920s. She would get up before seven in the morning, feed the horse, fix the harness, load up the cart, give her companion for the day another carrot and go out on her own as she strived to make a living. It didn't matter if it was hail, rain or shine, this incredible character simply went about her business; sometimes leaving when it was pitch black and coming home in the same conditions. Her name was Margaret Diamond Devlin. I got to know her rather well several years later.

Margaret worked for her father in the family business and, as luck would have it, a Glaswegian turned up on their doorstep one day as he searched for employment. There were no vacancies in Glasgow, so he travelled around scouting for work elsewhere. For someone without his own transportation, Girvan was a long way off, but it was a case of needs must for this guy. He got the job – and, eventually, Margaret's hand in marriage. His name was Joe Auld. And without them I wouldn't have a tale to tell. How I loved those two extraordinary human beings – my mum and dad.

Robert Auld made his entrance onto the planet on 23 March 1938, ready to take my first steps down the road for the rest of my life. I was the first son in a family that would eventually stretch to eight. I was brought up in a two-bedroomed council house at 95 Panmure Street in Maryhill. We even had an inside toilet, unlike so many tenements in the city at the time where so many neighbours had to share a communal loo on one of the landings. My mum followed her husband back to Glasgow in 1934 where they lived in a flat in Abercromby Street in the Calton before they were decanted across the city to the West End. A year and a half after my birth, World War Two broke out. To be honest, I don't recall too much about the war; it seemed to be something that was taking place elsewhere. Every now and again, when I was a little older, my mum would open the bathroom window and we could hear sirens, probably coming from the Clydeside or Clydebank. Sometimes we could hear what we thought was the drone of enemy aircraft.

My dad was never out of work. He was a crane-driver during the war and he always found something to turn his hand to – it didn't matter what. My mum was a great provider, too. She may have brought up and cared for a huge family, but it didn't prevent her from continuing to work. She became a hawker. Now I realise that many in this century will have no idea what that means. Basically, a hawker was someone who went round the doors selling their wares. Remember, there were no such things as supermarkets back then. There were little corner shops, but they normally closed around five o'clock. So if, for whatever reason, you found yourself without milk or tea or something to put on the dinner table, then you required an alternative. My mum was that alternative. She would sell just about everything, from fish to fruit, and became a well-recognised figure on the streets of Maryhill as she did her rounds.

My dad had a variety of jobs as I was growing up. He was a pipe-layer, brickie's labourer and he also worked as a general handyman in a foundry between Firhill, home of Partick Thistle, and our flat in Panmure Street. My dad was only about 5ft 6in, but he was as wiry and as tough as they came. He would often be found going about his business with the inevitable cigarette dangling from the corner of his mouth. One of his many employments saw him traipse around the streets with a giant metal bucket of warm tar as he maintained the potholes in the road. He would slap a great dollop of tar into these craters and then stamp on it until he had levelled that area. I once asked him why he didn't get a wheelbarrow to help in his chores because, believe me, these tar buckets were heavy beasts. My dad looked at me with a faint shake of his head. He took another puff of his cigarette and, in a voice that obviously took pity on me, answered, 'Son, if I get a wheelbarrow I'll get the jobs done at least four times as fast.' Then he added with a grin, 'And I'll be out of a job at least four times as fast!'

I had a great time in Panmure Street. I enjoyed every minute of my time growing up there. We weren't rich, but we weren't poor, either. Certainly, we never went hungry. My mum made sure of that when she returned with her baskets carrying the stuff she didn't sell. We had potatoes with everything. It didn't seem to do us any harm. What I remember most is a happy household and, as a family, we all enjoyed each other's company. We looked out for each other and when I signed for Celtic for the first time in 1955 I couldn't have found a prouder bunch of people on this earth as I returned with my dad after agreeing to join Jimmy McGrory's side.

My mum was a Roman Catholic and my dad was a Protestant and I, and the rest of the family, were brought up in his faith. There was never any chance of bigotry getting in the front door of the Auld household. Quite right, too. And the last thing my mum, who was educated by nuns, would say to us every night was: 'Remember to say your prayers.' We spent an hour or so most Sundays at the local Salvation Army where we could have a cup of tea and a scone. After that, decked out in our best gear, my mum and dad would take us a long walk around Maryhill. We always got an ice cream at the Terminus Café and the trick was to keep it away from my father. 'Let's have a little taste, son.' I would hold out my ice cream and my dad had a tongue that would not have looked out of place in the mouth of a snake! He would scoop up half the ice cream in one go. Then we would make our way back to Panmure Street where we got into our other clothes and my brothers and I were allowed out to play some football.

I really enjoyed my upbringing in Maryhill. It was such a close-knit community and there was a lot of warmth among the neighbours. As I recall, there seemed to be enormous families; everyone seemed to have at least five or six children. There was one neighbour, a Mrs Mucklewee – honest! – who, my sister Margaret, who is six years older then me, insists, had nineteen kids. I think that might just be a slightly inflated figure. If we had problems fitting eight plus my mum and dad into two bedrooms, how on earth would Mrs Mucklewee manage nineteen plus herself and her husband? Maybe she stuck them to the wall overnight! Mind you, there may be something in Margaret's memory bank that might be accurate. I'm sure Mrs Mucklewee went to get the bread in the morning with a pillowcase!

Everyone mucked in together, such was the camaraderie of

the place. I could be out kicking the ball around the street when a window would open and I would hear the shout from a neighbour, 'Bert, come on up – I've just made a big pot of soup.' It was like that everywhere you went; everyone was so kind.

My first school was Springbank Primary and I loved it there. There weren't too many televisions in those days and all my pals seemed to be out kicking a ball about the streets until it got too dark and we had to go home. We could also play under the gas street lamps until they were snuffed out by the lamp-lighter. I recall we could start a wee kick-about among, say, four boys and, about half an hour later, there were about twenty-two on each side and you were lucky to get a look at the ball never mind a kick at it. Sometimes we would play until the winner would be declared as the first team to score twenty-one goals. If there were two good goalkeepers playing that night you could be in for a long evening. No wonder extra time never bothered me when I was playing as a professional.

It helped also that our house in Panmure Street backed onto Ruchill Park and me and my mates would climb the railings to get in once the parkie had closed the gates for the night. We had the place to ourselves and we could actually play on grass. The cops turned up every now and again to chase us, but we were too fast. I did get caught once, though. I had injured my left arm and had it in a plaster cast. The cops duly turned up one night, we took flight, but, as I was walking down the street minding my own business, they approached me and told me they had seen me playing in the park. I protested my inno-cence, 'Wisnae me, officers.' They laughed and pointed to my arm. 'How many kids around here have a plaster just like that one, son?' I was done like a kipper.

I continued my education as I moved to East Park Secondary

which was situated in Bilsland Drive. I was never too far from Panmure Street. My top subject was woodwork, but, naturally enough, I wanted to be a footballer – I fancied myself as a centre-forward in those days. To be honest, that seemed as likely as me having the ability to walk up Ben Nevis backwards in a frogman's outfit. I wasn't particularly exceptional and there were a lot better players around than me. I played for the school team, but I was never in with a chance of being selected for Glasgow Schoolboys or anything like that. To this day, I could come up with a list of players from that era who you would have put your last penny on going on to making a name in professional football. Maybe I just got lucky and was in the right place at the right time.

After leaving school at fifteen I combined playing football with Panmure Thistle with my first real job as a joiner and shop-fitter. Actually, before that, I had a very brief career in a butcher's shop. It was called Halliday's and I will always remember the slogan on the board outside the shop. It read, 'Always pleased to meet you and always meat to please you.' Brilliant! On my first day I might have realised this was not the job for me. I was handed this enormous ox's tongue and told to scrub it. I have to say I felt a bit queasy as I went about my task. A couple of days later I was given a pig's head and told to take the eyes out of it. Easier said than done. I hadn't a clue as to how to go about this particular order. One of the other butchers came along and, with a flick of the wrist, suddenly two eyes were shooting across the shop. After the fourth day, my mum wakened me up as usual and said I would be late for work if I didn't get a shift on. She was greeted with, 'Maw, I'm no' going!' That was the end of that particular career path. Football was a hobby at the time and I was simply content in trying to hold down a regular place for Panmure. If you lost your first team spot it could be an awful long time before you got another opportunity. I hate to admit it, but you hoped maybe someone would pick up an injury – nothing life-threatening, you understand – but just something that would open the door. On other occasions our manager would spot a player who had possibly overdone the beer the previous evening and was showing signs of a hangover. Even better was the bloke turning up still drunk. Those guys were dropped and you were in. Even back then, I was taught you had to be disciplined if you wanted to play football.

Actually, I have to admit I was a bit spoiled by my mum and dad as I was growing up; the first-son syndrome, I think it's called. Leather footballs were few and far between and kids used to play on the streets with a tennis ball – or tanner ba', as we called them. Now that helped you hone your ball control skills, believe me. Especially with about twenty opponents trying to take that little sphere off you. However, my parents must have saved their pennies because I remember I always had a proper football and, more often than not, that meant I could get first pick of the players when the street teams were assembled. The name Bertie Auld was prominent in the early selections!

So, I got plenty of practice and I just wanted to play. I even turned out for Panmure as a goalkeeper. Remarkably enough, I can't recall the score on that particular occasion. I shifted around the team and older Celtic supporters will surely be surprised that I played right-back for the reserves a couple of times. Even I find that hard to believe.

I must have done enough at amateur level to attract the attention of the Juniors. I was called up by Maryhill Harp and, after a whirlwind spell, I was on my way to Celtic. It could happen like that back then. Celtic were actually looking at two or three other Maryhill Harp players at the same time and, luckily enough, I must have caught the scout's eye. My brothers were all reasonable at football, too, but, for whatever reasons, didn't make it in the pro ranks. Alan and Ian played Juniors while William was content to perform in the Amateurs. Actually, the best footballer in the house was my younger sister, Annette. What a player she was and, remember, this was long before people accepted women should even be allowed to play football never mind develop their own World Cup tournaments in years to follow. My pals used to come to our front door and ask if Annette wanted out to play for their team. They weren't interested in me or my brothers. My goodness, she was one of the best players in Maryhill never mind just the Auld household!

Annette was one of four girls in the family, the others being Esmeralda, who was the eldest, Margaret and Marion. Esmeralda, as she was later to discover, was the daughter of my mother's sister, Annie. Honestly, I don't know all the ins and outs of that particular situation, but I know my mum and dad took in Alda, as we abbreviated her name, as a baby. She grew up being loved just as much as any of us, I can tell you that. Alda Auld? We never found it odd.

Alda, who was born on the same day as the Queen on 21 April 1926, was the first to get married, to a guy called Albert McMillan who had an interesting tale to tell. He had signed up for the army at fifteen years old and had been sent out to Africa to join the Desert Corps. Apparently, he became the youngest prisoner of war in the British Army and he returned after the war to meet up with Alda and get wed. He used to joke with my sister – I once inadvertently introduced her as my stepsister and was given a stiff rebuke – that the only reason he travelled to see her was to raid my mum's larder which was always bulging with all sorts of grub.

I can tell you that the food was fresh. My mum would give me and my brothers and sisters our duties and, more often than not, I found myself plucking chickens that would be sold around the streets of Maryhill. Another of the chores was to polish the apples – and they had to be done perfectly. We used to scale the fish as well. I'll tell you that put me off that particular dish for some considerable time. I still can't bring myself to watch *Jaws*!

Goodness knows where it came from, but we actually possessed a piano. My mum Peggy, as she was known, and dad weren't bad singers and this guy Eddie Connelly used to rattle the old ivories in fine style. It was either live entertainment or the wireless because we didn't have a television set. My parents used to duet to 'By the Light of the Silvery Moon' which was a popular song by Doris Day and Gordon MacRae at the time. I will always recall one of our neighbours, a nice man by the name of Bobby Elliott, who used to go into the toilet when it was his turn to sing. It had nothing to do with acoustics or a weak bladder, either. He was a shy chap and he used to go to the bathroom, leave the door open and then belt out his song. He would come back in to rapturous applause. I couldn't see him taking his show on the road, somehow. The Empire and the Pavilion weren't ready for his stage act, I don't think.

When I got a bit of reasonable money as a professional footballer, I bought my mum a wee shop that was situated nearby. Actually, I got a loan from Celtic as I had just missed out on bonus money. You had to play a certain number of first team games after so many years to get £750 and I just failed to qualify. I think I was loaned something in the region of £450 by the club in 1959. My dad was doing three extra shifts a week and I thought the shop might bring in more cash and he could have some time off. He was having none of it – that money he earned was his and that allowed him to go for a pint and buy cigarettes.

The shop did reasonably well, but there were a lot of renovations being carried out around Maryhill at the time and my mum was told she would have to close her premises for about three months or so. We didn't have an argument as the building was still owned by the council. My mum putting her feet up and doing nothing for about twelve weeks? No chance. A couple of my brothers and my mum would then fill in the blanks by delivering the Sunday newspapers. They would go down to the local newsagent and stack up a pram with the day's news and take off on their rounds. At that time I picked up a Ford van for my mum so she could go to the cash and carry twice a week to pick up fish and fruit for her deliveries. Well, that was the original idea. It wasn't long before my mum was back working a full week and dealing from the van.

She would 'invite' me to go down to the Glasgow fish and fruit markets, sitting side by side, to give her a hand picking up provisions. She was well aware, as a Celtic player, I was beginning to get recognised on the streets. 'Hi, Mrs Auld,' the traders would say. 'Is that your boy, Bertie?' And with that they would throw in a few apples for free. Then it would be the guys selling oranges, bananas and suchlike. After that, it was the turn of the fish market guys and we went through the same routine. It showed the generous side of Glaswegians. My arms were breaking by the time we hauled the fish and fruit back to the van before the journey home to Maryhill.

Afterwards, I bought my mum a single-decker coach from which she could sell her goods. It made life that little easier and, naturally, I was happy to help out. I remember I was back in Glasgow during a close-season break from Birmingham City when I drove the van for my mum. We were in Drumchapel one day when a young lad came up to me and said, 'You look like that guy Bertie Auld who used to play for Celtic.' The kid was flabbergasted when I revealed I was, in fact, that very fellow. The youngster turned out to be an East Stirling player called Eddie McCreadie who would go on to have such a marvellous career with Chelsea and Scotland. He played left-back the day Scotland became 'world champions', beating England 3-2 at Wembley in 1967!

My mum then got the opportunity to pitch her van – simply called Auld's – in the shadow of the high-rise flats overlooking Firhill. She was loved by the community. She looked after the kids, made sure they got the correct orders and then always handed out sweets. Ironically, to this day, I get people, grownups now, of course, who approach me and tell me stories about Auld's, the place where the nice lady always gave you chocolate and sweets for free. It was hard work, but she enjoyed it. You will undoubtedly find this hard to believe, but my mum could go out at seven in the morning and roll in at ten at night, a straight shift of fifteen hours. She thought nothing of it. One of my sisters was working with her one day and asked, 'When do we close up, Mum?' She replied in a matter-of-fact manner, 'When the last customer has been served, dear.'

My dad was taken into nearby Ruchill Hospital in the mid-1940s for a wee examination and they kept him in overnight for observations. My mum, who had been downstairs hanging up her washing, breathlessly raced up the stairs and her face was as white as the sheets she was putting on the line.

'Your da's deid,' she exclaimed. 'He's deid.'

This news rather startled the family and she got our full attention.

'What's happened, Mum?' one of us asked.

'I've heard his voice – it was coming from the heavens. He was shouting, "Peggy, Peggy".'

Thankfully, my mum had overreacted somewhat. Actually, what had really happened was that my dad, who had sneaked out of his ward, had clambered onto the wall of the adjoining Ruchill Hospital, just up the back from our house, and was yelling at my mum to bring him some cigarettes! 'Peggy, Peggy, get me some fags,' was his plea. He loved his cigarettes. Sometimes he would get up in the morning and ask Mum for his first puff of the day. If there weren't any, he would say, 'Nae fags, nae work,' and then he would go back to his bed! That didn't happen too often as my mum made sure cigarettes were in plentiful supply so her Joe would get to his work.

My dad was a real character. He was of the old school and enjoyed a pint and a dram with his mates down the local. He had a pal who stayed across the road and, late in the evening, my mum would post me at the window to see what condition her husband was in as he made his way home. I recall one night he went out and was wearing a rather smart hat – the kind former Prime Minister Neville Chamberlain used to sport – and a long black coat. Happy with his attire, he was now ready for a few pints with his chums. As usual, he stopped off at his pal's flat on his way back. He probably needed another drink as much as a drowning man would require a glass of water. I was at my usual post, watching out for my dad. 'Maw, da's across the road,' I informed my mum. 'Keep your eye on him, son,' came the reply. So, given my orders, I stood by the window and waited for my dad to reappear. About half an hour or so later, sure enough, there was my dad ready to come home. I noticed he appeared to have his hat on back to front and even his coat looked as though it was the wrong way round. 'Is he coming across the road?' asked my mum. I replied, 'Honestly, maw, I don't know whether he is coming or going!'

Anyway, holidays back in those heady days were spent in Girvan. Honestly, it was a genuine adventure just getting on the bus at Buchanan Street and making our way to our destination in Ayrshire. Girvan just seemed so exotic in those times and to see the beach and the tide coming in with those little colourful boats bobbing around are treasured memories. It was a lifetime away from Maryhill. There always seemed to be a relation who managed to put up the Auld entourage for the holidays.

My mum was a great dancer, but my dad didn't have much time for ballrooms and the like. He preferred to go down to the pub, have a pint or two and talk football with the locals. So, it may seem odd these days, but my mum thought nothing of going to the dancing with my father's dad, Robert, as a partner. At least it made sure she always got home safely!

Back at Panmure Street, it was often musical beds. The youngest always got to sleep with our parents, so that left one bedroom among the rest of us. The boys had bunk beds and we slept two on top and two at the bottom. The girls must have found a corner somewhere. The kitchen, or scullery as we called it all those years ago, had a pulley where my mum would hang up her washing in an attempt to dry the clothes. Someone once suggested that she would pull it down at night and the boys could lean over it and go to sleep. Believe me, it was never quite as bad as that. One thing I do recall is that the first up was the best dressed. There was a collection of clothes left out for us as we got ready for school and, if you were last up, you weren't exactly going to look like something paraded in the windows of one of those fashionable big stores in Sauchiehall Street. I thought I had pulled a masterstroke when I would often go to bed with my vest, underpants and socks on. That cut down the time it took to get prepared in the morning and I could be first through to the front room to take my pick of the gear. But it didn't take long before Ian, Alan and William cottoned on.

Glasgow, of course, had a reputation as a breeding ground for so-called hard men as I was growing up. If you displayed any sort of fear on these streets you were in trouble. I hated bullies. Luckily, I was quite tall for my age, but I think I stopped growing sometime after my third birthday! I remember an evening when I was getting into my glad rags as I prepared to go the dancing up at the nearby Woodhill Halls. I recall exactly what I was wearing that evening and, I can tell you, the local lasses were in for a treat when they clapped eyes on the sartorially elegant Bertie Auld. I had a light fawn suit and a brown shirt with a huge collar. I also had this favourite tie, a cream and red effort with huge bands going across it. To complete the picture, I had these brown suede shoes with three-inch crepe soles. I believe they were called brothel creepers in their time. Anyway, I set off from Panmure Street on my own and was looking forward to the night's entertainment. No-one could fail to be impressed.

I was strolling along the street when I noticed a bunch of local neds who were hanging around a tenement close. I did my best to ignore them, but they were having none of it. I was summoned to come over and meet their leader. I didn't know his name, but I was aware that he had a reputation as a hard case. I walked toward him and he sized me up. I was doing my utmost to prevent my knees from knocking together. He eyeballed me and growled: 'Ye know a guy called David Porter, don't ye?'

I was determined not to show I was afraid. His mates were gathering around, too. 'Never heard of him,' I replied, hoping I sounded reasonably composed.

'Aye, ye dae,' said the head hooligan, who, in fact, was quite correct because I did know the bloke in question. What happened next almost had me in a state of collapse. The guy produced a pair of scissors – the biggest pair of scissors I had ever seen. You could have trimmed garden hedges with these things.

I thought my time was up as this gorilla brought up these scissors to just under my chin. 'Tell Porter Ah'm looking fer him. OK?' he said. Then he grabbed my tie and cut it in two just under the knot. 'Now fuck off,' he advised. I didn't have to be asked twice. The dancing was off that night. I got straight home and locked the door behind me. The local girls missed out that evening, I can tell you.

Another incident that comes to mind was downright dangerous and could have proved fatal. I was just a kid, about ten years old, and I was dared to dive into the nearby canal, swim under some object that was in the water and get to the other side. There was always so much junk chucked into the water – prams, bikes, bedsteads, all that sort of stuff. Now I can think of more pleasant ways of passing the time of day and I would have preferred to have been anywhere else other than at the side of the canal that day. Once again, though, I knew you could not afford to display any sort of fear. I duly stripped to my underpants and threw my slight frame into the freezing-cold water. I completed the dare, but almost at a terrible cost. As I came out of the canal, I looked down at my stomach and noticed I was bleeding. There was a scratch of about eight inches stretching down my belly. Obviously, I had scraped across something sharp and probably rusty while I was underwater. It could have been much worse, of course, but I knew I could never display a lack of courage. I was never going to have anyone call me a 'feartie'.

Reputations like that stuck with you in my part of Maryhill and any refusal on my part to accept the challenge would have swiftly got round the school. Life wouldn't have been worth living. It was utterly foolhardy, of course, and I shouldn't have done it, but I also knew the consequences of lacking courage in front of your mates. Mind you, I had to disguise the wound when I was either getting up in the morning or going to bed at night. If my mum had seen that I really would have shown fear!

I didn't watch a lot of football as a schoolkid. I much preferred to play the game, but you used to be able to get into Firhill about ten or fifteen minutes from time when they opened the gates to allow the fans out. My pals and I used that option often enough. There was another way of watching Partick Thistle take on their opponents on matchday without having to pay in. There was a mound of ground across the canal known as Miser's Hill. If you stood on your tiptoes you could see both goals, but the rest of the playing surface was completely blocked out by the stand. So, you could take in the action, not have a clue how the game unfolded, but, at least, know the final score!

But, as I have emphasised, I was too happy being involved in kicking the ball around to watch the game. I was beginning to carve out something of a reputation as a player which was as much a surprise to me as anyone else. Maryhill Harp came calling and, after only six games at Junior level, I was suddenly being transported from Panmure to Paradise.

2

PARADISE FOUND

Clyde offered me £60 to sign professional forms for them in 1955. Partick Thistle offered me £50. Celtic offered £20. Yes, TWENTY pounds. So, of course, I joined Celtic. How on earth did that happen? Let me explain.

My dad Joe and I had already met with officials from Thistle and Clyde and they had made their bids. They both wanted the young lad who was making a bit of a name for himself at Maryhill Harp and both were offering £2 and 10 shillings per week (£2.50 in today's money) in wages. Celtic, too, wanted to talk to me. I remember the day I was told to turn up at Celtic Park for a meeting. It was a Sunday and there weren't too many trams running in the city on the Sabbath. A smashing guy called John McNellis, who doubled as the Maryhill Harp secretary and local coalman, came to the rescue. Unusually, for that part of the world, he actually owned a car. He told my dad, 'Don't worry, Joe, I'll come and pick you and Bertie up at the close and take you over. Happy to help.'

It seemed most of the neighbours turned up that morning to wave us off on our travels. The Panmure Street grapevine had been in action and it seemed everyone knew that young Bertie Auld was going to have talks with the great Glasgow

Celtic. I felt like a prince as I was ushered into the back seat behind Mr McNellis while my dad sat in the front beside him. It was an old Austin and was Mr McNellis's pride and joy. Sitting behind him, I couldn't help but notice that, no matter how he must have scrubbed himself to get clean, there was still coal dust all over his neck. No matter, he was a splendid fellow who was about to do me one of the greatest favours of my young life.

I had never even been to Celtic Park before as we drove up Kerrydale Street, but the stadium certainly looked daunting and the club had an obvious worldwide appeal. I wasn't a particular fan of any team as I was growing up. I may have gone to a Protestant school and people could have automatically thought Rangers were my team. Where I was brought up in Maryhill, that didn't necessarily follow. Funnily enough, although most of my schoolmates were followers of local side Partick Thistle, there were a few who favoured Celtic. So, I was there to talk to Celtic and see what they were prepared to put on the table.

That lovely gentleman Jimmy McGrory, the Celtic manager, greeted my dad and me. Now I believe legend is a word that is often overused these days. Mr McGrory had earned his status as an icon as you can understand when you take a quick peek at his goalscoring record for the club – 410 goals in 408 league games! In all, he scored 550 goals in a playing career that spanned fifteen years up until his retirement in 1937. He was famous for his bullet-like headers, but he once scored eight goals in one game against Dunfermline in 1928 – all with his feet. There must have been a good reason why this guy only played seven times for his country. Anyway, was it any wonder that I could detect my father was in awe of this imposing man with the broad shoulders?

Mr McGrory shook my hand and looked me straight in the eye. He took us through to the Celtic boardroom and I was impressed immediately. It was fitted out with all this antique furniture and I had never seen such old world grandeur. We were shown to our seats at this beautifully crafted oak table that ran from one end of the room to the other. There were about ten or twelve seats set out. I wondered how many people would be turning up to talk to me. Thankfully, it was only Mr McGrory, and, still puffing on his pipe, he drew up a seat beside my dad and me. Rather surprisingly, the Celtic manager then asked me if I fancied a glass of whisky. My dad almost went ballistic. He said, 'What do you think you are doing? My son's only sixteen.' He calmed down immediately to say, 'I'll take one, though!' Mr McGrory was happy to oblige and poured a generous measure for my dad before taking his seat again.

He looked at me and said, 'We've been receiving good reports about you. How would you like to join Celtic?'

Before I could answer, my dad countered with his own question, 'What are you offering?'

Mr McGrory, who I would later find was a true gent, took another puff on a pipe that seemed to be perpetually lit and answered, 'We'll go to £20 for a signing-on fee and £2 per week in wages. We'll also give him two shillings for his expenses.' Celtic must have worked out exactly how much it would cost for me to travel by tram from Queen's Cross to Kerrydale Street and back. They were spot on with their calculations.

As I sat there slightly stunned – and more than just a little bit disappointed – with Celtic's offer, I heard this voice beside me say, 'We accept! You've got a deal.' I didn't utter a word. Clyde had put £60 on the table. Thistle had come up with £50. And here was Celtic making a bid of £20 and my dad was

19

accepting on my behalf. Celtic's offer was a third of what Clyde were prepared to pay and here we were accepting it without the merest hint of negotiations. I was also going to be ten shillings a week poorer in my pay poke. Incredible. Looking back on everything I have enjoyed at the club over so many years and the treasured memories that will never leave me, I can only say, 'Thanks, Dad. You got it right, as usual.' It only seemed natural back then to leave everything to my dad. He was the head of the household, after all, and I always looked up to him. He never did me wrong at any time.

Mr McGrory – I never brought myself to just call him Jimmy – got me to sign forms which he put in a safe. I was too young to actually put my signature on those papers, but it would be OK in a fortnight or so's time when I turned seventeen. Those forms would have remained locked away in that safe until the time was right to register yours truly as a Celtic player.

My dad and I were asked if we had ever seen Celtic Park. We both had to admit we had never had the opportunity. Mr McGrory decided to act as our tour guide. I always remember this Celtic legend opening the doors for my dad and me as we passed through. He took us out onto one of the terracings and I almost fainted. The sheer size of the place was awesome – simply breath-taking. I had been inside Firhill which could probably have held 30,000 or so, but this was an entirely different ball game. This was the big time even if the signing-on offer didn't quite match that from Clyde or Partick Thistle. Ach, it was only money.

After being shown all round the place, we returned to the boardroom where the Celtic manager asked me, 'Have you ever seen a new £20 note, Bertie?'

I answered, 'I've never even seen an OLD £20 note, Mr McGrory!' The note – brand, spanking new – was passed over and I clutched it firmly in my right hand. I folded it over neatly so as not to crunch it. A £20 note back then was so huge it could have papered my mother's kitchen. It may not have been what was on offer elsewhere, but it was still an awful lot of money. Remember, my dad would work all week for £7 per week and that was to help raise a family of eight. You could buy a bungalow in the posh area of Bearsden in Glasgow for around £500 at the time.

We made our way out of Celtic Park, with the money still tightly grasped in my right mit, and got into my dad's pal's car. For the second time that day my father surprised me. He always called me son. He said, 'Right, son, did you see that place they called the Jungle? That's where you will find the fans crammed in when you are playing. You can make these guys love you. You perform for them and they'll repay you. This support has got a great knowledge. They'll encourage you and they'll never forget you.' I was a bit taken aback. I had never heard my dad talk like this. It wasn't bad for a wee labourer to make such a stunning prediction over half a century ago.

He then said another thing I have never forgotten. I thought Mr McGrory's large whisky was taking effect when he said, 'It's kick and be kicked now, son,' and repeated, 'Kick and be kicked.' I soon got the message.

I was now going into a footballing environment where no quarter would be asked or given. Playing for fun was a thing of the past. I knew I could still enjoy myself, but I was now a committed team man. I realised that I would be kicked. Look, it's a contact sport, as far as I am concerned. There will be physical collisions and there will be hard tackles. It's a man's game. But if anyone set out to deliberately kick me, then he was going to get some of the same back, I can assure you. Take the kick, remember it and, when the opportunity arose, let the guy know you hadn't forgotten. If I was done, you could be sure I was going to do him back at some point. Kick and be kicked. It was something that I remembered throughout my career. If you allowed someone to kick you and you didn't respond then you had just given him licence to kick you all day. He knew you wouldn't come back in kind. Anyone who booted me soon realised I would return with a like-for-like answer.

As I sat in the back of Mr McNellis's Austin I couldn't stop myself from looking at this £20 note, still firmly clasped in my right hand. I was so proud and I couldn't wait to get home to present it to my mum. We duly arrived at 95 Panmure Street and said our thanks to our accommodating chauffeur for the day. It was great to see that the whole family had assembled to congratulate me on signing for the famous Celtic and, at last, I allowed the £20 note to escape from my grasp.

'That's for you, Mum,' I said and duly passed it over.

She looked at it and I'm sure a wee tear came to her eyes. 'Thanks, son,' she said. 'I'll make sure you have a treat tonight.' Then she started to ask me about Celtic. 'Are you happy with the move? Is it right for you? Will you enjoy yourself at the club?' Suddenly I realised she was addressing me as an adult for the first time. Previously, I had been Wee Bertie, her son. Now I was Bertie Auld, Celtic player. It was a wonderful day in my life.

I wondered what the promised treat might be. We had our tea and did all the usual things our family did on a Sunday although this was hardly a normal day for me. I waited and waited. Then it was time to go to bed. I was getting prepared and I had to ask, 'What about my treat, Mum?'

She said, 'I haven't forgotten, son. You get to choose which side of the bed you sleep on tonight. That's your treat.'

Well, one of my brothers had a wee bit of a problem holding his water sometimes – it was known as an 'accident' – and I immediately said, 'I'll take the shallow end!'

My early days at Celtic were simply marvellous. I thrived on mixing with players such as Charles Patrick Tully, Willie Fernie, Bertie Peacock, Bobby Collins, Sean Fallon, John McPhail, Bobby Evans and a guy called Jock Stein. I'm sure we will hear a little bit more about this individual later! They were all household names – guys you read about in the newspapers every day. Charlie Tully, bought for £8,000 from Belfast Celtic in 1948, was an amazing character. There was nothing he couldn't do with a football. I would have paid to get into training just to witness this guy's skills at close range. He was a born entertainer. I have to say he wasn't the best trainer at the club and I also have to admit I don't recall him ever doing laps round the pitch. That wasn't for Charlie. Instead, when the manager and the coaches weren't around, he would merely sprint the six yards or so between the dug-outs. I wondered what this was all about at first. Then the penny eventually dropped. If any of the training staff were coming down the Celtic Park tunnel all they would see was Charlie racing past at full pelt. When they emerged trackside cheeky Charlie was puffing and panting and looking as though he had just completed about twenty laps. And that was him for the day.

I'm not sure the Celtic training staff knew what Charlie was up to, but he was such a character that I think they would have let him off with anything just so long as he turned it on on matchday. And he did that often enough, take it from me. You know, I don't think he was ever properly fit. You can only wonder what he might have achieved if he had been 100 per cent. I recall one time, Celtic were taking us down to Seamill, in Ayrshire, for some pre-season training. Someone ordered the bus driver to stop about halfway to our destination and we were told we would have to run the rest of the way. Eric Smith and I teamed up and set off running to the hotel. Everyone was doing fine but after about thirty minutes or so there was no sign of Charlie. Then, about halfway to our destination, we heard the spluttering of a moped. It passed us and there was the bold lad himself, perched on the back seat and waving to his team-mates. Priceless!

I was part-time at that stage, mixing football with joinery, and our training was normally at six o'clock at night when most of the first-teamers had long since departed the place. My mum wouldn't have been happy if she had ever found out, but every now and again her errant son used to duck his daytime job to train with the first team squad. It was well worth it in the long run.

The fans adored Charlie. He has a special place in Celtic folklore after displaying a typical piece of impudence and no little skill in a Scottish Cup tie against Falkirk at Brockville in 1953. Charlie swung in a corner-kick that completely bamboozled the unfortunate keeper and swept directly into the net. The referee wasn't impressed, though, and, for reasons known only to himself, decided to rule out the 'goal' and order a retake. Charlie simply shrugged his shoulders, placed the ball in the arc and took another kick. Once more the keeper was left helpless as the ball soared over his head into the net – once again directly from the corner. This time the match official allowed the goal to stand. You get the impression if he had ordered another retake Charlie would have sent that into the net, too!

How could you fail not to be inspired by this outstanding, irresistible personality? Younger supporters won't remember too much about him and, sadly, there isn't a lot of footage around to show you just how skilful he was. You'll have to take my word for it and I am not exaggerating when I say there was a mix of the best of Jinky Johnstone and George Best in Charlie Tully. Yes, that's how good he was. By the way, the Falkirk keeper obviously didn't do his homework on Charlie. I should point out that he scored two goals in Northern Ireland's 2-2 draw with England in Belfast the previous year and, yes, one was direct from a corner kick.

Naturally enough, a young and impressionable Bertie Auld adored these guys and I hoped I could emulate them at some stage. I could always dream. I signed a full contract on 2 April 1955 and made my debut against Rangers on 1 May, two years later. In between, I had a season-long period at Dumbarton and I can reveal now that I am unique in Celtic history – I am the only player to sign for the club THREE times. When I went to Dumbarton it was supposed to be on loan but there was some sort of problem with the contract and the Boghead side actually had to pay a nominal fee to sign me. It would only have been a token and Celtic promised to return it in a year's time.

When I heard Celtic wanted me to go to Dumbarton I, naturally, consulted my dad. Once again he didn't hesitate: 'Take it, son. You'll get first team football there. It's part of your education.' I returned to Parkhead and the transfer was done and Dumbarton got their money back at the end of the season.

Around that time I was called up for my national service. I was put through a rigorous examination and, as a sports enthusiast and as you might expect, I passed with flying colours. I was rated Grade One. My mum wasn't having any of that –

her boy wasn't going to be taken away by the army. She knew a doctor who had a practice in Possil and, rather amazingly, I was suddenly found to have flat feet and that put me down to Grade Three. It was known as a deferment – whatever that actually means. So, there was no place in the frontline for me and it was business as usual at home.

Something always seemed to be happening to me and I recall a funny incident shortly after I had put a string of games together in the first team. We were due to play Hearts at Tynecastle and the coach was ready to leave Glasgow at eleven in the morning for the journey through to Edinburgh. I was getting prepared as usual, trying to look neat and tidy, and my mum Peggy was fussing around as she always did on matchday. 'Have you brushed your teeth? Is your tie straight? Have you polished your shoes?' All that sort of thing. My mum made me my breakfast which I made short work of in my normal fashion. 'Have you had enough to eat? Do you want another sandwich?' On this particular morning she seemed more determined than ever to fatten up her first son for the rigours that lay ahead – so much so that I was late for the coach which left for Edinburgh without me.

'Oh, hell,' I thought, 'what am I going to do now?' I could just imagine even the normally placid Jimmy McGrory hitting the roof when he discovered I was missing. There was nothing else for it – I would have to get a taxi and try to catch up with the rest of the lads at Tynecastle. I waved down a black cab on the street and asked him to take me to Hearts' ground. He eyed me up and said, 'That'll be three quid, son. Have you got the cash?' I had exactly £3 on me and I showed him the money. Satisfied, he nudged the vehicle into gear and set off for our capital city where, later in life, I would have such an eventful period as a player, coach and manager of Hibs.

It seemed to take an eternity to get from Glasgow to Edinburgh that day although, of course, the traffic is nothing like as congested as it is today. I recall it was just five days before Christmas, so there was the usual rush on at the shops. We eventually reached our destination, luckily enough, just as the team coach was pulling in. I got out of the taxi in a rush before mingling with the rest of my colleagues as they got off and headed for the main entrance at Tynecastle. Boy, was I relieved. I'm not too sure how the Celtic bosses would have viewed it at the time, a young player missing the official team bus. I don't suppose they would have accepted the excuse that my mum delayed me because she wanted me to eat another bacon buttie!

I was excited at the prospect of playing a very good Hearts team who had strong characters in the likes of Dave Mackay and John Cumming. These blokes were two of the hardest men in football, but were always fair. They would go in for a 50/50 ball like their lives depended on it. You knew you were tackled when these two guys hit you. But, as I said, they never went over the top. They were just a pair of very committed professionals and I have always admired that in people. I would like to think I was every bit as dedicated to the Celtic cause. Anyway, there I was at Tynecastle, when the team sheet was read out. You can imagine my surprise when the name Auld wasn't on it. I had been dropped. I had just spent a week's wages haring from Glasgow through to Edinburgh and my reward was a seat in the stand.

Before being dropped, I had played the previous fifteen games, netted eight goals, and was in the line-up that hammered Stirling Albion 7-3 the previous week. I thought I would get the nod again, but a fellow called Matt McVitie was named at outside-left that afternoon. We managed a 1-1 draw and I returned the following week for a 3-1 triumph over my one-time suitors Clyde. I still wonder if Jimmy McGrory had noted my absence on the bus going through to Edinburgh and dropped me as some sort of punishment.

My wages had gone up ten shillings since my signing and I'm sure my weekly earnings of £3 made made sure the family of a certain Glasgow cabbie had a wonderful Christmas at my expense.

My mum, on hearing of my lack of travelling facilities, thought it would be a good idea to buy me a car, a Vauxhall Velux. There was only one snag – I didn't possess a driving licence at the time. The vehicle was duly delivered to Panmure Street and my brother-in-law, who could drive, told me he would teach me. Another little problem – there was no petrol in the car. I think my mum had spent everything on buying the Vauxhall, so we had to get money from somewhere. That normally meant the pawn, those quaint establishments that no-one ever admitted to using but everyone seemed to know where they were. Well, no-one was ever going to say they were hard up, were they?

Margaret, my big sister, had bought me a new suit when I started to go on my travels with Celtic. I think Marion also chipped in to buy this new checked outfit. I'm not too sure what it would have cost, but Margaret and Marion, who both worked as bus conductresses, must have saved up a few quid to spend on their wee brother. I was wearing it one day when I got a tap on the shoulder from a Celtic official. 'Those trouser bottoms are too tight,' I was informed. Drainpipes were all the fashion back then, with trousers that tapered all the way to your ankle. I didn't think they were that tight, but Celtic didn't agree and I knew that was the end of the argument. My prized suit went back into the wardrobe.

When we were exploring ways to make dosh to put petrol in the car, I had a sudden thought. The suit would never be worn again, so why not take it down to the pawn and see if we could get two quid for it? I got the OK from my sisters so my brother-in-law and I set off for the pawnbroker's, to give them their proper title. We wrapped up the suit in a big brown parcel, tied it up with string and off we went. I had only gone about six yards when one of our neighbours, looking out of her upstairs window, spotted us. 'Bertie, are you going down to the pawn?'

I tried desperately to get her to lower her voice. I was a Celtic player, after all, and I was supposed to be rolling in cash. Anyway, she said she had her husband's nightshirt that might be worth two shillings (10 pence these days!) and could I take it down for her. She, too, wrapped up the garment in a brown parcel and then threw it down to me.

In Maryhill, the pawnshop was up a tenement close, so you always went through the entrance next to it and climbed over the wall behind it before entering the pawn via the back door. There were little cubicles in the place as about three or four employees worked behind a long desk. They were probably put there to protect your privacy although, of course, everyone knew everyone else's business in Maryhill.

The bloke behind the desk asked, 'Name?'

I whispered, 'Auld.'

'Sorry?'

I kept my voice low again, 'Auld.'

Suddenly this big guy from the next berth looked round the partition and said in an ear-splitting roar, 'Bertie Auld, of Celtic! What are you doing here?'

I mumbled something and the guy at the desk took the two parcels. He opened mine, looked it up and down, inspecting both the jacket and the trousers. 'How much?' he asked.

'Two quid?' I ventured. He said nothing. He opened my neighbour's parcel. He shook the nightshirt and I noticed it had been slightly soiled.

Again, he was quiet and merely asked, 'How much?'

I swiftly disowned the garment. 'My neighbour's looking for two bob,' I replied.

'OK,' he said, slamming down some cash with a receipt.

'Two quid, suit, jacket and trousers,' he said and then, unnecessarily in a louder tone, added, 'Two shillings, shirt and shite!' My brother-in-law and I picked up the money and got out of there as swiftly as possible. Maybe the bloke was a Rangers fan!

It wasn't all a barrel of laughs, though. I well remember the shock of being omitted from the Celtic team sheet on a quite remarkable afternoon at Hampden on 19 October 1957. We were due to take on our oldest foes Rangers in the League Cup Final and I have to say I thoroughly enjoyed Old Firm encounters. The atmosphere, the rivalry, the fierce competitiveness, the lot – I loved it. Once more, without sounding conceited, I thought I would be in the side. After all, I had played in the previous League Cup matches against East Fife (6-1), Hibs (2-0), Third Lanark (6-1) and Clyde (4-2). I had also chipped in with two goals along the way. The gaffer, Mr McGrory, decided to recall Neilly Mochan who hadn't played in the competition since we lost 3-1 to Hibs in the qualifying section in August. The League Cup format at the time was divided into groups and we qualified on points after eight games. Then it became a knockout tournament at the quarter-final stage.

There we were at Hampden, I was looking forward to the entire occasion until I was taken aside and told I wasn't playing. The more experienced Mochan was taking my place. Actually, I really liked the guy who was known as Smiler for the way his face lit up when he scored a goal. He later became a trainer at the club, of course. A lovely bloke, but I could have seen him far enough that day. Jimmy McGrory put out this team: Beattie, Donnelly, Fallon, Fernie, Evans, Peacock, Tully, Collins, McPhail, Wilson and Mochan. There were no substitutes in those days and I wasn't even at Hampden to witness the spectacle. I was sent with the reserves to play Queen of the South in Dumfries. Yes, I wanted to be out there in the hoops at Hampden, but I wasn't grumbling when the news was relayed that Celtic had won 7-1 in truly overwhelming fashion. And it could have been worse for Rangers – we hit the woodwork three times as well. Mr McGrory's decision to leave me out was vindicated when Smiler flashed in two excellent goals.

As I travelled back to Glasgow that day I wouldn't have believed that the success over Rangers would be Celtic's last piece of silverware until we returned to the Mount Florida district of Glasgow in 1965 to meet Dunfermline in the Scottish Cup Final in an extremely fateful afternoon for yours truly when I definitely played my part. More of that unforgettable, rollicking occasion later.

However, something very strange occurred on the evening of 26 April 1961. Celtic lost 2-0 to a Dunfermline side managed by Jock Stein in the Scottish Cup Final replay at Hampden. I played for the reserves against Hearts at Tynecastle the same evening, scored five goals and agreed to leave Celtic the following day.

3

PARADISE LOST

An immaculately dressed individual in a beautifully tailored camel-hair coat stood in front of me in the Tynecastle dressing room. He was about 6ft 2in tall, sported an expertly trimmed moustache, and he fixed me firmly in his gaze. He said, 'I want you to join my club. I'll be talking to Celtic about you. Expect a call tomorrow.' Honestly, I didn't recognise the dapper gentleman who had taken such a shine to me. More than just a little bit bewildered, I made my way home that evening. Who was this mysterious stranger?

The following day I turned up for training as usual. Obviously the mood in the camp was one of deep despondency. Celtic had been massive favourites to beat Dunfermline in the Scottish Cup Final replay the night before. They had failed spectacularly against a club that wasn't long out of the Second Division. A 2-0 defeat wasn't in the script that April evening in 1961. Obviously, I couldn't have realised it at the time, but my one and only appearance in the national tournament that year would be my last first team outing for Celtic this time around. I was in my usual berth at outside-left when we beat Falkirk 3-1 in the first round on 28 January. Actually, I had played in the three previous league matches, a 3-1 victory over Aberdeen, a 4-0 triumph over Airdrie and a 2-1 defeat from St Mirren. I didn't play in every match, but it would be fair to say I was something of a fixture in the first team squad. I had absolutely no thoughts about leaving the club – none whatsoever. Someone at Celtic had other ideas, though.

I was awaiting the call that the manager wanted to see me. In his normal forthright manner, Jimmy McGrory told me an English First Division club wanted to buy me. They had offered £15,000 and the directors were willing to accept the bid. To be honest, it was a shattering blow to discover that Celtic were quite content to allow me to leave. I felt sick in my stomach. I was then informed that the club who wanted to sign me were Birmingham City. The suave gent from the night before had been none other than their manager, Gil Merrick, the former England international goalkeeper. I should have recognised him, but he looked completely different without his football clobber on. He certainly scrubbed up well.

I found myself in a quandary. What should I do? I didn't want to go but something within me told me I didn't want to hang around someplace where I wasn't wanted. What went wrong? Why was I being moved on? My old Parkhead chum Paddy Crerand had a theory that might not be too far off the mark. He insisted, 'Those in power at the club at that time wanted rid of Bertie. He was a typical Glaswegian and wasn't afraid of answering back. That was to be his downfall at Celtic. Bob Kelly didn't like his style.'

Yes, I admit I wasn't slow to give my opinion. If I didn't agree with someone I was hardly going to sit there and nod my approval. I'm not a particular fan of yes men. If you are in a dressing room and someone is spouting something you think is not quite right I don't see much wrong in throwing in your tuppence worth. Footballers aren't robots, you know. You can't program them, wind up the key and send them out to play. We are human beings and, as such, I always thought I could contribute something extra to the thought process if or when it was possible. That wasn't welcome at Celtic at the time. There was an almost puritanical streak at the club. The directors would frown when they saw an individual fly into a tackle. It didn't matter that it was perfectly fair and all above board. Their idea was to play football in an almost Corinthian fashion. 'Play up and play the game.' All that sort of nonsense.

The directors would take their usual seats in the stand and witness their own players being kicked black and blue by their opponents. Yet you knew if you went in hard and someone from the other club was hurt then there was every chance you wouldn't be playing the following week as a punishment. It was so naive of our directors at that time. They had a vision of how the game should be played but you can't do much if you don't have the ball. Unless your opponents are in a very benevolent mood and give you the ball constantly, you've got to go and win it. Simple? You would have thought so, but others, who really didn't know too much about the game, had different ideas and I didn't always agree with them. The easy option was to remain silent as a lot of others did. Ironically, Paddy was similarly minded and that's probably why Celtic allowed him to go, too! Mind you, he went on to do great things at a team called Manchester United.

Although things weren't quite right at the club, I still loved Celtic. They were my team, but there were some puzzling aspects of being a Celtic player back then. Who, for instance, picked the team? Obviously, it should have been the manager, but no-one was quite sure. Mr McGrory would put up a team sheet on a Thursday night after the weekly board meeting and it would be a changed line-up by Friday afternoon. You didn't require Sherlock Holmes-like qualities to detect the chairman, Bob Kelly – later to become Sir Robert – had the final say.

Here's an interesting wee story. The players used to gather in a room on matchday at Celtic Park at about one-thirty in the afternoon if it was a three o'clock kick-off. We would play snooker and so on. I would make some sort of excuse about going to the loo or something and duck out. I would go to the home dressing room to see if my boots had been looked out and were in the No.11 position. I would be happy when I saw them there. I would nick in half an hour later just to make sure they were still in place. Somehow they would have found their way to the No.7 position. At least I was still playing. Then the team would be read out and there was no Bertie Auld in it. After all that, I wasn't playing. Thankfully, things changed rather dramatically when Big Jock arrived in March 1965. There was only going to be one person picking the team after that and we all knew exactly where we stood. It was Jock's way or no way and the board got the message. There was to be no more meddling in team affairs. About time, too. It's my belief that most directors' knowledge of football could be written on a fly's backside and there would still be space for some more!

Bob Kelly's influence on team selection was emphasised one afternoon on 1 October 1960, as our team bus was wending its merry way to Broomfield, the quaint home of Airdrie Football Club. The chairman recognised one of the Celtic supporters, bedecked in a huge woolly green-and-white scarf, walking towards the same destination. 'That's one of our reserve goalies, isn't it?' asked Kelly. It was, indeed, an individual called Willie

Goldie, and Kelly ordered the bus to be stopped. Goldie was invited on board and he didn't only get a lift to Broomfield, he also played! Kelly was so impressed with his commitment to Celtic that Goldie suddenly found himself in goal. John Fallon, who had been in position for the previous four league games, was dropped. Just like that. Celtic duly lost 2-0. By the way, Goldie got plenty of opportunities after that to support the club from the terracings – he never played in the first team again! Actually, I owe him a big thank-you for helping restore me to the first team. I missed the game against Airdrie with Alec Byrne playing outside-left, but I returned for the next match and scored two goals in a 4-2 victory over St Mirren.

Yet, even in the midst of these bizarre team selections and other odd goings-on, I still wanted to remain a Celtic player. I knew Bob Kelly had tried to get rid of me earlier when Bobby Collins was about to join Everton. Our chairman tried to persuade the Goodison Park side to make it a double deal and throw me in as well. But I was having none of it. For a start, I was in love! I had met this fantastic girl called Liz at the Locarno Ballroom in Sauchiehall Street, Glasgow, one Saturday night and it was love at first sight. She is now Mrs Auld and we married on 28 January 1963 at St Andrew's Church in the shadow of Birmingham City's ground. At that time, though, we had just started going out with each other and I realised a transfer to Merseyside would mean the end of our all-too-brief relationship. That wasn't going to happen and no-one was going to force me into leaving Celtic or Glasgow. When Birmingham City came on the scene it was a different proposition. Liz and I were an item, as they say, so a shift across the border wasn't out of the question if we both agreed it was the right thing to do.

After talking to Jimmy McGrory, I decided the very least I could do was to speak to the Birmingham City manager. I was sad in my heart, but I thought it was only polite to meet again with Gil Merrick. At least this time I knew his name. I was immediately impressed by the man. He gave me the impression he only wanted me – no-one else. He knew exactly what he wanted me to do for his club and he was exceptionally persuasive. I found myself thinking maybe it wouldn't be a bad idea if I looked into this a bit more carefully. He was offering me the opportunity to go to England and play against the likes of Spurs, Manchester United, Chelsea, West Ham and so on. There were so many personalities down there at the time. There was my old mate Denis Law at United, Dave Mackay had joined Spurs and West Ham had youngsters such as Bobby Moore, Martin Peters and Geoff Hurst beginning to emerge. Of course, that trio would win the World Cup with England some five years later. After a quick word with Liz, I decided to move to Birmingham City. Genuinely, I thought it was the way ahead for me. Exciting times were around the corner, but my career at the St Andrew's outfit almost didn't even get off the ground. But for a chance happening, I would have been on the train back to Glasgow only hours after meeting the board of directors.

Honestly, they couldn't have been more welcoming. The men who owned the club and the directors couldn't have been more accommodating. Gil Merrick, too, was there as the red carpet was rolled out. Actually, Birmingham City reminded me so much of Celtic in a sense. It was like one big family and I was impressed by the mere fact they actually cared about me. I had travelled down by train on my own, utterly convinced I was doing the right thing. Liz had packed my holdall, two pairs of socks and two pairs of underpants. She must have listened to my mum who continually insisted, 'Always have fresh underpants – you never know when you might get hit by a bus!'

Gil Merrick and one of his coaching staff, a chap called Don Dorman, accompanied me from the football ground at St Andrew's to the Midlands Hotel which was situated near the railway station. Gil, as ever, was kindness personified. 'If there's anything you need, Bertie, just let me know.' Nothing was too much trouble and I really appreciated that. Once they departed, I thought I would go out and have a walk around the city where I would be plying my trade to a whole new set of supporters. But it almost didn't happen.

I was walking up Corporation Street and caught sight of my reflection in the window of a giant store called Rackham's, which looked like Birmingham's version of Glasgow's Frasers. I stopped and looked at myself. Suddenly, I thought, 'Ach, what am I doing here?' And with that, I turned on my heel and headed back to the hotel where I had every intention of picking up my holdall and getting on the first train back to Glasgow. Then fate stepped in.

As I was preparing to leave my room, someone knocked on the door. I answered and there was Don Dorman standing in the hallway. He said, 'Do you mind me in your company?' I was more than just a tad bewildered. He admitted things weren't quite right at home and he and his wife were going through a rough patch. I invited him in. What on earth was I going to do? Don had no inkling that I was about to quit his club and get back up the road as swiftly as possible. We went for a coffee and then a bite to eat. If Don had been even five minutes later in coming to that door, I would have been off and my career would have been in jeopardy. That's if I still had a career. Birmingham City had just paid £15,000 for me and they held my registration. I don't think they would have been too pleased with my disappearing act and they could have put me out of the game altogether. Who could have blamed them?

Thankfully, that rather awkward situation did not develop. Don sidetracked me and I stayed the night in the Midlands Hotel before reporting for training the next morning. Remarkably, I made my debut for Birmingham in the Inter-Cities' Fairs Cup Final against Italian side AS Roma a week or so afterwards. I couldn't have asked for a more glamorous occasion in which to perform at St Andrew's for the first time. Before the game, Gil Merrick and his coaches – one of whom was Spanish, I seem to recall – were talking to the players in the dressing room. They were meticulously going through our team and telling us what they expected of each individual. They were talking tactics and suchlike and I was mesmerised. This sort of thing did not happen at Celtic, believe me. At Parkhead, I would be given the No.11 shorts and told to beat the full-back, get down the wing and hurl in crosses for the main strikers. If I chipped in a goal or two myself, all well and good, but my priority was to serve the frontmen with a steady stream of balls into the penalty box.

Now I was sitting in a different dressing room and it might as well have been a different world. Our manager was talking about set pieces, systems and so on. I was transfixed. He would take time out to point to an individual and tell the rest of the team how they should treat him. 'Get the ball to Bertie,' he would say. 'He'll bring a new dimension to our play. You will all like what you see from this player.' I sat there, drinking all this in, and I couldn't wait to get started. There was one problem, though – the Birmingham City shirt was BLUE! Bertie Auld in Rangers' colours? What a shocker! I made sure I put on a vest under that blue top. Only joking!

My first game, watched by a reasonable crowd of 21,000 at St Andrew's, finished in a 2-2 draw in the first leg and we lost the return 2-0 in Rome where 60,000 fanatical Italian supporters turned out to create a magnificent atmosphere. I had desperately wanted to repay everyone at my new club for their faith in me, but it wasn't to be. However, I would have better luck against another Italian team in a European Final six years later, of course.

I became a better player for my experience in English football, I am convinced of that. I was mixing with so many good players and learning from them. Birmingham City fans were passionate about their team although not on the scale I experienced at Celtic with their supporters. Mind you, you would have to travel far and wide to find a set of fans like the Celtic crowd. I really mean that. My dad was absolutely right when he said they were the most knowledgeable in the game. I thought that the day I signed first time around and I still believe it to be true today.

At Birmingham, I was encouraged to come inside a bit more often. Gil Merrick left before I returned to Celtic and a guy called Joe Mallett took over. He was the first manager to encourage me to move in from the touchline. At Celtic, as I said earlier, my job was to get down that wing and thump over as many crossballs as I could in ninety minutes. But the supporters in England were a bit different in their outlook to the game. Instead of haring down the touchline all day, they would applaud you if you hit an accurate long-range pass across the pitch to switch play. I found myself venturing inside a bit more often than in my days in Glasgow. I enjoyed it, too. It was adding a new dimension to my play and I was getting a bigger and clearer picture of what was developing all around me. It was an education and I thrived on my new responsibilities.

I'll tell you this, though, and I wouldn't blame you one bit if you didn't believe me, the day I left Celtic I instinctively knew I would return. And so, of course, it proved.

4

PARADISE REGAINED

The shrill of the telephone in my Birmingham City club flat demanded an answer. I picked up the receiver and was more than just a little taken aback when I heard the immediate question, 'Do you want to come back to Celtic?' Without a hint of hesitation, I asked, 'When? Tonight?'

I was on my way back to Paradise, a place I had always regarded as my spiritual home. The moment I had yearned for had arrived – as I still maintain I knew it would. I had left in April 1961 and it was now January 1965. I had enjoyed my experience in Birmingham, but Celtic were always my club and I had no problem in agreeing to rejoin them. My wife Liz, though, must have thought I was going off my head. We were settled in a beautiful flat in Solihull. I had just become a father with Liz presenting me with our gorgeous daughter, Susan. I was a first team regular with Birmingham City, they were still treating me really well and I got on with the supporters. Yet I still wanted back to Celtic. I even agreed to take a £5-per-week drop in wages and, believe me, that was a fair amount of cash all those years ago. No wonder Liz thought I was going doolally!

But what can you do when the love of your life – after Liz, of course! – comes calling? Now a lot of people have asked me if I agreed to go back to Celtic because I knew Jock Stein was also about to return after his impressive managerial stints at Dunfermline and Hibs. Listen, the man in the moon could have been on the verge of becoming Celtic boss, it didn't matter. I was returning to Celtic and that was the main thing. Yes, of course, I had heard the speculation that Big Jock was about to take over from Jimmy McGrory. Actually, Big Jock should never have been allowed to leave in the first place, but that's another story. Celtic agreed to pay Birmingham City £12,000 for me – £3,000 less than the Midlands outfit had forked out in 1961 – but they knew my feelings and, thankfully, weren't difficult to deal with. I thanked the management for all their kind assistance, said my farewells to my team-mates of four years or so, picked up my boots and headed back to Paradise. Little did I know what lay in store for me this time around.

So, who actually bought me? Was it manager Jimmy McGrory? Was it his assistant Sean Fallon? Or was it Jock Stein? I've never revealed this until now, but I have to say it was Big Jock. Technically, he should not have been allowed to have any say in matters concerning Celtic because, after all, he was the manager of Hibs. However, he certainly had something to do with my return, maybe dropping a word or two in the right ear. That call asking me to return to Celtic just happened to come from a bloke called Dougie Hepburn. Would you be surprised if I told you he was a close friend of Jock? I didn't think so. The following day Birmingham were due to play West Ham in an English Cup tie and I was overjoyed to see Sean outside the ground with another guy I knew, Tommy Reilly. He had driven the Celtic assistant boss down to Upton Park and, as soon as I saw them, I knew it wasn't a wind-up. I was, indeed, heading home.

I recall bumping into Big Jock when he was down in Birmingham to take in an English League v. Scottish League game around about that time. He was accompanied by Bob Kelly. The Hibs manager with the Celtic chairman? Draw your own conclusions. Anyway, he was quite chatty and said, 'How are things going, Bertie? Enjoying yourself?' I answered honestly, 'I'm having a great time. I've just become a father, too. Everything is wonderful.' Big Jock rarely indulged in small talk, but, on this occasion, he seemed genuinely interested in what was going on in my life, on and off the pitch.

Anyway, I arrived back in January and, of course, Big Jock returned two months later. Six weeks after that we were both celebrating a 3-2 Scottish Cup Final victory over Dunfermline at Hampden on 24 April in front of 108,800 fans. I was lucky enough to score two goals with Caesar – our skipper Billy McNeill – netting the winner with a trademark thumping header from a left-wing corner-kick by Charlie Gallagher, who was always so precise with his deadball kicking. That triumph didn't seem likely when I made my second debut for Celtic on a cold afternoon on 16 January against Hearts at Parkhead and we toppled to a 2-1 defeat. There have been more spectacular comebacks in sporting history, I suppose. I wasn't caring, though. I was wearing that famous green-and-white hooped shirt again and I knew things would get better. How much better I just couldn't have dreamed.

Tommy Gemmell, Billy McNeill, Jimmy Johnstone and Bobby Murdoch also played in that defeat against the Edinburgh side. Who would have believed that TG, Caesar, Jinky and Chopper as well as yours truly – Ten-Thirty to you – would all help the club conquer Europe six years later? If you had even dared to make such an outrageous suggestion you would have been put on strong medication for the rest of your life.

If I needed to impress Big Jock in his first match in charge, I would like to think I achieved that target. We were playing Airdrie at Broomfield on the evening of 10 March and we walloped them 6-0 and I claimed five. I had scored five times as many in one game as in my previous five matches since coming home. Talk about good timing! That was the problem with Celtic back then – an awful lack of consistency. Over the years when Celtic had won nothing they still had fabulous, entertaining players. On their day, they could beat the best. A week later they could lose to the worst. It was something Big Jock was going to address and if he needed a reminder of the hard work that lay ahead then he got it in his next game when we lost 1-0 at home to St Johnstone. A week later saw a 3-3 draw against Dundee at Dens Park and immediately after that we went down 4-2 to Hibs in Glasgow. That sequence of results just about summed up Celtic. One minute wonderful, the next woeful.

Big Jock had plenty to contend with as he attempted to awaken the club from its slumbers. I was ready to do my bit.

5

BHOYS' OWN

There once was a time when I answered to Sammy D. That's what my Celtic mates called me and I doubt if some people out there will have a clue as to how I came about my unusual nickname. As I have surely emphasised already, my colleagues – plus a certain Jim Baxter – were all genuine characters.

At that time there was the Hollywood ratpack led by Frank Sinatra and consisting of actors and singers such as Dean Martin, Peter Lawford, Cesar Romero . . . and Sammy Davis Junior. Sammy, a fabulous crooner, was unusual in that he was a black Jew. I used to have a very heavy growth and had to shave about twice a day. We had no black players around at the time and, without too many alternatives, that's why I was named after Sammy Davis. I hope that's not politically incorrect in this sensitive day and age. By the way, Sammy only had one eye and I'm fairly certain more than a few of my team-mates thought I did, too, after some of my performances!

So, Billy McNeill became Cesar after Romero because he was the only one who possessed a car and did all the driving. Romero, a good-looking leading man of his era, appears to have been given a similar task for Sinatra and his chums, so Billy was duly named Cesar. You will see throughout this book that I continually refer to my old captain as Caesar, note the different spelling, which I think is a lot more fitting. Well, who would you want to be called after – a chauffeur or a Roman emperor? I always thought Billy had that magnificent presence about him that marked him down as something special. Just think back to that famous photograph when he is standing up in the gods holding aloft the European Cup with the sun streaming down from the heavens in Lisbon. You'll see what I mean.

Mike Jackson, an old-fashioned inside-forward who could score a goal or two, thought he could sing. Note the word 'thought'. He wasn't shy to grab a microphone on a night out and he became Dino after Dean Martin, a smooth American-Italian singer and actor whose stage act used to be played out with him kidding the audience he was sloshed. He always seemed to have a huge glass of what looked like straight gin as he ambled through his performance. He had a great line when someone asked him for a cure for a hangover. Immediately, he responded, 'Simple – stay drunk!' Actually, a lot of that was sheer kidology and Dean Martin was one of helluva singer. Our Dino might have grudgingly admitted he was just a wee bit better than him!

John Colrain, a big, powerful frontman, was known as Oceans. Frank Sinatra was a lead in the movie *Ocean's Eleven* about a mob of guys who were plotting to rob a Las Vegas casino. George Clooney and Brad Pitt starred in the remake much later. Sinatra was Danny Ocean and so Colly took up his film name. I loved the story I heard about the making of the movie. Sinatra was outlining the plans to knock over the casino when Dean Martin broke in and said, 'To hell with the movie – let's do the heist!'

I was very friendly with Dino, Colly and Paddy Crerand back in the early days and we used to have some great nights out on the town. I recall one day we decided to go to the dancing, the Locarno in Sauchiehall Street, as I recall. Dino, Colly and myself had a change of clothes, but Paddy seemed to be wearing the same shirt he had had on all week. 'Give me half an hour and I'll get ready,' he said. We all trooped over to his mother's house at Thistle Street in the Gorbals. His mum, a lovely lady named Sarah, had lost her husband during the war, but she always appeared such a cheery person. She greeted Dino, Colly and me with her usual warmth and charm. Paddy went off to change his shirt and we noticed the Crerands actually possessed a television set. Now that must have been unique in the Gorbals in the Fifties and I mean that as no disrespect to the citizens of that area back then. There was a lot of poverty and deprivation around. For someone to have a television set was a big deal, believe me.

We also noticed this array of chairs set up in the living room pointed towards the TV. There were probably about four rows of five, I seem to recall, and there was a wee chap sitting there, wearing a bunnet and a huge coat, watching something on the box. As we waited for Paddy the little guy got up, thanked Mrs Crerand and walked down the stairs. 'Same time tomorrow, Sarah,' he said. I asked who this fellow was. 'Oh, I think he's a neighbour,' answered Mrs Crerand. Obviously, anyone was allowed to watch her television and, remember, these were the good old days when you could leave your front door open and not be scared of being burgled. They may not have had a lot of money back then, especially in the Gorbals, but they were honest and respected each other. Paddy duly returned and it looked as though he had simply turned his shirt inside-out!

Anyway, we did go to the dancing and had a splendid time, as we always did.

There was a superb bonding among the players and maybe some people at the club thought there was too much going on off the pitch. We had a good time, I'll admit, but we were 100 per cent professional in our training and playing. No-one could ever say otherwise. However, it was no surprise when I was sold to Birmingham City, Paddy to Manchester United, Dino to Third Lanark and Colly to Clyde over a fairly short period. Someone was trying to break up football's version of the Rat Pack, but we all remained good pals. Nothing was going to end our friendships.

Just over a year after I returned, Big Jock did something I am certain did so much to set Celtic off on their unstoppable glory run that would see nine successive League titles, among so many other honours, sweep into Parkhead. He arranged a trip to America where we would stay for five weeks and play eleven games. We met Spurs three times, beat them twice and drew the other. We drew 2-2 with Franz Beckenbauer's Bayern Munich, drew 0-0 with Bologna and beat the Mexican champions, Atlas, 1-0. We played in places such as New York, Los Angeles, Bermuda, New Jersey, St Louis and San Francisco. Those were exciting times and we came up against a few select teams along the way, hammering all sorts of opposition. Tommy Gemmell actually badgered Big Jock into allowing him to play at centre-forward in an encounter with a Hamilton Select. TG did OK – he netted a hat-trick in an overwhelming 11-0 success. The star of the trip, though, was undoubtedly Bobby Lennox who scored nineteen goals!

You think you know a team-mate when you are training with him most days and playing in games. It doesn't even come close to the camaraderie that emerges on a trip such as that. The players were just about living out of each other's suitcases. Obviously, as I have said, we were constantly on the move and someone might have forgotten to get his laundry done. So, Stevie Chalmers or anyone could come to your hotel room and see if they could borrow a shirt or trousers or a jacket. Guys of the size of Caesar and TG must have done a few swaps with each other. These are just little things, of course, but it does help you get even closer to your team-mates.

If that was the aim of Big Jock when he put the tour together then it was a massive success. We were close before we stepped on that plane to take off on our great adventure. We had completely bonded by the time we got home. We played a few friendlies as we prepared for our record-breaking 1966/67 season. The main one was obviously the visit of Manchester United to Parkhead. Now I have heard it said that the Old Trafford side were under-strength for that meeting. I believe my pal Paddy Crerand has gone on record as saying they were without Bobby Charlton and Nobby Stiles, who had won the World Cup with England that summer.

Paddy, my old chum, your memory is playing tricks on you. The guy who wore the United No.6 shirt that afternoon looked an awful lot like Nobby Stiles and the bloke in the No.9 jersey was the spitting image of Bobby Charlton. They played against us that day and so, too, did Denis Law and George Best. I've got the video evidence to prove it. It was a top side Sir Matt Busby fielded against his pal Big Jock and we still slaughtered them 4-1. We were exceptional and, believe me, United gave it all they had. They would go on and win the English Championship that season and then emulate our feat of lifting the European Cup a year after us.

However, we took them apart with a quite marvellous exhibition of attacking play that left Crerand, Charlton, Stiles, Law, Bestie and all their other international stars in the shade. There was no stopping us after that.

6

THE CUP THAT CHEERED

My dad Joe would never have claimed to be one of life's great philosophers, but there were occasions when he would make a remark that would make you sit up and take notice. After we had started the silverware landslide by beating Dunfermline 3-2 to lift the Scottish Cup in 1965, he said to me in a matter-of-fact tone, 'You know, son, if Celtic keep playing like that, I'm going to be forced to leave an hour earlier to get my place in the Jungle on a Saturday.'

He could have said something vague along the lines of, 'Celtic are playing well,' and that would have been enough, but he always enjoyed putting his own particular spin on things. My dad and his pals had their own special place on the terracing opposite the main stand. Older fans will surely remember the rusting ramshackle Jungle with affection. Supporters used to cram in there and Celtic, for decades, never did anything to upgrade the place. A fan I knew said he could have found his place in this part of our ground blindfolded if it was raining. 'How?' I asked innocently. He answered, 'Because there's been a huge hole in the roof above me and it's been like that for years. I get soaked when it's pouring down.' I countered by

saying, 'Why don't you shift?' and was met with an incredu-
lous stare. 'Because it's MY spot!' My dad, you should know,
could have got seats in the stand courtesy of his son, but he
never took me up on my offer. He preferred to be with his pals
in the Jungle.

I've touched on our victory over Dunfermline all those years
ago and, for me, it was the breakthrough to all the good things
that were awaiting us. Actually, that was one helluva game that
see-sawed throughout a dramatic ninety minutes. I couldn't
have had a clue as to what was around the corner when we
went a goal behind in only fifteen minutes of that Cup Final.
Our defence failed to clear their lines and the ball fell kindly
for Harry Melrose to hammer into the net past our grounded
keeper John Fallon. We could have thought, 'Here we go again.'
Things, under Big Jock, had changed somewhat dramatically,
though. I looked at my team-mates and I realised they felt to
a man just like me. 'We're going to win this one' seemed to be
the unified message. Sixteen minutes later I was lying on my
backside in the Fifers' net, but I wasn't one bit upset. The ball
was also sitting there beside me. I had equalised. I remember
the goal like it was yesterday. John Clark slid a pass to Charlie
Gallagher and he took a couple of steps forward, shaped to
play it wide, changed pace and then sent a thunderbolt of a
shot towards their goal from about thirty yards.

Jim Herriot, the Fifers' extremely competent goalkeeper who
would become a team-mate of mine at Hibs later on, threw
himself at Charlie's effort, but he failed to divert its course and
it thumped against the face of the crossbar. I saw my chance
as the ball swirled high into the air. Herriot was on the ground
and was desperately trying to get back to his feet as I moved
in for the kill. The ball seemed to be suspended by an invisible

hand. It appeared to be up there for ages. I was aware of their right-back Willie Callaghan coming in at speed from my right. He was wasting his time – I was never going to miss this opportunity. The ball came floating back down after what seemed an eternity and I launched myself at it to head it over the line. One–one – game on!

It was never like this Celtic side to do anything the easy way. It even took us a replay against Motherwell to reach this stage; drawing 2-2 in the first game before winning 3-0 in the second encounter. Once again, we gave ourselves a mountain to climb when we gave away a daft free kick smack in front of goal about twenty yards out. There was only a minute to go until the interval. Could we hold out? No-one should have been unduly surprised when Melrose touched the ball sideways and their big centre-forward John McLaughlin toe-ended it through our crumbling defensive wall. From where I was standing, it still looked saveable, but it managed to elude the grasp of our keeper, low down to his right. Bang on half-time is an awful time to hand the initiative to your opponents for all the obvious reasons. They go in buoyed up by the goal and we get to the dressing room wondering if the fates are conspiring against us again. The one thing I recall vividly in the interval team-talk is that not one of us believed we would lose. The worst we thought we could get was a draw and another game as they had replays in those days. Thankfully, we didn't need it.

'Get that early goal,' ordered Big Jock as we left the dressing room for the second half. 'Get that early goal and we'll win this game.' Prophetic words, indeed. Seven minutes into the second period and Tommy Gemmell turned the ball to me and I swiftly passed it to Bobby Lennox. He took off like a sprinter on the left and I chased into the penalty area. Bobby couldn't have hit a sweeter pass into the danger area and I arrived on the button to first time a right-foot shot low past the helpless Herriot. Two–two – we're going to win!

It couldn't have been scripted better. With nine minutes remaining we were pushing for the winner and it looked as though the Fifers were the ones who would have been happier with a second chance. We won a corner-kick out on the left and Gallagher trotted over to take it. We were all making nuisances of ourselves in the box, darting this way and that, in an effort to leave a gap for Big Billy to expose. Charlie duly delivered with sublime accuracy, Billy was exactly where he should have been and he did precisely what we wanted him to do. Our skipper soared high above everyone to get his head to the ball as Herriot frantically grasped thin air behind him. There was perfect contact with head and ball and there was the very satisfying thud as the sphere reached its destination and strangled itself in the net. Three–two – we've won the Cup!

I've always maintained that was a massive victory for Celtic. I will never think otherwise. It shows you how much things have changed in football when you look back at the crowd for that game – 108,800 was the official figure, but I think more than a few extra thousand must have scaled the walls. The receipts were a record at the time – £36,973. Celtic and Dunfermline each got £14,397. An average Premier League player wouldn't get out of bed if that was his weekly wage these days.

This victory was not about cash, though. It was about bringing back that winning feeling to Celtic Football Club. We succeeded and that sparked the most sensational and spectacular period in the club's history. I'm glad I got to play a part.

7

BIG JOCK AND ME

So, there I am, pinned against the dressing room wall with Big Jock's huge left hand around my throat and he is threatening to wallop me with his right. If he was trying to get some sort of message across, it was working, take my word for it.

We had just come off the pitch after beating Clyde 3-0 at Shawfield and I knew our manager wasn't greatly enamoured with some of my antics. My sin? I sat on the ball three times during the game. OK, it's a highly unusual tactic when you are hoping to tempt a team into your own half. Clyde, though, refused to budge that afternoon. We were three goals ahead and you might expect them to open up and have a go at grabbing some sort of salvation. Not that day. The Clyde players seemed wary of even crossing the halfway line. They appeared to be content to keep the scoreline as it was.

I chased back to the eighteen-yard line to collect a throw-out from Faither, Ronnie Simpson. I looked up and, sure enough, there were the Clyde players refusing to come out of their own half. Quick as a flash, I decided to sit on the ball, hoping to spur at least a couple of their players into action. Nope, they weren't buying it. I got up, rolled the ball back to our keeper and asked him to return it. Faither duly did and I sat on the ball again. Still nothing stirred from our opponents. I staged an action replay immediately and parked my backside on the ball for a third time. Still, Clyde didn't want to know.

I looked around the Shawfield Stadium and the Celtic fans were cheering and applauding. They loved this piece of show-manship, but I wasn't doing it to belittle our rivals. Genuinely, I wanted them to make a game of it and they just didn't want to know. I glanced over at our dug-out and that was when I saw Big Jock in full ranting mode. Not a pretty sight. Now whoever designed the dug-outs at Shawfield would never win any award for services to architecture. For a start, you had to take a step down to get into them and that left you getting a worm's-eye view of the action. All you could see were ankles flying past and there is no way you could actually witness the game unfolding. It was the worst view in the house.

But there was Big Jock, with all his bulk, trying desperately to clamber out of that small confined space. There was a slab of concrete across the top of the dug-out that acted as a roof. Jock slammed his head off it – not once, not twice, but three times – as he attempted to climb his way onto the track. He was furious and I thought, 'You're for the high jump here, Bertie. Let's hope he calms down at full-time.' I could always hope. There wasn't a chance of that happening. Once Big Jock went up like Vesuvius it took an awful long time for him to come back to earth. Maybe a week or two!

When the final whistle went, I took a gulp and headed for the away team's dressing room. I wondered if there was any chance I could have a shower, get changed and get on the coach before Jock emerged. I prayed for someone to stop him and have a chat before he could get to the dressing room.

Headbutting a speeding train would be preferable to incurring the wrath of Jock. I knew I was in for an ear-bashing, but I didn't anticipate what happened next. Jock, with that heavy limp that ended his career, stormed in behind me as quickly as he could. Now, the pegs in the changing area at Shawfield must have been put up by some fairly tall joiner. They were so high up the wall that we used to have to put Wee Jinky on our shoulders when he was hanging up his gear!

Big Jock must have thought it was a good idea to hang yours truly on one of those pegs that afternoon. He grabbed me with that massive mit of his and lifted me off the floor. 'Put me down, boss,' I squeaked as his clenched right fist looked a wee bit too close to my nose for comfort.

'Don't you ever dare do that again,' he bellowed. 'Don't you ever treat a fellow professional in that manner.' My feet were dangling by this stage as I attempted to plead my case. Jock wasn't interested. 'Do that once more and you'll never play for this team again as long as I am manager.' Thankfully, after a while, he released his grip and I slumped to the floor. Then he turned to Faither, who thought he was going to get away with his part in my impromptu tactic of trying to entice our opponents to cross the halfway line. 'The same goes for you,' said Jock. 'You encouraged him.' At least our veteran goalkeeper was spared being suspended by the throat for a minute or two.

Did I tell you our boss had a temper? Life wasn't dull when Big Jock was around. He was the gaffer and he let everyone know it. He could be a complex character. He could be irrational. He could be inspirational. He could be humorous. He could be hurtful. He was impossible to second-guess. There were occasions when you might expect a rollicking and, instead, he would put his arm around your shoulders and give you a little pep talk. 'OK, you weren't at your best today, but don't worry. It'll come back in the next game, I guarantee you.' Then, when you least expected it, he would give you a dressing-down in front of your team-mates and leave you utterly baffled.

I'll give you an example. We had beaten St Johnstone 4-0 at their old ground at Muirton in Perth on the Saturday and before training a day or so later I was taken aside by Neilly Mochan, our trainer, and told that Big Jock would be having a meeting with the players. I didn't think I had anything to worry about because I believed I had actually played quite well against the Saints. Neilly warned, 'Big Jock is going to have a go at you. Don't say anything back. He's going to single you out because your mates know you had a fine game. He's going to wind them up and make certain no-one gets complacent. So, play the game, take in what he says and he'll move on to someone else.' I thought, 'Fair enough if it helps the team's cause.'

What followed surprised even me. Jock did, indeed, start with me. He also ended with me. He ranted on for what seemed an eternity. I was on the receiving end for about fifteen minutes as I slumped deeper and deeper into my seat. Then, after his tirade, he simply said, 'Right, everyone – out on the park, we've got some training to do.' And, with that, he turned on his heel and left the room. There was silence all round until someone piped up, 'Thank Christ we won on Saturday!'

Jock, if the mood took him, could be savage in his criticism of some of his players. He was never slow to make some salient points right in front of your team-mates. We were all adults, but he treated us like children sometimes. There was nothing to do but accept it. I also recall shoving the ball through the legs of my pal Willie O'Neill in training one day. 'That's enough of that,' came the cry from the sideline. I did it again and the next minute I found myself being ordered to stand behind one of the goals and to face away from the pitch. 'I don't want to find you looking round,' said our boss. 'Keep facing the other way.' It was a rather weird punishment, but, as I have said, you just had to take it. There I was, a seasoned professional, with a wife and weans, being treated like some naughty schoolkid.

People often said Big Jock would have been different if he had taken a drink. You might even have thought with his mining background he would have fancied a foaming pint of ale after a day's work down the pit. But I never once saw him take a drop of alcohol. The champagne corks could fly all over our dressing room after an important victory, but Big Jock refused to indulge. I remember talking to him one day when we were travelling to an away game. 'If we win, will you have a drink with us afterwards?' I queried, rather mischievously. Jock thought about it and replied, 'OK, you're on. Just make sure you win.'

We duly went out and got the triumph and on the way home I asked Jock when he was coming out for a drink. Again, he remained silent for a moment before replying, 'Would you think more of me if I went for a drink?'

I answered, 'I couldn't think any more of you than I do just now, boss.' He never went for that drink.

He may not have liked a beer, but he certainly loved sweets. He never knew this, but the players' nickname for him was Sweeties. Mind you, no-one ever called him that when he was within hearing distance. He was forever dipping into his pockets and bringing out some kind of confectionary and popping it into his mouth. He seemed to have an endless supply. Maybe he had shares in Rowntrees!

Jock was a difficult guy to negotiate with when your contract was about to be renewed. Remember, these were the days before the Bosman Ruling. The clubs kept your registration and if you didn't accept the deal on the table that was just tough luck. If they said you were going nowhere, then you were going nowhere. Everything was heavily weighted in the club's favour and Big Jock held all the aces. You would have thought he was dealing with his own money and not Celtic's. He also knew no-one wanted to leave the club. I was Celtic through and through and so were most, if not all, of my team-mates.

We loved the place, the rapport with the supporters and, generally, everything that entailed being a player with Celtic Football Club. Jock was aware of all of this and that was why he was on a winner even before anyone asked for a wage hike. My God, I was the guy who took a pay cut to join Celtic, such was my desperation to get back to Parkhead. However, I still believe Celtic and Jock could have treated the players a bit better on the financial front. No-one was looking for a fortune. We just wanted what we thought we were worth and, naturally enough, we heard about extravagant wages being paid by mediocre English clubs who were hardly close to the stature of Celtic and had nothing like our fan base. All this didn't wash with Jock, though. I thought he might have fought our corner a bit better with the board. He didn't and I think that was wrong.

In those dark, old days the club could offer you new terms and if you refused to sign then they placed you on the absolute minimum for the year. That could be as little as £250 and if you had a family, house and car then you would have to resign yourself to the fact you weren't going to eat for the next twelve months! Clubs would send you a new contract by registered mail with 1 May the cut-off date. I know a few players who waited for that letter to arrive and when it didn't they realised they had been given a free transfer. That's the way it worked back then.

Players, naturally enough, will always inflate their wages and there was talk of Rangers getting £100 per man when I think we were on £65 at the time. I'm not too sure about the discrepancy, but we always earned more because of our bonus structure and Rangers didn't get too many bonuses back then! But you had to be in the squad. If you were injured, suspended or out of form, you dropped back to the absolute basic. That was sore.

I recall a day when Jock came into the dressing room to announce we were going to either Bermuda or the Bahamas to play a local select. It was a wee five-day break in the sunshine and he thought it would freshen us up. One of our players, I think it was Jim Brogan, asked: 'How much are we getting?'

Jock turned round, 'What do you mean?'

The player replied, 'Well, presumably the club are getting something for making the trip, so how much are we getting? What's our cut?'

Jock's jovial mood changed dramatically. He said instantly, 'You're getting nothing – the trip's off!' And that was the end of it. We never got on that plane and I think our place was taken by Chelsea. Lucky sods!

I've already said I don't think Jock should have been allowed to leave Celtic back in 1960. We could all see how revolutionary he was in his methods when he was working with the reserves. He was a football man – he wasn't just going through the motions to pay his mortgage or top up his pension. He continually sought out new ideas, fresh methods, varying tactics. He delved into things in minuscule detail. He was hungry for knowledge and he took in games the length and breadth of the country as he followed his passion. You would hear him talk to Neilly Mochan or Sean Fallon after training. 'There's a player at Cambuslang Rangers I want to see. They've got a game on tonight. I'll just pop over.' His dedication was boundless and he expected the same from his players.

Neilly, by the way, could have been a top-class manager in his own right – I am convinced of that. Jock brought him back from Dundee United where he had finished his playing days and he was a smashing guy to have around. He was brilliant in the dressing room before games. Now I don't know if he was an unconscious comedian or he knew exactly what he was doing, but he could certainly relieve the tension with some of his remarks. He would say something like, 'Get out there and let them do it to us before we do it to them!' Another favourite was, 'People in glasshouses shouldn't throw tomatoes.' Or, 'There are too many Indians and not enough chiefs.' We would start to fall about and he would stand there wondering what he had said that was so funny. Fans must have realised we were confident of getting a victory those days when we would emerge from the tunnel still laughing.

Jock, of course, was forced to hang up his boots in January 1957 after a London specialist told him his ankle would never be repaired to the extent that he could return to a sporting pursuit. He was thirty-four years old at the time. Celtic obviously saw something in Jock and offered him a scouting position. Bob Kelly even afforded him the accolade that he liked his 'influence' around the club and hoped he would learn the managerial side of things from Jimmy McGrory. Kelly, with what would turn out to be a masterly understatement, said:

'We hope that will stand him in good stead for the future.' Stein became manager of the reserve team a few months later and I was in the side that beat Rangers 8-2 over two legs in the final of the Scottish Second XI Cup. We actually won 5-1 at Ibrox to add to our first leg 3-1 success on our own ground. Over 40,000 fans saw both matches.

Even back then, he had a great eye for detail. He changed a lot of small things. When he came back in 1965, for instance, he got rid of our old training gear – and not before time. The stuff we used consisted of heavy woollen jumpers you would more often see being worn by trawlermen and baggy and well-worn shorts with the backside hanging out of them. When you arrived for training these garments were lying in a pile in the middle of the dressing room. I think they were washed about once a year. They were filthy and you were forced to train in them no matter the weather. One day we turned up and there were lightweight modern sweatshirts waiting for us. We rarely, if ever, wore tracksuit bottoms because Jock believed we would run about a bit more in shorts to keep warm if it was cold! Everything was washed regularly, too. Just a wee thing, I suppose, but it underlined that fresh ideas were being put in place at a club that had been stuck in medieval times for too long.

Another change that marked Jock's early days was the removal of the snooker table from the recreation room. We used to meet there before games and have a wee knock-about on the green baize. Jock saw that too many players were standing around with nothing to do while two, or sometimes four, other guys played on the table. Jock introduced table tennis and that meant more of us were involved with the games because they were being played at a ferocious pace. He also reckoned table tennis sharpened up your reflexes. He liked to play, too, but it was always a good idea to let him win! Again, a small point, but it did show everyone that no detail, however minute, would be overlooked in his quest for perfection.

And yet Celtic still allowed this visionary man to quit Parkhead and take over as manager of Dunfermline in March 1960. I know he agonised over his decision to leave Celtic. He was very friendly with a journalist called John Blair, of the *Sunday People*. He confided in John and arranged to meet him in Glasgow Green to talk over Dunfermline's move for him. John later admitted he told Jock to take it – it was too good an opportunity to turn down. Celtic did little to persuade him to stay and that, obviously, was a mistake of monumental proportions. Six days later he managed the Fifers for the first time and, would you believe, they beat Celtic, of all clubs, 3-2 at East End Park! Just over a year later Jock came back to haunt Celtic again when he steered unfancied Dunfermline to an astonishing 2-0 Scottish Cup Final replay triumph at Hampden.

His stock was high and it looked only a matter of time when he would step up from Dunfermline. Would Celtic, looking as though they were going nowhere, make a move? Yes, he did leave East End Park to a team that wore green and white, but it was to be no homecoming to the east end of Glasgow, of course. Instead, he joined Hibs in April 1964. I know the Hibs players were gutted when he agreed, at last, to return to Celtic in January 1965. He kept his word and remained in Edinburgh until March when they got a new boss in Bob Shankly, the brother of Jock's pal Bill, manager of Liverpool. Actually, Celtic almost lost out on Jock because he let it slip to Kelly that he had had an approach from Wolves. Whether or not Jock, who could be as daft as a fox, deliberately imparted that information to activate the Celtic chairman, we'll never find out. But he did drop it into the conversation and, thankfully, Kelly made his move. Not before time.

At first it was mooted that Sean Fallon would act as joint manager with Jock. It had been thought by many that the Irishman had been groomed as the successor to Jimmy McGrory and he did take charge of the team on numerous occasions. But Jock was having absolutely none of that and I mean that as no disrespect to Sean. It was going to be Jock's way or no way. He was the main man and he wasn't going to share the duties 50/50 with anyone.

As everyone is surely aware, Jock liked a gamble. Kelly might have believed he was bluffing. He might have thought Jock couldn't possibly knock back his club. There was an impasse for a few days and Jock wouldn't budge. Eventually, the directors saw sense and a compromise was reached with Sean becoming assistant manager. I recall Jock saying, 'This is what I have always wanted – a return to Celtic. I'm back where I belong.'

I had a fair idea of what to expect when Jock arrived. I knew all about his desire to be successful, his determination to win things at the club. His ruthlessness in pursuit of silverware was legendary. Second was nowhere to this guy. Any player who didn't match up to his expectation levels soon found themselves plying their trade elsewhere. Take Hugh Maxwell, for instance. He had been bought by Jimmy McGrory from Falkirk for £15,000 in November 1964. He was an old-fashioned inside-right with a nice touch, but, to be honest, he was a bit on the frail side. Jock played him twice and, unfortunately for Hugh, Celtic lost both games – 4-2 to Hibs at Parkhead and 5-1 to Dunfermline at East End Park. That was the end of his Celtic career. He was on his bike to St Johnstone for £10,000 in the summer.

Johnny Divers got similar treatment. He was a more than useful inside-right with a lot of skill. He started in the first team in 1957, played over 200 games and scored something in the region of 100 goals. Not bad going at all, but Jock thought otherwise. Johnny has admitted he had a conversation with Jock shortly after his return from Hibs and agreed he may have lost a bit of his enthusiasm. Jock immediately said, 'Then you're no use to me.' Poor Johnny. He played against Rangers in a league match at Ibrox early in the season and missed a good chance near the end with us losing 2-1 and trying desperately to get back into the game. If memory serves correctly, Caesar nodded the ball down into his path and it looked a goal all the way. Johnny swung his boot at it, but the ball bounced awkwardly and he connected with fresh air. The opportunity was gone and the game was lost. Jock, as you will discover later, absolutely abhorred losing to Rangers. He was far from impressed.

It was then, I believe, he had his conversation with Johnny and, there and then, the player could have packed his bags and quit the club. He trained on his own for about three months and was then injured in training when Willie O'Neill accidentally stood on his foot. That was his season wrecked. He knew his time at Celtic was over when he picked up a newspaper and there was the story informing everyone that he was to be given a surprise free transfer. Well, it would have been more of a shock than a surprise, I would think. There must be better ways of discovering you're on your way. However, that was typical of Jock. Personalities meant nothing to him. He wasn't interested in popularity contests. It was all about Celtic and the players he believed could do a job for the club. You might have questioned his methods, but what wasn't up for debate was his success. Johnny, by the way, gave up football altogether shortly afterwards following a spell at Partick Thistle, and John Clark remembers spending part of his £1,500 European Cup bonus on a car from Johnny's showroom in Bearsden!

Of course, there was a warmth about Jock, but if you crossed him you knew you were in serious trouble. He could be vigorously protective of an individual if he believed the situation warranted it. But he could be more than robust in his criticism if he thought it was deserved. I don't think he ever forgave Big Yogi, John Hughes, for missing a wonderful opportunity right at the start of extra time in the 1970 European Cup Final against Feyenoord with the score balanced at 1-1. He and Willie Wallace were sold to Crystal Palace a year later. I know Yogi, in particular, didn't want to go. Jock simply informed him, 'You've no choice – you're going.' Yogi was only twenty-seven at the time and reluctantly accepted it was all over at Celtic. He went to Palace, but clearly his heart wasn't in it. I think he lasted about eighteen months in London and then had a short spell at Sunderland alongside his brother Billy before chucking it. That was a criminal waste of talent. I believe Yogi was so upset at his treatment that he didn't attend Jock's funeral. Sadly, that says it all.

John Fallon, too, was rather hastily removed from Celtic when Jock decided he had to go. Fallon, who had been in goal in Jock's first Scottish Cup triumph over Dunfermline in 1965, was told by a team-mate one afternoon that he was being transferred. This was after training on 27 February 1972. The keeper thought someone was pulling his leg. You can imagine his surprise, though, when he got home to Blantyre to find the boss sitting in his living room.

'You're going to Motherwell,' he was informed.

'No, I'm not,' replied Fallon.

'You're going and that's the end of it.' Fallon, after almost fourteen years at the club, left two days later.

You might have thought Fallon would have been happy to 'escape' from Big Jock. Our gaffer had a great distrust of goal-keepers – I honestly don't think he liked them! It was FOOTball we were playing. Why were guys allowed to use their hands? I'm sure Jock would have played without a keeper if he thought he could have got away with it. I really mean that. Possibly he had a bad experience with goalies during his playing career. He certainly bought enough of them in his thirteen years at the club. I lost count of the number of keepers who came and went in those years. Jock could make up his mind in an instant about an outfield player, but he definitely swithered over goalkeepers. It was rather ironic that the No.1 who was his most consistent by far was Ronnie Simpson, who, of course, was transferred to Celtic by Jock when he was manager of Hibs.

Jock made some fairly strange decisions when it came to picking his keepers. I recall he played three different goalies in three consecutive games back in September 1965. He fielded Fallon in an 8-1 League Cup quarter-final win over Raith Rovers and a week later an Irishman called Jack Kennedy played in the second leg which we won 4-0. Three days after that Ronnie was between the sticks in an emphatic 7-1 triumph over Aberdeen. Folk often said if Jock had an Achilles heel it was over his last line of defence and they may have something there. By the way, that bloke Kennedy never played in the first team again. He is the only goalkeeper in Celtic's history who never lost a goal. What a claim to fame!

At least he had a bit more luck than a certain Dick Madden who made his debut in a league game against Kilmarnock at Rugby Park in March 1963. I was with Birmingham City at the time and I gulped when I saw the result in my local newspaper. It read: Kilmarnock 6, Celtic 0. I don't know if the keeper was to blame, but he, like Kennedy, never played again. It wasn't all bad news for Madden though, because his family won the football pools that week. I heard that one of his teammates said to him, 'Why don't you buy a pub, Dick? You could call it the Lets Six Inn!' Footballers can be so cruel.

Big Jock used to take great pleasure in putting his keepers through the mangle in training. I recall a training session when we were down at Largs preparing for our 1965 Scottish Cup Final. Fallon was the man in possession and training pre-Jock was a fairly gentle workout for the keepers. There could be a lot of larking about, but Fallon's face was a picture when Jock grabbed one of these huge nets filled with balls and said to him, 'Right, let's you and I go out for some practice.' And he put the keeper through all sorts of punishment as he belted balls at him from all angles for over an hour. Fallon probably saw as much action in that session as he had all season playing in the first team.

My old midfield mate Chopper – Bobby Murdoch – didn't have too much of a say in the matter, either, when the end came for him at the club. Jack Charlton, then the Middlesbrough manager, phoned Jock to ask if he knew of any middle of the park players who might do a job for his club. He must have thought our boss was joking when he replied, 'Bobby Murdoch's your man. He'll do you a turn.'

The Boro gaffer could hardly believe his ears. Jock was prepared to let him go for nothing. Chopper was only twenty-nine at the time and still had a lot of football left in him. He had played 484 games for the club and scored 105 goals. But Jock was starting to change the system at Celtic. He brought in players such as Stevie Murray, from Aberdeen. He had already signed Tommy Callaghan, from Dunfermline, a few years earlier. Murray performed on the right, in Chopper's position, and Callaghan played on the left, in my position. Both were entirely different types of players to Chopper and me. We preferred to pass the ball around, picking out team-mates from all sorts of ranges. Murray and Callaghan were runners with the ball. Jock had been toying with the idea of freshening things up and changes were in the wind.

Chopper, like so many before him, didn't want to move. Celtic was his club and he must have thought he would bring down the curtain on a splendid career in the green-and-white hoops. Jock didn't see it that way and Chopper was off to Boro where, I'm delighted to say, he had a wonderful career and helped bring through a young Scottish midfielder who listened and learned from my former colleague. That youngster was Graeme Souness. Chopper also had a spell as manager of the club when Charlton moved on, but you always knew he hankered at 'getting back up the road', as he put it.

Davie Hay, still a friend to this day, recalls being told by Jock that it was his time to go after he returned from a very successful World Cup Finals with Scotland in West Germany in 1974. Davie played really well in our games against Brazil (0-0), Yugoslavia (1-1) and Zaire (2-0). I remember he had gone on strike for better pay conditions earlier that season. I think he was out for a fortnight and Jock tried to sell him to Spurs around that time. Davie was having none of it and said he had no intention of going. Now Davie Hay is not a greedy guy, I can tell you that. He wanted what he was worth, but Celtic, back then, weren't interested. Davie told me he returned from the World Cup Finals and was ready to settle his differences with the club.

He admitted he had made that perfectly clear. He would accept what was on the table and get on with playing for Celtic. However, Chelsea had been alerted by his superior performances in West Germany and they had offered £250,000, a lot of money back then, for the versatile Hay. Celtic took it and Davie was told to report to Parkhead. The offices were closed, but Jock was waiting for him in his car at the front door. Davie was convinced Jock wanted to try to persuade him not to go. They sat in Jock's Mercedes in the car park and Davie, one of the most honest blokes you are ever likely to meet, was told he was on his way this time.

He admitted he had been hurt that they were willing to let him leave – just as I was all those years ago when Birmingham City came on the scene. Davie did, indeed, go to Chelsea where I believe his wage packet soared from £65 per week to £210. Wee Louie – Lou Macari – had gone to Manchester United the previous year for £200,000. Both would be followed by Kenny Dalglish, who went to Liverpool in 1977 for a then-British-record fee of £440,000. George Connelly, a genius with the ball, was lost to the game altogether as he quit with off-field problems. I think he was twenty-six years old at the time. That was a travesty. But what a team Celtic could have had around that time if they had spent the money to keep these players at the club. They might even have won another European Cup or two. That wouldn't have been out of the question with those guys around.

If Jock was ever hurt by having to release a player then he hid it well. Maybe he did these things in private, but there was never a public show of emotion. Once a player had served his purpose, it was time to move on to the next stage. Jock wasn't slow to let you know there were other players out there who could come in and do a job in your position.

Back in the Sixties, our reserve team was known as the Quality Street Gang. They had fabulous youngsters such as Kenny, Davie, Louie and George as well as Danny McGrain, Vic Davidson and John Gorman. They were all beginning to emerge and Jock liked to take them down to Seamill every now and again before a big European game to give them a taste of what it was like to be part of the first team squad. It also acted as a reminder that these guys would soon be knocking on the door and wanting your place in the team. It kept us all on our toes, believe me. A hint of complacency and you were out and they were in.

Jock always insisted, 'A manager is as happy as his unhappiest player.' So, Jock simply eliminated his unhappiest players. Anyone stirring it up would find his P45 coming towards him at the speed of light. Another of Jock's saying was 'Play to your strengths and disguise your weaknesses.' He would always cut to the chase in his observations. 'Football is nothing without fans' was another of his favourite sayings.

He was a great man for kidology, too. When the referee was in the dressing room before the match checking your boots and so on, Jock would make sure he heard him say, 'This is Mr Smith and he has got a tough enough job today, so don't make it any more difficult. Be on your best behaviour throughout.' The match official would listen to all this, but as soon as he went out through the door, Jock would say, 'Right, get stuck in. Let's make sure that we win every 50/50 ball.' He never advocated kicking anyone, but he let you know there had to be no shirking when it came to tackling. Anyone ducking out of a challenge would be told in no uncertain fashion that it was totally unacceptable. The player would, in all probability, find himself sitting in the stand the following week, too.

Sometimes Jock would have a word in your ear as we were getting ready to go down the tunnel. 'Bertie,' he would say, 'that No.8 of theirs isn't a bad player, but let's see how brave he is. Find out if he can take a tackle. Let him know you are there. OK?' Message received and understood.

It was a far cry from my early days at the club when the directors frowned on the physical aspects of football. Jock changed so much. Even in training we were more aware of what the game was really all about. 'Fail to prepare then prepare to fail' was another motto. Before Jock took training it was just a shambles. It was all about lapping the park. We rarely saw a ball and that can't be right. We would run round the pitch for about two hours and it was absolute tedium. We were bored witless and I never ever met a player who enjoyed running around endlessly. Put all those miles together and I've probably lapped the world about three times! Jock transformed that aspect so much that we actually started to enjoy training.

For a start, we got balls to work with. Believe it or not, that was innovative. Pre-Stein we might have got one ball thrown into our midst at the end of our running sessions. There would be about forty players present and we had to make do with one ball. Sometimes, believe it or not, it was a medicine ball that we got to play with. Have you ever tried to kick a medicine ball? Take my word for it, don't bother. There are other ways of breaking your foot!

Jock would painstakingly go through all sorts of routines. Corner-kicks, free-kicks, defensive formations, attacking options. He would go over and over it until he was certain you knew exactly and precisely what was expected of you. He was meticulous in everything he did. Look at our winning goal in the European Cup Final, for instance. People may have thought it was a bit of a fluke as Chopper hammered a ball across goal and Stevie Chalmers deflected it into the net. That goal came straight from the training ground at Barrowfield.

The players would be assembled in groups with Chopper, Cairney, Jinky and others out on the right thumping balls across the six-yard line. Stevie, Wispy, Lemon and Jose were all expected to knock the balls into the net. Then it would be the turn of myself, TG and Big Yogi to wallop over crosses from the left. Again the strikers would be asked to convert them into goals. This went on every day in training. I felt sorry for opposing goalkeepers back then if they spilled a shot. Suddenly, there would be about four of our frontmen right in on top of them, looking for the rebound. I lost count of the number of goals we scored like that. They might not have been too spectacular, but they were effective.

Jock was a good psychologist, too. He knew how to coax you to get the absolute best out of you. He knew which players would respond to different types of cajoling. 'What are you doing in the reserves?' he would say. 'You should be in the first team. Sort yourself out.' He could make you feel ten feet tall, but he could cut the feet from you whenever you did something to displease him.

Down at Seamill, as we prepared for important games, he would get the tactics board out and go through the opposition. Every now and again he would ask, 'Any questions?' A player, usually me, would pipe up and say something. Then he would just ignore you and wave that big left paw at you. 'I'm the manager and we'll do it my way.' That was so typical of the man.

He rarely showed any favouritism, but we all knew he really liked Caesar, whom he had signed for the club as a youngster from Blantyre Vics, his own former Junior team. But our captain could get a dressing-down as well as anyone else if it was perceived he had stepped out of line. I think he was a big fan of Jinky, too. Mind you, that didn't stop him from almost punching him good-looking one day.

Jinky was angry at being substituted in a league game against Dundee United at Parkhead one afternoon. As he raced off the pitch he threw his jersey towards the Celtic dug-out. Not the brightest thing our wee winger had ever done! Jock was fizzing. He leapt to his feet and chased after Jinky. The Wee Man told me later, 'I was angry and frustrated. I just didn't think when I chucked my shirt onto the track. But I almost fainted when I ran up the tunnel and heard this roar behind me, "Johnstone – I want a word with you!" I looked over my shoulder and there was Big Jock moving faster than he ever did as a player.

'I thought he was going to do me. What was I going to do? I could run into the dressing room and try to hide. Or I could just keep running, straight out the main doors and head for Parkhead Cross!' Could you imagine that? A world-class foot-baller racing through the streets of Glasgow just in his football shorts, socks and boots? With Jock Stein in hot pursuit! Thankfully, Jinky managed to get the door closed and locked by the time Jock was hammering on it. Jinky told me, 'What was I to do? So I said, "I'll let you in if you promise not to hit me." Then there was silence and then, remarkably, the sound of laughter. I was relieved when I heard that. The boss obviously saw the funny side at that moment.' Afterwards, Jock did get round to giving him a verbal blast and also fined him. Jinky accepted the punishment. It could have been much worse, after all. No Celtic player threw their shirt into the dug-out ever again. Not surprising, really.

You know, I could have been manager of Aberdeen back in the Seventies, but for the intervention of Big Jock. I was perfectly happy at Partick Thistle, of course, but the Dons job would have interested me. Dundee also wanted me to become their gaffer after they parted company with Davie White, who, by the way, was the left-half at Clyde when they refused to be lured into enemy territory the day Jock thought it would be a good idea to demolish the Shawfield dressing room with my head. I did have a chat with Dundee chairman Ian Gellatly, but I turned him down to remain at Firhill. I told him their captain, a certain Tommy Gemmell, had all the makings of a good manager and I'm happy to say he took my advice and appointed TG as White's successor. What a friend gets is no loss, eh?

But back in 1975 there was a chance of going to Pittodrie, with the Dons looking for someone to take over from Ally MacLeod who had replaced Willie Ormond in the Scottish international post. The Aberdeen chairman, Dick Donald, approached Jock to seek his advice. This happened quite a lot. Jock had a massive influence and people listened to him. Now I don't know what went on in that private conversation between Jock and Dick, but I do know that Aberdeen dropped their interest in me. For whatever reason, Jock didn't give me his recommendation. I'll never know why.

Jock actually telephoned me to tell me what he had done. I was extremely hurt that he didn't recommend me but he insisted he was just being professional and honest. Actually, he also realised that I would have got to know all about his chat with Dick Donald. You don't keep things like that quiet for too long on soccer's grapevine. So, what had I done to be treated in such a manner after all the service I had given Jock and Celtic? Nothing, as far as I was concerned. The Dons job, of course, went to Caesar who had only been in management a matter of months with Clyde. I thanked Jock for the telephone call and we never mentioned it again. I wonder how my managerial career would have panned out if I had gone to Pittodrie. It's all conjecture now. Billy wasn't with the Dons too long, either, as he replaced Jock as Celtic boss in 1978. Now that was a job in which I would very definitely have been interested!

Jock may have been a fairly dour, no-nonsense, defensive-minded centre-half, but, conversely, he liked his football played with flair and adventure. He was always on at the players to remember to win while also entertaining the crowd. 'Let's get out there and bring those fans some enjoyment,' he would say as you prepared for a game. 'Entertain – don't forget. These guys have worked hard all week and they want to be entertained. They've been down mines, they've been up scaffolding, they've been repairing this, that and the next thing. Entertain them – you all have the ability to do that. So, let's give them a right good time. They've been looking forward all week to seeing their team in action on a Saturday. Don't let them down.' And, as the players trooped out of the dressing room, you would hear the words one last time: 'Let's entertain these guys.'

One victory that was always designed to put a massive smile on Jock's face was a win over Rangers. Publicly, he would tell everyone it was just another game. Privately, he thoroughly enjoyed putting one over on our oldest rivals. I would go as far as to say Jock detested Rangers. As I have said earlier, you could still get a rollicking off the boss even after a triumph. However, that never happened if we had beaten the men from Ibrox. It didn't matter how we achieved it. We might have ground out a victory and possibly not played at our best. We might even have been extremely fortunate. That didn't matter to Jock. The only thing that was on his mind was a victory. How he loved to beat them. It was so important to him. In fact, you could say he was obsessed about winning these games and he never let you forget how important they were to him. If you wanted to save your ears from receiving a right bashing all you had to do was beat Rangers. That was all.

Jock always wanted to know what was happening over at Ibrox. He was as surprised as anyone when they sacked Scot Symon and replaced him with the aforementioned Davie White in 1967. White was just thirty-four years old and had only been manager of Clyde for a short while. The appointment smacked of panic and Jock sensed it. He was a bit unhappy as the press talked up the tactical ability of White and Jock, clearly, wasn't quite in total agreement with any of that. As ever, he would show respect and every courtesy to a fellow sportsman, but, deep inside, we all realised he wanted Rangers' new boss to discover real pressure. Anything he had encountered at Shawfield would be infinitesimal compared to what was waiting for him at Ibrox. Especially in Old Firm confrontations.

The first time Jock pitted his wits against his latest Old Firm rival he didn't just want to dent White's credibility with the Rangers support – he wanted to obliterate it. It was 2 January 1968 at Celtic Park and Jock was looking forward to the match with even more than his usual enthusiasm for these encounters. I've covered this particular game in another chapter, so let's just say it didn't quite go according to plan after two terrible goalkeeping blunders from Fallon allowed Rangers to snatch a 2-2 draw. Jock saw it as an ideal opportunity lost. But there would be a next time. And that was the 1969 Scottish Cup Final when Rangers were well and truly put in their place with us running out 4-0 victors. Not only had Rangers been destroyed, but so, too, was the reputation of White who could never get to grips with his wily opposite number. Six months after that devastating defeat, White was sacked and replaced by Willie Waddell. And the mind games started all over again.

Here's something that may surprise you – Jock wasn't a bad singer. He liked to get up, grab the microphone and batter out some Sinatra songs to startled guests at some of the many functions we used to attend. The gruffness was gone as he belted out some numbers and let his hair down. But, back at the park the following day, it was business as usual. Looking back, I can now heave a sigh of relief and give thanks that there wasn't such a thing as karaoke around then. We would never have got Big Jock off the stage!

I had a few run-ins with Jock, of course. I recall one day storming out of Celtic Park after a particularly bad fall-out between us. I had been a substitute on the Saturday when Celtic drew 3-3 with Partick Thistle during a Scottish Cup tie at Firhill in January 1969. I didn't get on that afternoon, but I thought there might be a chance of getting the nod in the replay. Not only was I not in the first team, I wasn't even on the bench. I had been ditched without kicking a ball. I was more than just a wee bit incensed as well as puzzled.

I went to see him in his office. As a seasoned pro, I thought I deserved better treatment than that and I told him so. He could have pulled me aside at training and told me what he was going to do. I would still have been bewildered, but at least it would have softened the blow. But he never uttered a word – not one. Then when the team sheet went up there was no sign of my name. I couldn't bite my tongue on this occasion. I was angry. After I told him how unhappy I was at his selection process, I just got out of his room before he could even say a word. I went straight out of the ground, jumped into a taxi and went to a restaurant in Glasgow city centre. Stevie Chalmers – there was only one outfield substitute in those days – took my place as twelfth man and Celtic didn't seem to miss me as they won 8-1!

Things were more than a little strained after that. If only he had taken the time to explain his actions. Look, I've fallen out with many players while being a boss at Partick Thistle, twice, Hibs, Dumbarton and Hamilton. No-one likes to be dropped and everyone likes to play. Big Jock realised how much it meant to me to be out there with the rest of the lads doing my best for the club. I loved playing the game and he knew it. I would even turn out for the reserves if it meant getting a kick at the ball. So, I admit I was furious that evening and it was better for all concerned that I removed myself from the immediate vicinity. But I still ask myself why he didn't take the time to let me know I wouldn't be involved. There were four days in between the first game and the replay and he had lots of opportunities and numerous occasions to tell me the news.

Jock could be like that sometimes. He could make you look more than a wee bit silly in front of your team-mates and he certainly ruled with an iron fist. I could accept all that, but I repeat he knew only too well how much actually playing meant to me. He knew he would hurt me by leaving me out completely without a word of warning or explanation. I missed the next two Cup ties that season, wins over Clyde and St Johnstone, but, strangely enough, I came back for the 4-1 semi-final success over Morton and I kept my place for the final – the famous 4-0 drubbing of Rangers. Jock was all smiles after that one.

I wasn't at Celtic when he had his near-fatal car crash on the A74 in July 1975 when he was returning from Manchester Airport after a family holiday in Minorca and his Mercedes was in a head-on collision with a car coming directly towards him on the wrong side of the motorway. He was ordered to take a year out, but friends at the park told me he was there shortly afterwards although it was clear that Sean was in charge of the team on matchdays. Thankfully, he made a full recovery, but those close to him said he was never quite the same again. Possibly so, as he now had new priorities, and who could blame him?

I was watching Scotland's World Cup qualifier against Wales in Cardiff on 10 September 1985 on television in my pub, the Buccaneer in Hamilton, when he collapsed and died shortly after the game. I was numb. The footage only showed the viewers that there was some commotion around about the dugout area before the programme ended. I wasn't sure what on earth was going on. Telephone calls were made all over the place. Then the news bulletin came on and told us Big Jock had passed away. I felt as though I had lost a true friend, despite all our ups and downs. Big hard guys in the pub that night just broke down in tears. And yes, I cried too. I had to close early that evening and the blokes in the bar just accepted it. It was a very emotional evening for us all. Jock's funeral at Linn Crematorium a few days later was one of the saddest days of my life. Football had lost a legend.

As I have pointed out, Jock could be complicated on occasion, but how can you ever doubt that his methods, controversial or

Bertie Auld's schooldays. Can you spot me in this Southbank Primary School class photograph? I'm the cheeky chappie third from the left in the second back row.

Happy Families. A night-out with my wife Liz and mum Peggy and dad Joe who, as ever, has the inevitable cigarette in his hand.

Wedding day bliss. Liz and I tie the knot at Birmingham's St. Andrews Church on January 28, 1963.

A dog's life. Liz, with pet poodle in pole position, and I pose for the cameraman during my days at Birmingham.

Christmas joy. Daughter Susan and son Robert are all smiles in the Auld household on yet another special day for us all.

Old Firm action. Here I am about to challenge Rangers goalkeeper George Niven with Ibrox captain Bobby Shearer, a fierce opponent, looking on.

Birmingham's 1961 line-up. It's just as well this team group photograph is in black and white because that's me wearing blue second from the left in the second row. The dapper gent in the middle of the row is Gil Merrick, who signed me from Celtic.

Happy homecoming. Celtic manager Jimmy McGrory looks on as I complete the signing form to take me back to Paradise in 1965.

Me and my guiding light. That's my dad Joe in the background watching over me as he always did – on and off the pitch.

Dream come true. It's my boy Robert in a Celtic strip as we play at home while Susan joins in. Two Robert Aulds playing in front of those wonderful supporters on matchday at Parkhead would have been quite remarkable. Sadly, it never happened. It's a lovely thought, though.

In the net. This is one of my favourite goals as I sit alongside the ball after scoring the equaliser against Dunfermline in the 1965 Scottish Cup Final. I'm about to be congratulated by Stevie Chalmers while rivals Jim Herriot, the goalkeeper, and right-back Willie Callaghan don't quite share my joy. It got even better for me as I netted another and we won 3-2.

Joy unconfined. I join Bobby Lennox and John Hughes to congratulate Billy McNeill on his winner against Dunfermline – a landmark triumph for Celtic.

What a treble. My good chum Bobby Lennox and me with the Scottish Cup after the 1965 victory. I'm convinced that win sparked off Celtic's glorious run.

The race is on. Tommy Gemmell is about to go overlapping down the left as we break into attack. Big TG was easily one of the best left-backs in the world in his heyday.

No slacking. I go through a training routine with my Celtic team-mates under the watchful gaze of manager supreme Jock Stein. That's Joe McBride and John Hughes behind me.

On the attack. I put the pressure on grounded Dundee goalkeeper Ally Donaldson with Joe McBride backing me up. Funnily enough, Ally was a keeper at Hibs when I was boss there.

Jumping for joy. John Hughes, Stevie Chalmers and Charlie Gallagher take to the air, but I decide to sit it out with Bobby Lennox, Jimmy Johnstone and Willie Wallace.

I won three Scottish international caps in my Celtic career first time around. Here I am with some friends, Billy McNeill, Mike Jackson, John Colrain, Paddy Crerand and Alex Harley.

Job done. I'm congratulated by trainer Neilly Mochan as we draw 0-0 with Dukla Prague to reach the 1967 European Cup Final. Stevie Chalmers, John Clark, Tommy Gemmell and Jimmy Johnstone celebrate too, along with assistant boss Sean Fallon and physiotherapist Bob Rooney. Another fantastic day.

Lisbon here we come. Jock Stein and I can't contain our joy at getting through to play Inter Milan in the Portuguese capital. A memorable day was around the corner.

otherwise, brought dividends? Just take a quick look at his trophy haul – ten league championships, nine Scottish Cups – one with Dunfermline – six League Cups. Oh, and a little matter of the European Cup. Jock Stein gave Celtic back their belief.

Above everything, he taught us what it was like to be a winner. I hope he would accept that as an appropriate epitaph.

8

THE AULD FIRM

Nitro often merged with glycerine when Celtic met Rangers. Old Firm games weren't always classics, but I believe you could say without fear of contradiction that they were most certainly always confrontational. They could be enjoyable; they could be exasperating. And, yes, they could be explosive.

I never needed any extra motivation to go out and give my very best when I was playing against anyone. Just pulling that green-and-white hooped shirt over my head was enough to get me fired up and raring to go. I always remember signing for the club first time around and Jimmy McGrory insisting, 'You must be able to fill that jersey, Bertie.' Even as a seventeen-year-old I knew exactly what he meant. However, there was always something extremely energising when a match against Rangers was coming up.

I have heard all about the other derby occasions such as the Merseyside, Manchester, Milan and Madrid encounters. Of course, I've also been involved in the Midlands version. There are games throughout the world that people insist is THE derby. With the greatest of respect, forget those observations. I don't think for one fleeting second any other match on this planet could hold a candle to the Old Firm games. You've got to be involved in them to appreciate what these contests are all about. Passions from the fans would rocket through the stratosphere and some of these tussles should have carried a Government Health Warning such was the ferocity at which they were played. Celtic supporters would be coming up to you days before the game and imploring, 'Beat them for us, Bertie.' Or 'Don't let us down, please.' And so it went on. No pressure there, then.

I loved that rivalry. I thrived on these head-on collisions where no quarter was asked or given and the fans on both sides conjured up their own special – if that's the right word – atmosphere. Bonhomie deserted Glasgow when these games took place. Instead, it was replaced by bedlam. If you were not prepared mentally or physically for these ninety minutes of combat they would overwhelm you. Both sets of supporters gave it pelters and you could hear the racket that was being generated down in the dressing rooms as you prepared for the game.

You came out the tunnel and it never ceased to astonish me what I was about to encounter. In those days the games were played with the Celtic supporters in one half of the ground and their Rangers counterparts in the other half. It was a 50/50 split. That's changed nowadays, of course, with so many ticket holders at both clubs. The away fans are herded into a section behind a goal and, of course, they are heavily outnumbered in the chanting stakes. You knew you were going to get stick when you played in these confrontations. There seemed to be an ignorance among a fair percentage of the Rangers support who didn't seem to realise that my parents, Peggy and Joe, had actually been married a few years before Robert Auld Esq. debuted on this planet. And I've got the birth certificate to prove it. Did I find it offensive? If they were screaming abuse at me at least they were leaving some other player alone. Embarrassed? I'm a Glaswegian – you couldn't give me a red face with a blowtorch!

You got the distinct impression that Old Firm fans just lived for these games. To some, it didn't matter that their club didn't win any silverware – just so long as they beat their illustrious rivals when we locked horns. The vitriol bounced around the ground and created a din from start to finish. I'm fairly sure that a huge percentage of those fans parked their brains outside the ground before the game and picked them up afterwards. But forget all the bigotry and the like that is associated with these clashes. Believe me, both sets of players, ourselves as well as the Rangers lads, didn't get involved in any of that. We both wanted to win. It was as simple as that. If you were an over-sensitive wee soul then Glasgow on derby day was not the place for you. The faint of heart were advised they would be far better off staying indoors when these games loomed on the horizon.

Obviously, I've got some fabulous memories of these games, including my debut first time around against the Ibrox outfit in a Glasgow Cup tie in 1957. I was playing at outside-left and was up against the legendary Geordie Young. He really was an icon, captain of club and country, and he was a monster of a man. But he played me fairly that evening, I have to say that, and, if memory serves correctly, we lost 1-0. For me, though, it was such an extraordinary occasion. The first of many I'm glad to say.

I recall another Glasgow Cup tie at Ibrox in 1966 when I wished a black hole would open up and I could throw myself into it. I was ashamed of my performance that night which was rather strange because Celtic won 4-0! We did well as a team and Lemon – Bobby Lennox – netted a fabulous hat-trick with skipper Billy McNeill getting the opener. But I wasn't satisfied with my display on a personal level. It was just ninety minutes when I could do little right and I was growing increasingly frustrated with myself as passes went astray all over the place. I was playing like I had just been introduced to a football for the very first time a few minutes before the kick-off.

We went into that game absolutely determined to beat Rangers. In fact, we wanted to hammer them, to rub their noses in it. We had played our old foes in the Scottish Cup Final only a couple of months beforehand and had somehow contrived to lose 1-0 in the replay after having the bulk of the play and possession over the two games. Our name wasn't on the Cup that year. I believe Rangers had one shot at goal in the entire three hours of the two encounters. It was from their Danish right-back Kai Johansen and his 25-yard effort simply flew past a startled Ronnie Simpson. There were only about fifteen minutes or so to go at Hampden and we were stunned, to put it mildly, that we were losing 1-0. Big Jock later blamed Yogi – our outside-left John Hughes – for not tracking back and picking up Johansen. That was a wee bit harsh because we shouldn't even having been playing that night – we should have finished the job in the first game that ended goalless. Caesar came closest to scoring in the Saturday clash when he hit the crossbar with a header. I missed that game, but I returned instead of Charlie Gallagher for the second match.

So, as well as everything else, we had revenge on our mind in that Glasgow Cup tie at Ibrox. It didn't matter in which competition we were playing – and no-one could claim the Glasgow Cup was the most glamorous tournament – we were hell-bent on making our rivals pay big-style for stealing the

Scottish Cup. Caesar got the opener with a shot from close range after Rangers failed to clear a corner-kick and then Lemon took over with a tremendous hat-trick. So, our supporters were delirious at seeing the Rangers keeper Billy Ritchie pick the ball out of his net four times while Faither, in our goal, could have taken out a deckchair and read a good book such was the inactivity around our penalty area.

I still wasn't satisfied, though. I did make one lung-bursting run that took away a couple of defenders and allowed Lemon to score one of his three goals. Big Jock always possessed the ability to surprise you with his observations and he made a fuss of that run from me. 'Excellent work there, Bertie,' he said. Maybe he knew I wasn't happy at my overall performance and was just geeing me up. Mind you, he could put you down, too. If you were caught swaggering around believing you had just put in a world-beating display, he was there to remind you of the things that hadn't worked out. No-one was going to get big-headed with that bloke around.

Ibrox was the setting for another game where I came off the pitch a bit demoralised. It was back in the early Sixties and we lost 2-1. It wasn't the defeat that got to me, though, it was the fact I had been involved in a sickening collision with their left-back Davie Provan that saw him carried off with a broken leg. I was horrified when I realised the Rangers defender was so badly injured. To this day TG – Tommy Gemmell – insists he could hear the awful crack as Provan's leg gave way. And he was on the other side of the pitch, too.

There are always a lot of wild stories and insinuations when a player is seriously injured and, with the Old Firm, there are always added ingredients. You are on the receiving end of some outrageous claims and, naturally enough, some of the Ibrox support believed I had 'done' their player. Absolute nonsense. I had switched over to the right for a brief spell as Chopper – Bobby Murdoch – moved to the left. We did that every now and again just to freshen things up and give the opposition something else to think about. I remember chasing a ball down the right flank at the Celtic end of the ground that afternoon. I was very much aware that Provan was coming across to tackle me. I got there a fraction before him to send over a right-foot cross. Just as I delivered the ball, the Rangers player's outstretched left leg appeared on the scene. I couldn't stop my momentum and, equally, he couldn't pull out of the tackle. There was a crunch as my boot made contact with his leg and he went down. I knew immediately it was a bad one. I felt sick, but it was a complete accident. Later, in another Old Firm derby, Rangers skipper John Greig broke Bobby Lennox's leg and, as I said earlier, Celtic fans were far from convinced it was purely accidental. Again, that wasn't fair on Greigy. Lemon was the first to absolve the Rangers player of all blame.

I should say here that Davie Provan was a player for whom I had massive respect. I saw him play against Jinky on loads of occasions and I don't think he ever kicked our winger. He might have been given the runaround, and I hope he doesn't mind me saying that, but he never stooped to underhand means to stop Jinky. It must have been frustrating facing the Wee Man when he was at his tantalising best. Being taken apart in front of thousands watching on cannot be too pleasant. But Davie never lost the rag and never tried to boot our player. You could not say that about too many left-backs Jinky came up against back then. In fact, I rated the Rangers lad so highly as a person as well as a professional that I gave him a job on our back-room staff when I was manager of Partick Thistle. And, just to underline how well we still get on, Davie was a guest among the Lisbon Lions at my surprise seventieth birthday bash at the Burnside Hotel in Rutherglen in March 2008.

He reminded me that night of the story of how he reckons he saved Jinky's life! Some nutcase managed to get onto the pitch at Ibrox and made a beeline for our player. Davie is convinced the yob was carrying some sort of object in his hand. You could be certain he wasn't about to make a presentation to Jinky to congratulate him on another fine performance. However, as he raced past the Rangers player, Big Davie did a quick bit of thinking and grabbed the would-be assailant. He wrestled him to the ground and the police eventually frog-marched the intruder off the field and up the tunnel. Well done, Davie!

I've got loads of happy memories too, of course. Back on a gloriously sunny evening in August 1967 we faced our old foes in a League Cup tie. We knew a victory would put us through and a defeat would knock us out of the tournament that we had won the previous year when a goal from Lemon gave us a 1-0 triumph over Rangers in the final at Hampden. I'll talk about that game in a moment. We were smack in trouble, though, as Rangers took the lead on our ground and were then awarded a penalty kick deep into the second half.

Something remarkable happened after that and it gave us all the wake-up call we urgently needed. Kai Johansen stepped up to take the kick and thumped it high past Faither. But the ball crashed against the underside of the crossbar, bounced down and a posse of Rangers players raced into the box to get to the rebound. Johansen was first on the scene and got his head to the bouncing ball. I'm sure there were a couple of other Rangers players in the vicinity who also wanted to finish off the job. The referee immediately awarded Celtic a free-kick because Johansen had two consecutive touches of the ball without the opposition getting a kick. Every Celtic player took a deep breath. We knew we had been let out of jail.

Having been given a second chance, we grabbed it. Willie Wallace levelled after their goalkeeper Erik Sorensen failed to clear a corner-kick and, in rapid succession, Chopper put us 2-1 ahead and Lemon finished it with the third. The Rangers players looked aghast and who could blame them? They were twelve minutes away from a 2-0 victory and then, in a whirl-wind spell, we had completely turned it around and finished 3-1 winners. I'm glad to say we went on to beat Dundee 5-3 in the final to retain the trophy.

A year before there was another occasion when Rangers didn't know what hit them and were two goals down inside the first three minutes. These games were normally quite tight as the opposition weighed each other up in the opening spell – just like two boxers in the first round. On this occasion, though, I scored in the first minute and Chopper flighted in a gorgeous second from the edge of the box. I had a good laugh when I scored and my old mate Joe McBride – Jose to his friends – won't thank me for this recollection. Wee Jinky fired over an inviting cross from the right and it looked as though Jose was certain to score. He lashed at it and got a fair chunk of fresh air. The ball carried through to me and I planted it behind Billy Ritchie. Now Jose didn't know whether to congratulate me or burst into tears. He is one of the biggest Celtic fans you are ever likely to meet, but, and I believe I am right here, I don't think he ever scored a goal for us against our Old Firm rivals. Yet the guy was so prolific against just about every other team in the league. He racked up thirty-five goals in 1966 before sustaining a horrendous knee injury against Aberdeen at Pittodrie on Christmas Eve. That was the end of the season for this genuinely lovely bloke yet he still finished as the top goalscorer in the country.

Jose didn't even get on the scoresheet in the 3 January game in 1966 when Celtic beat Rangers 5-1. Stevie Chalmers snatched a hat-trick with Chopper and Gallagher adding two more. The extraordinary thing about this match was that our Ibrox pals had led 1-0 at half-time after a ninety-second goal from Davy Wilson. Talking about Gallagher, I must say he was a very clever and cultured player, but Big Jock didn't believe we could play in the same formation. That was more than a little strange because Charlie and I played in the 1965 Scottish Cup Final success over Dunfermline and combined to score our first goal. Jock stuck to his guns, though, and, therefore, we rarely teamed up in midfield. Charlie, of course, could have gone elsewhere and been guaranteed first team football, but he loved Celtic so much he decided to stay and hope he would get his opportunity. When he was called up, I can tell you he never let the team down. Not once.

Games against Rangers never passed without incident, take it from me. I recall getting a telling-off from the Celtic management after a daft wee incident against Rangers. Their big defender Harold Davis scored an own goal in a Glasgow Cup tie at Parkhead in 1960 and I couldn't prevent myself from ruffling his hair as I raced past him. It was meant to be playful, but Davis, who was built like a heavyweight boxer, didn't find it amusing. I must have been on the brave pills to have done such a thing because Davis never took any prisoners when he was out on the pitch. I think he had been decorated in the war, too. As I ran back up the park I looked over my shoulder and there was the Rangers defender, red-faced with steam coming out his nostrils, chasing after me. I didn't realise I could run so fast. Thankfully, he didn't catch me and simmered down shortly afterwards. My Celtic bosses didn't see the humour in the incident, either. 'That is not the Celtic way,' I was told. 'That is not the way we expect our players to behave.' Ach, I was only having a laugh.

Actually, the same thing happened in reverse in a Scottish Cup tie at Parkhead in February 1970. This time Cairney, Jim Craig, put the ball behind Evan Williams to net for Rangers and Willie Johnston patted our disconsolate right-back on the head. Cairney, thankfully for the Ibrox forward, didn't possess a short fuse on his temperament and at least didn't race after him all the way to the halfway line. It didn't matter in the end as we won 3-1 with goals from Jinky, Lemon and Davie Hay.

The fans up in the stands or on the terracings who roar their heads off and those who spit bile and venom from start to finish at Old Firm games would never believe it, but there were moments of levity among the swinging boots in these torrid encounters. Big TG knew he was always in for a tough time of it when he was up against wee Willie Henderson. He was a pacy right-winger who was always at his happiest running directly at defenders with the ball. TG used to try to show him inside and pass him on to one of the other defenders to stop him in his tracks. I think Willie would be the first to admit his left foot was only for standing on.

There was one game when TG and Willie were going at it hammer and tongs. The challenges were thundering in all over the place and on one occasion my big Celtic pal caught the wee Ranger and sent him flying. The raging Ibrox support was demanding the referee send off TG and I saw Willie having a bit of backchat with my team-mate. I sidled up minutes afterwards and asked Tommy, 'What was the wee man complaining about?' Tommy laughed and answered, 'He was just saying if he had known he would be up in the air so much this afternoon he would have brought a parachute!'

On another occasion, Greigy, who also revelled in these encounters, went over to the Celtic end to fetch the ball for a throw-in. A voice exclaimed, 'Greig, I didn't realise you were such a dirty bastard.' The Rangers captain swiftly replied, 'Have you not been watching me all season!'

Between 6 September 1958 and 1 January 1960 I played four league games against Rangers and Celtic didn't win one of them. We drew the first 2-2 at Parkhead with goals from Eric Smith and Bobby Collins. The next was on 1 January 1959 and, despite a goal from Bertie Peacock, we went down 2-1 at Ibrox. The next came on 5 September the same year and we lost 3-1 with Mike Jackson getting our consolation effort. And the misery continued in the New Year derby when I played inside-right in a team beaten 1-0 at Parkhead.

Around that period Rangers regularly beat Celtic and you can't argue that they were the better team with better players. They were also organised which certainly wasn't the case at Parkhead until Jock returned to sweep through the place with the force of a hurricane.

Thankfully, I had better fortune against the boys from Govan during my second spell at Celtic. I remember a smashing League Cup Final against them on 29 October 1966 when 94,532 crammed into Hampden. We all realised beforehand it was going to be a fabulous piece of skill or a huge blunder to break down the barriers both defences would undoubtedly erect. Luckily, we conjured up something fairly early into the contest to get the only goal of the game. I sent over a nice pass and Jose McBride magnificently back-headed the ball into the tracks of the inrushing Lemon. The wee man from Saltcoats took the ball first time in his stride and it was in the back of the net before the Rangers keeper, Norrie Martin, could move. Jose might not have scored against our deadly rivals, but he more than played his part in helping us to beat them back then.

Another Cup Final that will never be erased from the Auld memory bank was the meeting for the Scottish Cup on 26 April 1969 at the national stadium which again was packed. Rangers had been playing well and had overwhelmed an excellent Aberdeen team 6-1 in the semi-final. We had beaten a more modest Morton side 4-1 on our way to Hampden. I believe our rivals were favourites that day. They were without the suspended Colin Stein, who had been scoring so many goals since his £100,000 transfer from Hibs. However, we were also going to be going into the game minus the skills of Jinky who, like his Rangers counterpart, was banned from the occasion. John Hughes, too, was sidelined with injury.

The match turned into a stroll for us in the most remarkable of circumstances. Lemon took a corner from the left wing in the second minute and flighted in an inviting cross. Now everyone and their auntie knew about our skipper Caesar's prowess in the air. He was virtually unbeatable and his timing was impeccable. He surely couldn't have believed his good fortune when he got the freedom of Hampden to leap unchallenged, snap his neck muscles, make immaculate contact and send the ball soaring past the static Martin and into the net off the post. I'm told the Rangers manager, Davie White, had detailed a guy called Alex Ferguson to pick up our captain at set pieces. However, there was no sign of their centre-forward when Caesar timed his run into their penalty area to complete perfection. The Ibrox bosses couldn't have been happy with Ferguson because he never played another first team game for them. I wonder whatever happened to him!

We simply rolled all over our opponents that day and were an incredible three goals up before the half-time whistle sounded. Lemon, so often the torturer-in-chief against the Ibrox side, rolled in the second and George Connelly got the third with astonishing assurance from such a youngster who was hardly a first team regular. Rangers made a complete mess of a goal-kick. The keeper knocked it to Greigy and he carried it about six yards before shaping to pass the ball. Big Geordie anticipated the actions from the Rangers skipper and intercepted the ball. He then waltzed round his startled opponent, strolled away from centre-half Ronnie McKinnon, walked the ball round Martin and plonked it in the pokey. It was such impudence from a young boy from Fife who probably wouldn't have been in the side that afternoon if Jinky hadn't been suspended.

The fourth goal summed up our day as we made about six or seven passes to sweep the ball upfield. As I recall TG started the ball rolling with a clearance to me. I put it across to Chopper who gave it back to me. I waited for my midfield partner to advance and I passed it to him again and he delivered a defence-shredding ball into the path of Stevie Chalmers. Rangers hadn't a clue what was going on. Stevie, who had pace to burn, simply took off towards the unprotected Martin as McKinnon tried desperately to get back. Lemon, as you might expect, raced with Stevie in support, but his colleague was in no mood to share the glory. Stevie shaped to pass across goal and then nonchalantly flicked the ball off the outside of his boot and into the net at the near post. Rangers were well and truly routed. Happy days!

Of course, as I said earlier, it wasn't all sweetness and light on these occasions. I was left seething after a 2 January 1968 clash at Parkhead. Chopper and I had scored and we were the dominant force that day. Yet we dropped a point in a disappointing 2-2 draw and our keeper, John Fallon, had a howler. OK, your goalkeeper can make one mistake and you have to accept it. We are all human, after all, and there is often no way back for your last line of defence if he makes an error. John – or Peter as he was known and I'll tell you why in a moment – blundered twice to gift Rangers their result. The first was bad enough as he allowed a half-hit shot from Willie Johnston to go through his legs. However, we still thought we had done enough to rack up a victory when we were leading with about a minute to go. Johansen – that guy again! – tried a speculative shot from about forty yards out on the right.

I recall it was a foggy afternoon and I don't know if our keeper saw the effort properly. But it was a sclaffed shot from such a long way out and shouldn't have given him any trouble. He could have thrown his bunnet on it, as they used to say. However, Peter dived right over the top of the ball as it squeezed under him. Even the Rangers players couldn't believe it. I swear that neither of their shots that day had enough oomph even to touch the back of the net. They simply crawled over the line.

Peter was a dejected figure as he sat in the dressing room. He didn't need to be told he had performed miserably. At least, he lived up to his nickname! We called him Peter after a character called Peter Brady in the popular television series *The Invisible Man*. Fallon, who could be some shotstopper when he was on form, would often go AWOL. The defenders would look round and think, 'Where on earth has our goalkeeper gone now?' I think he enjoyed a wee walk about his goal area when it might have been a better idea to remain on his line.

There was another occasion when Rangers beat us and we should have thanked them for that. Let me hastily explain just in case you think I have taken leave of my senses. A goal from their Swedish winger Orjan Persson gave them a 1-0 victory at Ibrox in September 1967 and, as European champions, we were so sickened by the defeat that we didn't lose another league game throughout the campaign. That was only the second league match of the season, too. We were angry with ourselves. We didn't think we had done ourselves justice that particular afternoon and we all vowed to make sure there would be no more slip-ups. And so it proved. Celtic became the first club since 1935 to secure a hat-trick of titles and we did it by scoring 106 goals and conceding a mere 24 from 34 games. That was the best league campaign in Big Jock's years.

By the way, I am sorry to inform the Rangers support that they did not beat the European champions that day. I have heard it said many times that the Ibrox loss was the first by the Lisbon Lions, but that is not the case. Davie Cattenach, a talented utility player, was in at right-back for Jim Craig at Ibrox, so that was not the team that had conquered Europe. Thought I might just clear that one up!

Old Firm games, of course, were seen as the absolute acid test. You would swiftly discover the stature of friend and foe in these meetings. Some could handle it and others, unfortunately, simply disappeared off the radar. These games engulfed them and stifled their abilities. The intensity, the sheer insanity of it all, in fact, turned some legs to jelly. You could touch the electricity in the air in the dressing room before kick-off. The cacophony of noise, as I said, carried downstairs and you knew what you were about to encounter. Some could go out and show off. Others, alas, could go out and switch off. The entire atmosphere could suck the strength out of some players' muscles. There was a lot of excessive muscular activity around. That's nervous tension to you and me. Folk have said the ball was like a hot potato in these confrontations. Hot potato? More like a live hand grenade, as far I am concerned.

One Celtic manager was asked his views when a vitally important Old Firm match was only days away. The inquisitor wanted to know how he was feeling. In that special Glasgow sense of humour, he replied, 'It's time to look out the big nappies!' Strange way to answer the query, I suppose, but it got the message across loud and clear. There was absolutely no hiding place and a few backsides fainted at the prospect of the hurly burly that is unique to the Old Firm.

Each player handled the strain in his own particular fashion. Some, naturally enough, were more on edge than others. Big TG, for instance, could have been preparing to go out and smell the flowers as he got ready. Some players, like Stevie Chalmers, liked to be well prepared about an hour before the start. TG would be out dispensing tickets to supporters and chatting to friends before wandering into the dressing room looking as though he didn't have a care in the world. He was always one of the last to get dressed. That routine didn't seem to do him any harm at all. I read somewhere that a former player has admitted he used to put his fingers down his throat to help him throw up before going out to play. That seems a bit drastic.

I would like to think I stood up to be counted on these occasions. Back in Big Jock's days we went into these meetings brimming with confidence. We knew we had better players than Rangers and, if it came to a fight, we could also give as good as we got. One guy who never shirked an Old Firm game was my wee pal Jinky. There wasn't much of him, but he had the heart of a lion. Actually, Jinky was a really powerfully built guy. He had tremendous upper-body strength and that was because he trained so hard. He always reminded me of a light-middleweight boxer in his physical stature. He was strong, too. He was rarely injured and that suspends belief when you consider the amount of kicking he took during ninety minutes. The Wee Man enjoyed life, as we all did, but he never abused his body.

There was one game on 6 May 1967 at Ibrox when the Wee Man put on as spellbinding a display you could ever wish to witness. He was unstoppable that day and when you consider the conditions it made it even more astonishing. The game was played in monsoon conditions and it poured down from the heavens all day. The pitch quickly became a bog and you would expect someone who measured up to 5ft 4in to be swallowed up by the conditions. Not Wee Jinky. He decided to pirouette and prance all over the place while other players couldn't keep their feet on an extremely tricky surface.

We were due to play Inter Milan in the European Cup Final nineteen days later and their manager Helenio Herrera was in the stand that day to run the rule over his opponents. He couldn't have failed to be massively impressed by the Wee Man. It ended in a 2-2 draw and Jinky got both our goals. That draw also sealed the league title for us. I will always remember that awesome performance by our winger. He was skipping past defenders like they weren't there, setting up opportunities, scoring himself and generally just creating chaos in the Rangers rearguard.

The Ibrox side actually took the lead when Sandy Jardine rifled a long-range drive into the top corner. It was hit so well and with such marvellous accuracy that Faither didn't even bother going for the ball as it soared past him. Cue Wee Jinky to enter proceedings. Lemon smacked an effort off the upright and, before their keeper Martin could get back to his feet, Jinky came flying in to prod the rebound over the line for the equaliser.

His next effort was just a shade more spectacular. Rangers were making a real game of it because they didn't want their oldest foes to clinch a title on their own pitch. Also, they were a very good team at the time. They reached the European Cup-Winners' Cup Final that year only to lose 1-0 in extra time to the formidable Bayern Munich, Franz Beckenbauer, Gerd Muller et al. However, they just could not pin down Jinky. He was irrepressible as he weaved around the pitch with that wonderful mazy, snake-hipped style of his. It was still locked at 1-1 when he decided to come wandering inside; the ball, as ever, glued to his toe. Rangers backed off, their defenders wondering where he was going. The ball was on his left foot and their defenders seemed quite relaxed about letting him drift inside. That was a mistake.

Despite the atrocious conditions, the driving rain in his face and the pitch now a quagmire, Jinky, with his jersey soaking wet and flapping outside his shorts and socks down at his ankles, looked up and from about twenty-five yards sent a left-foot effort thundering high past the startled Martin. He made a super-human effort to stop the drive, but there has been no goalie born who could have kept that shot out of the net. Even Jinky's team-mates were left open-mouthed at this piece of genius. It was truly astounding and the watching Herrera must have had a sinking feeling as he saw this piece of magic from our diminutive winger. God knows where he summoned up the power to launch that blistering effort into the roof of the net. He didn't just beat the Rangers defenders that day, he also took on and beat the elements. They got a late leveller through Roger Hynd, but it didn't matter. We had all witnessed a virtuoso display by a genuine world-class player. And we also had our second successive title to boot!

You could always rely on Jinky rising to the occasion – as he did even as an eighteen-year-old in the 1963 Scottish Cup Final against Rangers. I was at Birmingham City at the time and would rejoin my old club two years later, but I was still keeping tabs on all things Celtic. I received reports that Jinky had been magnificent at Hampden and was hugely influential in helping the team to a 1-1 draw. Chopper scored the goal and Frank Haffey, one of life's truly eccentric goalkeepers, had a tremendous game to defy Rangers time and time again. But I was told Jinky had a stormer and worked the left-hand side of the Rangers defence all day with his outstanding dribbling.

The Wee Man must have been looking forward to the replay. Remember, Celtic had lost both their league games to their opponents, 1-0 and 4-0, that season. Jinky hadn't played in either of these defeats. So the 1-1 draw was a step in the right direction as everyone with Celtic at heart believed. The winger's reward for his scintillating performance in the first game? He was dropped! It could only happen at Parkhead back then. Rangers must have been overjoyed at the news. There was a lot of meddling with the team, of course, and chairman Bob Kelly would have had made that unfathomable decision. Into Jinky's place came a guy called Bobby Craig and he must have been as surprised as anyone that he got the nod over the Wee Man.

Jinky watched from the Hampden stand as Rangers ran amok and eased to a 3-0 replay triumph.

Why did Craig get the go-ahead to play in the second game? Your guess is as good as mine, but there was a train of thought that Celtic had paid a few thousand quid to Blackburn Rovers for him and they wanted to show it had been money well spent by a board of directors who would never become famous for throwing cash around. Now they were looking to get something back for their investment. It didn't quite work out and, in fact, Craig never played for Celtic again. Jinky missed a handful of games at the start of the next campaign, but was back in his rightful berth on the right wing for pretty much the rest of the season. Someone must have seen the error of their ways, but they never owned up!

I wasn't to know it at the time, but I would line up against Rangers in a Celtic jersey for the last time on 3 January 1970. After being involved in so many enthralling, engrossing, frantic, hectic Old Firm games throughout the years this one passed fairly quietly. It ended goalless and there wasn't much to note except it was a bitterly cold afternoon in the east end of Glasgow. What a way to say farewell to the most memorable and intoxicating fixture in the world.

9

LEGENDS IN LISBON

We conned the Inter Milan players rotten before we won the European Cup on that glorious occasion in Lisbon on Thursday, 25 May 1967 – a day and date that will live with me for ever.

It's often been said that Celtic beat the Italians in the tunnel at the Estadio Nacional when we burst into a rousing version of 'Hail! Hail! The Celts are here!' Our opponents definitely looked a bit bemused, even startled. They had never encountered anything like this and they must have thought they were about to take on a bunch of lunatics. It was highly unusual, of course, and it certainly got the message across that this wee team from Glasgow were not there just to make up the numbers.

However, I maintain we won the most prestigious trophy in Europe even before both teams reached the tunnel in Lisbon. I'm convinced they could have handed over that spectacular silverware the day BEFORE! Honestly, I really mean it. Let me explain. We were due at the stadium to go through our paces and, quite remarkably, Inter Milan's players, who had trained beforehand, hung around to watch us. That was a monumental mistake. What they witnessed would have terrified any opponent because we really gave it full throttle. They must have thought they were watching supermen. We were fit, yes, but we didn't need to go into overdrive that afternoon. However, for the benefit of our intrigued audience, that's exactly what we did. We put as much effort into that training routine as we would have done in an actual game.

We did everything at ferocious speed. Jinky was racing all over the place, Big TG was galloping up and down the wing in that lung-bursting manner of his. Even Chopper broke into a canter! It was all done for their benefit, of course. They must have wondered, 'If they are like this in training, what on earth are they like when they are playing?' We would glance over every now and again and we could sense the fear coming from Inter Milan. They were nudging each other, pointing to this player and that player. There were a few shakes of the head. We spotted them looking more and more worried the longer the turbo-charged session went on. They had sat on the terracing on an exceptionally warm day all smiles at the start. By the time we had finished, they looked more than just a shade perturbed. We were exhausted, but we were not going to let our rivals detect that. As the sun blazed down, we simply found extra reserves of energy to keep on going. It was the most punishing workout in history. And we loved every minute of it!

The Inter Milan players traipsed off back to their base and we knew we had already sent shock waves through their system. I later heard that Helenio Herrera, their esteemed manager, told the Italian press after our triumph that he thought we were invincible. On 25 May 1967, in a little piece of heaven called Lisbon, that's exactly what we were. Nevertheless, there's no doubt we conned our visibly startled onlookers the day before kick-off. It was gamesmanship, no doubt about it, but it worked a treat, didn't it?

I was privileged to play in that game. It was an absolute pleasure to watch my team-mates during that ninety minutes. We were not going to be denied what we knew was rightfully ours – the European Champions' Cup.

Jinky was immense that day. The Italians didn't really know how to handle him. They man-marked him with Tarcisio Burgnich, who was one of the best in the world at suffocating an opponent. Not on this occasion. Jinky came to me afterwards and said, 'I wish I had played better.' I replied, 'What are you talking about? You were Man of the Match.' And I meant it. Jinky did so much for the team against the Italians as he dragged players all over the pitch. It was a totally unselfish performance from the Wee Man who could have taken the spotlight if he had so desired in the biggest game of his life. It was a disciplined display from our mesmerising outside-right and I'm sure a certain Signor Burgnich would have readily agreed, albeit reluctantly. The great Portuguese player Eusebio was at the stadium to witness the performance of our diminutive winger and he admitted later, 'If he played for Benfica I would score a lot more goals. Who could fail with that sort of service?'

I looked around our dressing room before kick-off and thought, 'There's no way we can lose.' TG was wandering around, chatting away merrily, giving you the impression he didn't have a care in the world. And, knowing our cavalier full-back, he probably didn't. I honestly do not believe my old team-mate knew how good he was. Frankly, I thought he was the best left-back in the world at the time. And I'm not saying that because we are still good pals to this day. TG was formidable in full flight and he was a revelation as an attacking wide defender. The amount of running he did up and down that wing for ninety minutes during matches was literally breathtaking. He loved to launch himself into attack – I think he was a frustrated winger – and, of course, he possessed a shot of pulverising power.

Big Jock must take some of the credit for switching TG from right-back to left-back. Actually, Tommy started in the No.3 berth, taking over from the Prez, Jim Kennedy, in the early Sixties. But after a while he moved across to right-back with Willie O'Neill coming in to take his place on the left. Willie was one of those utterly dependable players you knew you could trust and rely on. Coming through at right-back, though, was Cairney, Jim Craig, and, like TG, he was a natural athlete. I never thought he received the praise he deserved. He wasn't as spectacular as his full-back partner, but, then, neither was anyone else on the planet. Cairney would just get on with the job, quietly and efficiently, and I don't recall too many, if any, wingers giving him the runaround.

Jock also knew TG was a naturally right-footed player, but, and you might find this hard to fathom, that worked against him when he played right-back. He would thunder down the wing as usual, but, of course, if he turned inside onto his left side he didn't have the same sort of goal threat. TG was two-footed, but there can be no argument that the better and more menacing foot was his right. So, consequently, when he was over on the left, he could come inside and terrorise goalkeepers with his thunderous shooting. Jock introduced Cairney on the right, switched TG back to the left and the rest is history.

Chopper was world-class, too. He was a lovely, beautiful lad and his chest simply expanded when he pulled on that green-and-white shirt. Like us all, he was so proud to be a Celtic player. What a guy to play alongside. His deft and exquisite skills used to baffle me. Here was this big guy, with that barrel chest of his, and he had the touch of an angel. Chopper didn't kick the ball, he caressed it. And, yet, when the situation warranted it, he

107

could give it one helluva dunt. If anyone ever got round to putting together a DVD compilation of spectacular long-range goals from TG and Chopper it would probably run for about a week – and that doesn't include the slow-motion replays!

Like Cairney, Wee Luggy, John Clark, didn't always grab the headlines, but what a vital component he was in our line-up. He was irreplaceable, if you ask me. He was a devotee of defensive duties and the fans used to call him 'The Brush' for the amount of cleaning up he did along the backline. If TG was caught up the pitch and I wasn't covering, you could always depend on Luggy to be in the right place at the right time to mop up. It took a special brand of player to sacrifice himself the way our sweeper did, but I never heard him complain. He was magnificent at reading play as it came towards him. If there was a break on from our opponents, in a two-against-one situation, Luggy was outstanding in forcing them to play the ball where it would do us the least damage. He would direct them into a corner or such-like. Luggy was a brilliant organiser and, please believe me, every one of his colleagues appreciated what he brought to our team.

We used to joke with him, asking if he needed a route map to show him how to get across the halfway line. He played 318 games for the club and scored three goals. Ironically, one of them was against Faither when Celtic beat Hibs, with Ronnie in goal, in a Scottish Cup replay at Easter Road. I saw film of it not that long ago and I have to say it was a whizzbang effort that TG or Chopper would have been proud to claim. Remarkably, it turned out to be the only goal of the game. I bet that date, 16 March 1961, is indelibly burnt into Luggy's memory banks! Luggy used to rib Faither about it every now and again, but our veteran keeper used to say, 'Luggy, son, you've got the wrong Ronnie Simpson who used to play for Hibs – I'm the good-looking one!'

In fact, Faither and Luggy were the only guys in our set-up who weren't expected to score goals. Jock demanded that everyone pitch in, but those two were excused goalscoring duties. As I have said elsewhere, Jock loved to entertain the supporters. We could go in 2-0 or 3-0 up at the interval and he would be urging, in fact, ordering us to go out and make it four or five. Faither and Luggy knew they had carried out their tasks if we finished the game with our opponents having a duck egg after their name.

Our goalkeeper didn't always get the praise he deserved, either, I have always felt. You look at Celtic in 1967 and you can marvel at the array of skills that are on display courtesy of Jinky, Chopper, Lemon, TG and, hopefully, yours truly. The cameras never dwelt on what was happening at the back because most of the action was centred around the other half of the pitch. But take my word for it, Faither was an exceptional goalkeeper – one of the all-time best. He may have been thirty-six years old when he won that European Cup medal, but age never diminished his outstanding reflexes. Faither was agile, supple and the possessor of uncanny anticipation. With Luggy and our keeper around, it gave the rest of us plenty of latitude to venture forward. If it hadn't been for an unfortunate shoulder injury, I am sure Faither would have continued playing well into his forties.

What can I say about our immaculate captain Caesar that hasn't been said before? What an inspiration he was for all of us. He had a presence on and off the pitch and was a born leader. So many people over the years seem to be astonished when I insist that the European Cup victory in 1967 was NOT the most important in Celtic's history. I genuinely believe our Scottish Cup win over Dunfermline two years earlier put down the marker for what was to follow. Without that success, we might have thought the gods were against us; we were fated to be also-rans. I scored two goals that afternoon, of course, but it was Big Billy who made sure the silverware was on its way back to Parkhead with a trademark header from a Charlie Gallagher left-wing corner-kick near the end. We celebrated like crazy – it had been seven years since the club had won anything – and it was a party that was to go on for another six years for me and three more after that for Celtic.

Another question that has come my way heaven only knows how many times is, 'Did the Celtic players think they had a chance of winning the European Cup in '67?' The answer is always the same, 'Of course we did!' That may sound arrogant and I can't be contradicted now as it's there in the record books for all to see. But I would have said the same back then when we were about to embark in our first-ever game in the competition against Zurich in Glasgow. Fair enough, if anyone wanted to write us off, but that would have been a huge error of judgement. For a start, we had played in the European Cup Winners' Cup semi-final the previous year and were ridiculously unlucky to lose 2-1 on aggregate to Liverpool. If anyone had witnessed our performances in those two games they would have realised what we had to offer and just how dangerous and professional we were.

We could even have gone into the European Cup as holders of the Cup Winners' Cup. No-one would have dismissed us then. We absolutely tore Liverpool to shreds at Parkhead, but could only muster a one-goal advantage with a typical Lemon whiplash effort in front of goal. The Anfield guys knew they had got off the hook big-style. If it had been 4-0 or 5-0 there would have been no grounds for complaint. Don't accuse me of exaggeration, either. We dismantled the team that would go on and win the English League that season and they hardly got across the halfway line in that first match.

And, as I recall, we were doing well at Anfield in treach-
erous conditions. It looked as though it had rained in Merseyside
for about a week, but we were still confident of getting the
result that would get us to the final which, ironically, was being
held at Hampden Park that season. What a double incentive.
It was goalless until around about the hour mark and Liverpool
were beginning to panic. Then they were awarded a free-kick
and up stepped Tommy Smith to belt one in from about twenty-
five yards. Faither looked to have it covered, but it whipped
up off the muddy surface and beat him at the post.

We could hardly believe it. Five minutes later we were left
thunderstruck – they had scored again. Geoff Strong, who was
a superb exponent when the ball was in the air, demonstrated
his aerial ability only too well when he rose to power an unstoppable header wide of our keeper. All was not lost, though. We
realised that a second goal for us would tie the aggregate at
2-2 and we would go through on the away goals rule. We started
to turn the tide and once again our opponents were hanging on
by their fingernails. Near the end there was utter chaos when it
looked as though we had got that crucial goal only for the referee,
a Belgian named Josef Hannet, to rule it out for offside. It was a
diabolically wrong judgement call from the match official.

Lemon had turned the ball wide of sprawling goalkeeper
Tommy Lawrence and their left-back Gerry Byrne was on the
line. The defender tried to handle it, missed and Lemon's effort
nestled in the back of the net. What a beautiful sight – Hampden
here we come. Or so we thought. The referee inexplicably wiped
it out for offside and awarded Liverpool a free-kick. You
wouldn't have to be a football anorak to know that if there is
a goalkeeper in front of you and an opposition player on the
goal-line then you cannot possibly be anything else other than

onside. It didn't do much for our simmering resentment when, a week or so later, Hannet, after viewing the 'goal' again, admitted he got it wrong.

Actually, Liverpool probably used up more than their quota of good fortune in the two games against us. They lost the final at Scotland's national stadium to Borussia Dortmund who won 2-1 with a goal in extra time. And it was a goal put into his own net by Ron Yeats! The West Germans snatched the silverware when their tricky little frontman Reinhard Libuda lobbed the ball over Lawrence from about thirty yards and centre-half Yeats, trying desperately to get back to clear, couldn't get out of the way of the rebound off the face of the crossbar. The ball struck him and then bounced over the line. If we had played Borussia that evening in front of a packed Hampden Park I am convinced we would have lifted our first European trophy a year earlier than we did. You would probably expect me to say that, though, wouldn't you?

When we took centre stage in the European Cup on a still evening in Glasgow on 28 September 1966, we could only guess at what lay in store. The European Cup had been won by only four teams – Real Madrid, who had succeeded six times, Benfica and Inter Milan twice and AC Milan once. These were giants of European football. It seemed you had to come from an exotic part of Europe to lift that trophy. Glasgow didn't seem to fit the bill! In fact, we were the first team from Northern Europe to gatecrash that particular party. So, what on earth were these upstarts from Scotland doing mixing with the hoi polloi of football? We were about to provide an answer, of course.

Big TG had the distinction of scoring Celtic's first goal among the European elite when he rocketed in a thirty-yarder in the sixty-fourth minute after the Swiss champions Zurich had proved to be an extremely competent group of players in the opening round of the competition. Big Jock, who was to celebrate his forty-fourth birthday four days later, had told us to keep calm at half-time. 'Keep moving the ball around,' he urged. 'Try to get round the flanks.' And so on. We had started the season in whirlwind fashion and were used to being in command by the time the interval arrived. Previously, we had taken eight off St Mirren and blasted in six against Clyde in League Cup ties. The three league games before Zurich had seen three successes – Clyde (3-0), Rangers (2-0) and Dundee (2-1). We were flying, but Zurich were doing their utmost to bring us back to earth.

TG came up with his wonder strike after the hour mark and their keeper, Steffan Iten, probably did himself a massive favour by getting out of the road of yet another piledriver. Five minutes later we doubled our advantage and felt a lot more at ease. Luggy broke up an attack, passed to Jose, Joe McBride, and he touched it on to me. I feigned to go one way and then back-heeled it into the tracks of Jose. He was a guy who never had to be asked twice to have a go at goal and he swept it into the net. It got a slight touch off a defender, but it looked good enough to reach its destination anyway.

And TG stole the thunder again in the second leg a fortnight later at the Hardturm Stadium when he walloped in two – one from the penalty spot – and Stevie added another. One thing I recall about that evening was the fact that Big Jock was convinced we would find it easier to play them on their own ground. They needed three goals to progress and had to give it a go. That would leave spaces for us to exploit. He was spot on again.

Next up were the French champions Nantes and this time we played the first leg away from home in their Malakoff Stadium on 30 November. The French, in typical Gallic fashion, fancied themselves and they had some excellent players, notably their main midfield man Robert Herbin, who had captained his country during the World Cup Finals in England the previous year. Robert who? I had him in my pocket in both legs, which we won 3-1 away with goals from Jose, Lemon and Stevie. They had actually taken the lead through Magny in the twentieth minute before we decided to put the tie to bed. Jinky gave Europe an advance warning of his glittering array of skills with a marvellous performance.

It was also 3-1 in the second leg at rain-lashed Parkhead where Jinky was once again simply unstoppable. He got the opener in the thirteenth minute, but all credit to the French as they refused to roll over and they levelled through Georgin. It was 1-1 at half-time and Nantes might have thought they were on the verge of pulling off a shock. No chance. Jinky meandered down the right wing, sent over an inviting cross and Stevie met it perfectly to send a header spinning into the net. It was *déjà vu* all over again for the French when Jinky staged a repeat performance with Lemon this time finishing it off.

I have to admit I didn't know an awful lot about our next opponents, Yugoslavia's Vojvodina Novi Sad. Their country was enjoying something of a renaissance and their national side had only lost 2-0 in a replay to Italy in Rome in the old European Nations Cup, now the European Championship, the previous year. Partizan Belgrade also reached the European Cup Final in 1966 before losing 2-1 to Real Madrid in Brussels. Dinamo Zagreb were to win the Inter-Cities' Fairs Cup, now the UEFA Cup, in 1967, beating Leeds United 2-0 on aggregate over the two legs. We also realised that Vojvodina had seen off the much-vaunted Atletico Madrid – who had overwhelmed their city rivals Real to win the Spanish title – in the previous round.

These days, at the flick of a switch, you can find out what's going on all over the world and watch players and teams in foreign leagues and have a good idea what they are all about. However, in 1967 that was not the case. You had to take the word of your boss and Jock let us all know that this was an exceptionally well-equipped team with quality players who were very comfortable on the ball. They also had a goalkeeper called Ilija Pantelic who was rated as the best in the world at the time. So, we had a fair idea what to expect when we took the field at their stadium on a cold evening on 1 March 1967. The pitch was rock solid and hardly conducive to football artistry. They were a good side all right, but we were holding out with only twenty minutes to play and they looked just a little bit despondent. They had tried all sorts of ways to get through our rearguard, but we were holding firm. A draw looked on the cards.

Then, horror of horrors! TG, so often the hero, was a bit wayward with a passback that dropped between Chopper and Luggy. Djordic, a speedy little attacker, nipped in, squared it across to Stanic who sent the ball wide of our exposed and helpless goalkeeper. Faither was well known for his infectious sense of humour. It deserted him at that moment, though. The Slavs celebrated like they had won the cup already. They arrived in Glasgow a week later and one thing I detected was that Jock and his Vojvodina counterpart, Vujadin Boskov, were never going to be big buddies. Boskov, who would later manage Real Madrid, was a cocksure character, that's for sure, and he had Big Jock sucking out his fillings when he said, 'We expect to win in Glasgow. Why not? We are the better team.' Oh, really? Wrong thing to say, comrade!

Unfortunately, I had to sit this one out through injury and Charlie Gallagher took my place in the middle of the park.

What a game he had, too. I'm not the greatest spectator you are ever likely to meet and it was murder sitting up in that stand watching this encounter unravel. The fans, and I make no apologies for repeating myself, were magnificent yet again. The encouragement they gave the side that night was simply awesome. But it didn't appear to be knocking the Slavs out of their stride. They were a solid, compact unit and extremely well drilled. I was talking to my big chum TG before the match and he was desperate to atone for his mistake in the first game. 'I've got to score, Bertie,' he said. 'I don't want the blame for us going out of the European Cup.'

TG didn't score, but he did the next best thing – he set up the equaliser just before the hour mark with yet another assault down the left wing. Yogi, at outside-left, played his part by dragging a defender inside and that allowed our full-back to hit the line and fire over a cross. Pantelic made to grab the ball, but he reckoned without the bravery of Stevie who launched himself at TG's effort to deflect it into the net. The place was in uproar. Jose and I were dancing up in the stand and the fans, all 69,374 of them, were delirious with delight. If they were overjoyed then, it was nothing to the state they were in just before the final whistle.

My replacement Charlie went over to take a corner-kick on the right wing as Caesar trotted into the packed penalty area. There was the usual jostling as players tried to block our skipper. They were wasting their time. Charlie flighted over as sweet a cross as you will ever see and Caesar, with his usual impeccable timing, soared high to meet it perfectly and arc a lovely header into the roof of the net. That was the signal for bedlam. The old Parkhead roof must have been close to being blown off such was the racket – and that was just Jose and me! And do you know how long there was to go – TWO SECONDS! Vojvodina just had time to kick off and the referee blew for the end of the game. If Caesar hadn't scored it would have gone to a replay because extra time hadn't yet been introduced. I believe it would have been in Rotterdam a couple of days later and anything could have happened against this gifted bunch. More and more I was becoming convinced our name was on the trophy. Now there was just the little matter of taking care of Dukla Prague in the semi-final.

The Czechoslovakian champions were captained by the wonderful Jozef Masopust who had been voted European Footballer of the Year in 1962 and had led his country to the World Cup Final where they were to lose 3-1 to Brazil the same year. Dukla had also beaten Ajax Amsterdam in the previous round – the same Dutch side that had annihilated Liverpool 7-3 on their way to the quarter-final. The Dutch were just emerging as a football nation at the time and were to offer us the delights of Johan Cruyff, Johan Neeskens, Johnny Rep and so many more in the years to come. However, Dukla had taken care of their threat and were in the semi-finals on merit. Once again, another tense occasion was just around the corner and, thankfully, I had overcome my injury to get my place back in the first team.

A crowd of 74,406 made their way to Parkhead on a fairly crisp evening on 12 April and they were about to witness another unforgettable encounter. Wispy Wallace had missed the games against Vojvodina because he hadn't been registered in time following his £30,000 transfer from Hearts in December. But he was more than willing and ready to go in this one. It wasn't a bad debut on the biggest platform European football had to offer – two goals in a 3-1 triumph. Once more the atmosphere was out of this world. I loved playing in these games; this was what football was all about. People used to say I was arrogant. No, I wasn't – I was big-headed. Seriously, I was afraid of no-one. They would have my utmost respect, of course, but once that whistle blew to start the game I was determined to show them who was the better man. It was an outlook that surged through the team.

Dukla, like Vojvodina, were a fine passing team, laced with a lot of clever players. I remember they had a beanpole centre-forward called Stanislav Strunc who must have been about 6ft 8in. Caesar was just about unbeatable in the air, but this skyscraper striker made it difficult for our captain all night. Everything looked as though it was going according to plan when Jinky opened the scoring in the twenty-eighth minute, which was justice after the referee had ruled out what looked like a perfectly good goal from Stevie earlier. Have you ever been in the middle of a crowd of over 74,000 people and been able to hear a pin drop? I have. Celtic Park was enveloped in an eerie silence just before the interval when the Czechs equalised. We couldn't believe it. Our defence got into a bit of a mess on the edge of the box as they tried to hack the ball clear. It didn't travel any distance and was being continually blocked by some part of a Dukla player's anatomy; it was bouncing around like it had a life of its own as it ricocheted all over the place. As luck would have it, it eventually fell to the towering Strunc and he slipped the offending article beyond Faither. Once more, some choice words were exchanged between the keeper and his defenders.

Enter Wispy! TG hammered a pass downfield in the sixtieth minute and Wispy, who had always been a real nuisance when he was playing against Celtic, made his run with Swiss-precision timing. The Dukla defence was caught square as he chased TG's ball into the box where a defender mistimed his attempt at a clearing header. Wispy anticipated the bounce superbly and then calmly lofted the ball with the outside of his right boot beyond the outrushing Ivo Viktor, their international goal-keeper. The ball floated nonchalantly into the net and it was time for our old ground to rock to its foundations again. Five minutes later it was shaking once more. A desperate Dukla defender pawed away a cross from Chopper and the ref awarded us the inevitable free-kick. It was about twenty-five yards out, fairly central and well within striking distance. Suddenly, for absolutely no good reason, something pops into your head that you think will work. I placed the ball down and was aware Wispy was at my side, on the right.

The Dukla defence erected its wall as Viktor, another fine custodian, watched nervously on his line. I stepped forward as though I was about to steady the ball with my hand, the defence must have relaxed for a split second and that was all I needed. Quickly, I withdrew my hand, touched the ball side-ways, Wispy arrived bang on time and clubbed an unstoppable effort wide of the open-mouthed keeper into the net. It might have looked impromptu, but, like so many things, it was a vari-ation on a move we worked on over and over again in training at Barrowfield. It's always nice when it pays off. It's even nicer when it puts you to within ninety minutes of the European Cup Final.

The grim and foreboding Juliska Stadium in Prague was the setting for the second leg on 25 April where we knew we had a date with destiny. I think there was construction work already underway in this vast bowl of an arena – it looked like chunks of the stands were missing. Fans appeared to be standing on a hillside. There was a huge police presence, too. If this was supposed to unsettle or intimidate us then they were wasting their time. Jock did the unthinkable that afternoon – he ordered us to play in a defensive formation. It was alien to anything we had been used to since he arrived when entertainment was very much the watchword. He went through everything with painstaking attention to detail, so no-one was in any doubt about his duties against the Czechs. Even Jinky was told to lie deep alongside Cairney on the right and Lemon likewise over on the left alongside TG. Wispy, our two-goal first leg hero, was given a man-marking role on Masopust. We were almost unrecognisable from the team that had faced Dukla only a fortnight beforehand although there was only one change in personnel, Lemon coming in for Yogi.

We all felt sorry for Stevie. He was given the lone striker's role and told to keep on the move for ninety minutes, to continually harry their defenders and let them know he was there. It was a hellish task that Stevie accepted with a smile on his face! He was fearless that day as he covered every inch behind enemy lines. We would thump the ball out of defence and there was Stevie haring after it, taking two or three defenders with him. It wasn't the most glamorous role he was ever asked to carry out on Celtic's behalf, but he didn't moan once. There was an occasion, deep in the second half when the Czechs were resigning themselves to their fate, when he got caught up in a melee deep in their half. About five or six of their defenders descended upon our solitary frontman and Caesar looked at me and asked, 'Do you think we should help him out, Bertie?' I answered, 'Naw, he'll be fine on his own!'

Faither had made a couple of fine saves when the Czechs had managed to get themselves free of our shackles and we were all mightily relieved when the referee decided to call a halt to the contest. His shrill whistle sounded and we all danced around like schoolboys. Celtic were in the European Cup Final. And, of course, it was to get even more magical and memorable. Out of the corner of my eye I spotted a disconsolate Masopust. He was standing there, looking at the ground and, now that he had reached the veteran stage, must have known his last chance of European Cup glory had surely gone. Wispy had made certain that Masopust contributed very little in the second leg. He never left his side and shadowed him everywhere, as instructed by Jock.

Masopust looked close to tears as Wispy approached him and offered to shake hands. Masopust didn't want to know – he refused the gesture. That was disappointing. Wispy had played him cleanly throughout the game and, of course, he was just following orders. Masopust trudged wearily in the general direction of the tunnel, making his way past elated Celtic players as he did so.

I'm glad to say there is a happy postscript. This fine Czech player, one of the world's first genuine superstars, must have realised how churlish he had been and came into our dressing room to seek out Wispy and offer him his hand in friendship. They duly clasped hands together and Masopust wished Wispy and the rest of us the best of luck for the final. We all appreciated that gesture.

Jock assembled the players around him afterwards and told us, 'I will never ask you to play like that again. That is a promise.' And it was a promise he kept.

If it had been barren in Prague, it was opulence all the way at the five-star Palacio Hotel in Estoril, a quite picturesque little coastal town to the west of Lisbon. This was to be our HQ as we plotted and planned to overwhelm Inter Milan and become European champions. The jigsaw was coming together.

Big Jock was meticulous as he drew up his plans for the big game. He warned, 'Watch yourself in the sunshine – the sun is your enemy!' He timed us when we were in the swimming pool, too. You were allotted such and such a time and then you were out. He patrolled the hotel like a headmaster. He wanted everything to be perfect. Big Jock had the habit of charging into your room without knocking on the door. He would always try to catch you off guard just in case you were getting on the outside of a bottle of gin. As if! The night before the game Jock came into my bedroom. 'Everything OK, Bertie?' he asked. 'No problem, boss,' I answered. 'Just reading a good book.' He looked around the room and, satisfied all was in order, closed the door and moved onto another unsuspecting team-mate. Actually, if Big Jock had bothered to look under my bed he might have got a bit of a surprise – he would have come face to face with my brother Ian!

My younger sibling had saved some cash to travel to Portugal to support us, but, being Ian, he hadn't bothered with the little detail of booking a room in a hotel. With the help of some of my colleagues, I managed to smuggle him into our HQ in Estoril. It was like something out of a Carry On movie as he ducked and dived to make sure he wasn't spotted by any of the Celtic powers-that-be, including our manager who wouldn't have been too pleased to discover someone had invaded our privacy. No matter how much Big Jock tried to silently creep up on you, we could always hear him coming. He still had that heavy limp that ended his playing career and you knew immediately that he was about to descend on you. I was playing cards with Ian the evening he decided to pay me an impromptu visit. The alarm bells went off in my head as I heard him approach. 'Quick, Ian, hide!' I said. 'Where?' he asked. 'Get under the bed. Now!' Honestly, it was hilarious. Ian scrambled under the bed, the door opened, Jock looked around and left without a clue as to the whereabouts of the uninvited guest.

As he prepared for Lisbon, Jock picked the same eleven who had performed in the second leg in Prague and no-one would have believed that the same bunch of players could undergo such an amazing transformation. We were going to conquer Europe and we were going to do it the Celtic way with the rest of the football world looking on. Inter Milan were masters of catenaccio, a defensive-minded formation that stifled all the good things in the game. They had won the European Cup twice in the previous three years and they had lifted the World Club Championship twice over the same period. They were dull, but they were successful. Other coaches, thinking it was the way ahead, copied their tactics. These coaches were strangling the life out of football, but it didn't seem to matter as long as trophies were being collected.

As I pointed out at the start, we must have frightened the pants off the Italians when they saw us storming through a training session twenty-four hours before the kick-off. We later spent the evening watching England play Spain in a friendly international in the hilltop home of a Scottish golfer called Brodie Lennox, no relation to Lemon, who had emigrated to this rather splendid part of the universe. We walked back down the hill in pitch darkness afterwards as we returned to our hotel to get a good night's sleep before the rigours that lay ahead.

So, there we are in the tunnel, ready to step onto that lovely, lush surface where we were about to put on the show of our lives. Wee Jinky was looking at the Inter Milan team and I have to admit they did look fairly impressive. They were immaculately turned out, hair gelled, teeth sparkling, tans twinkling in their smart, smooth strips. Jinky said, 'Look at them, Bertie, they're film stars.' I replied, 'Aye, Wee Man, but can they play?' He just burst out laughing. Inter Milan's expensively arranged team looked around quizzically at what was going on.

Jock had been remarkably calm in the dressing room before we had left to take our place in the tunnel. Collectively, he told us, 'Go out and enjoy yourselves, you've done the hard work. You've already made history by getting here. No-one can take that away from you. Just get on that pitch and let everyone see what you can do.'

Individually, he would put an arm around a player's shoulder and give him some words of wisdom. He knew how to treat us on a one-to-one basis. For instance, he would say to Jinky, 'Wee Man, I know you are going to win this for us. You're the star; this is your stage.' You could see Jinky growing in confidence. And so it went on as he prepared us for the biggest game in Celtic's proud history. We had come a long way from the team that had been turned over 5-1 by Dunfermline at East End Park and 6-2 by Falkirk at Brockville just over two years beforehand. A helluva long way – and we had yet to reach our ultimate destination. However, that was only ninety minutes away.

We took the field with yours truly, superstitious as ever, running out fifth in line. Don't ask me why – it just happened one day, I had a good game and it just stuck. Anyone wanting that fifth place would have had to fight me for it! We settled early, but were given a jolt when their main man Sandro Mazzola got his head to a Mario Corso ball in from the left and Faither had to make a smart save, diving to his left to push the effort away. A few minutes later we were in big trouble, though, when Cairney was adjudged to have brought down their bustling centre-forward Renato Cappellini and referee Kurt Tschenscher, from West Germany, had no hesitation in pointing to the spot. It looked as though the Italian had made the most of an awkward challenge from our right-back and Cairney, to this day, insists it was never a penalty-kick. Mazzola didn't hang around to argue – his simply despatched a perfect effort low into the net with Faither going the wrong way, diving to his left.

Funnily enough, I believe this seventh-minute goal acted against Inter Milan. They were known to withdraw into defence when they got any sort of advantage over their opponents and, not surprisingly, they were going to erect barriers in front of Giuliano Sarti, their goalkeeper who had been thought of as a weak link but was to disprove these theories with a fair degree of distinction. His display against us was easily one of the best I have ever seen in my life. However, the penalty goal invited us to take the game to the Italians and, with eighty-three minutes still to play, we more than welcomed the opportunity. As we trotted back to recentre the ball for kick-off, I said to Jinky, 'Give us a wee bit of magic, Wee Man.' He smiled, 'I'll do my best.'

We got to the fourteenth minute before the referee warned Sarti about time-wasting! Fourteen minutes! It was going to be a long day. Inter tried to dictate the pace of the game and slow down the tempo, but we weren't interested in following their script. We flooded forward and I knew we were going flat out when Caesar raced past me going down the old inside-right channel. I could hardly believe it as our centre-half rarely ventured across the halfway line unless, of course, it was for a corner-kick or a free-kick. I could only think he was acting as a decoy because there was no danger I was going to give him a pass! No disrespect, but Caesar's best work was done when the ball was airborne.

Celtic swarmed down on our opponents in relentless fashion and we knew something would have to give. I thought I had broken the barrier when I got into their box and chipped the ball over Sarti's flailing arm. My joy was stifled, though, when the ball smacked off the woodwork and bounced to safety. Then their keeper made an unbelievable diving save from a drive from TG that he wasn't even entitled to go for, never mind push round the upright. And so it went on. We drove forward and they reorganised in defence. It was getting monotonous, but we never believed for a fraction of a second that we wouldn't score.

As I recall, at half-time, there was a bit of shouting and cursing going down the tunnel and the match official was the obvious target for our anger. 'What a surprise – an Italian team getting a penalty-kick,' seemed to be the drift of our argument, although it might not have been put so eloquently. The West German ignored us. Jock was calmness personified once again as he talked us through half-time. We all agreed, a goal had to come. We had nine potential goalscorers out there and Inter had survived mainly due to the brilliance of their goalkeeper. It proved, at least, that we were getting through their defence, exploiting gaps and creating chances. Yes, it was only a matter of time.

Jock made few adjustments, but he did ask Cairney and TG to pull the ball back a bit across the box rather than fire it into the mix in the middle of the goal where the Italians were defending with plenty of bodies. Jock always liked to give his opposite number something to think about and he told Stevie to go and stand on the right wing with Jinky coming inside for the restart. Herrera, of course, had known that all five Celtic forwards had, at some stage in their careers, played as wingers. He had warned his team to expect us to attack with pace. Burgnich looked across for instructions after he had trotted over to pick up Jinky, as usual. He looked more than a little bit surprised to see Stevie standing there. 'What to do now, boss?' said the look on his face. It was just a bit of kidology, of course, and a few minutes into the second half, Jinky was back wide right and Stevie was in the middle. It unsettled them for a moment or two though. Jock was great at mind games.

One thing we had noticed during our interval talk was that Sarti was not taking any goal-kicks or, in fact, kicking the ball long. He would pass a goal-kick to a team-mate, pick up the return – you were allowed to do that back then, of course – and then throw it or roll it to one of his players. On the rare occasions Inter launched the ball upfield it was one of their defenders who took the kick. Basically, that meant there was a good chance we would be onside if we gathered the ball and made a swift counter-attack. It also showed the Italians were content to keep possession in their own half and try to hit us on the break. That might have worked against other teams but not with this Celtic line-up. If you handed us the initiative we would take it. And how!

The second period went much the same way the first had ended – with us rolling forward in numbers, playing the ball around, bringing Jinky into play and the Italians holding out resolutely. It was something at which they were extremely adept; something they were used to every week in Serie A. We were not to be denied, though, and, as everyone had realised, it was going to take something exceptional to beat Sarti. TG came up with the answer in the sixty-fourth minute. The ball was whisked around crisply before Chopper rolled it out to Cairney coming in from the right. He carried it, a couple of steps, I think, and then slipped it across their eighteen-yard line. TG came in like a whirlwind to meet it first time with that lethal right foot and Sarti, even the great Sarti, could not repel this raid. TG's strike strangled itself in the back of the net while the keeper was still in mid-air. We had equalised. Now for the winner.

At long last we had rattled Sarti's cage. He had looked imperturbable for most of the game. He was cool under pressure and his handling was excellent. Now, though, cracks were beginning to show in his facade. It was highlighted when he got into a shouting match with the photographers behind his goal when they returned the ball too quickly after it had gone out of play. He wasn't happy with them and, for the first time that memorable day, he was beginning to get a little flustered. The West German match official, so quick to award Inter Milan their penalty-kick, wasn't quite so swift in his decision-making when he denied us a stonewall spot-kick. It doesn't matter now, of course, but it was a penalty-kick all right and even Sarti seemed more than just a little puzzled at the bizarre decision by the referee.

TG sizzled in a low cross from the left, Sarti and a defender got in a real old fankle at the back post and Wispy nicked in to collect the ball. Just when he was about to roll it over the line from about two yards, Sarti, on the ground, wrapped his arms around his leg and sent him toppling in a somewhat undignified manner. Penalty? The whole of Europe must have thought so, but Tschenscher waved play on. Remarkable! Sarti got to his feet and at least had the good grace to look at Wispy and shrug his shoulders in that extravagant manner of the Latins. 'I don't know why he didn't give it either,' he could have said. 'Right,' I thought, 'we're not going to let them away with this – Inter Milan or the referee!'

We maintained the bombardment and we had them gasping as we continued to play the ball around at a spellbinding pace. TG flummoxed Sarti with a long, looping ball from the left that cracked off the crossbar and, once more, bounced away to a grateful defender who thumped it anywhere just to clear the danger. Five minutes remained on the clock when Stevie got the most valuable goal in Celtic's history – the European Cup winner. TG was involved again in an interchanging move with Chopper who slammed one into their penalty area from an angle and there was Stevie smack in front of goal to divert the ball past Sarti. They made a half-hearted claim for offside, but not even Herr Tschenscher, with Europe looking on, could nullify that effort. Inter did nothing to get back into the game. They were beaten and they knew it. I don't think they fancied the prospect of extra time even if they had got lucky and got a second goal. It was our day and everyone knew it.

Three minutes from time, I decided to help make sure the game was ours when I came inside from the left and could see Burgnich coming across. He had decided he had had enough of Wee Jinky. I could see he looked tired, even a bit bedraggled. Remember, this was one of the top defenders in Europe and, in fact, along with Inter team-mates Mazzola, Angelo Domenghini and Giacinto Facchetti, he would play for Italy in the World Cup Final against Brazil in Mexico three years later. I decided to commit him and I knew what would come next. Sure enough, I was clattered and I decided to show the Italians how it feels to see someone waste time as they had done continually against us. Eventually, I got back to my feet and TG said, 'Just give me the ball, Bertie.'

I asked, 'What are you going to do?'

He answered, 'I'm going to kick it as far over that bar and out of the ground as I can.' And that's exactly what he did.

Jock's tactics had worked perfectly and if I can take you through a few statistics they will underline this. Our boss had ordered Wispy, Stevie and Lemon to try to pull their defenders out of position to allow Chopper and myself to come from behind into spaces vacated by our opponents. They were also asked to make runs that would enable Cairney and TG to get wide on the wings. Would you be surprised if I told you we had THIRTY-FIVE attempts on goal with nineteen on target? TG, unbelievably, had nine shots on target. A left-back in a European Cup Final having so many attempts? Awesome. He could have had a hat-trick easily. He would have been due it.

Paradoxically, Stevie had only one shot on target – the winner! Wispy drew one save from Sarti and Lemon didn't hit the target at all. When you consider these guys had netted nine of our eighteen goals in the competition that season – Stevie with five, Wispy and Lemon both with two – it tells you how they curbed their natural instincts for the cause of the team. My God, they scored fifty goals in the league between them – Stevie hitting twenty-three, Wispy claiming fourteen and Lemon snatching thirteen. So, one look at those stats merely emphasises what they were prepared to do in our efforts to beat Inter Milan and, in doing so, conquer Europe. They were utterly dedicated, totally professional and completely unselfish. Chopper had four shots saved by Sarti while I had two on target, including the one that hit the bar, and Jinky chipped in with two, one a header that was expertly tipped over the bar for one of our ten corner-kicks. Inter Milan had three attempts at our goal, including their penalty-kick. Mazzola was the man who had all three efforts. They didn't force a solitary corner-kick. They may have been masters at timewasting, but I have to say they were not dirty. There wasn't a single booking in Lisbon. Did we deserve to win that European Cup? What do you think? The defence rests!

It would have been nice to have been able to parade our newly won trophy around the Estadio Nacional, of course, but that wouldn't have been too sensible since it had become a sea of green and white with our supporters taking over the place. We had been told beforehand by officials, in the event of a win, not to worry about a pitch invasion because there was a moat around the pitch. Listen, you could have filled that moat with sharks, crocodiles and alligators and you still wouldn't have kept our fans off that pitch. Who could blame them for their exuberance? Yes, a lap of honour would have been great, especially with Europe tuning in to watch the spectacle. But it wasn't to be and I'm not complaining. The main thing was to win that trophy and we achieved our goal with a bit of splendour, too. We went to the banquet afterwards and, surprise, surprise, Inter Milan didn't turn up until about a good hour later. Their players still looked shell-shocked.

We were sitting waiting for the event to begin when a UEFA official appeared with these two boxes and placed them at the top of the table. Then he simply walked off without saying a word. I looked at the boxes and shouted to Caesar, 'Is that the biscuits?' Our captain opened one of them and exclaimed, 'They're our medals! These are our European Cup medals!' As award ceremonies go, it was a bit of a non-starter. The players ambled forward, helped themselves, looked at these coveted little badges, stuffed them somewhere safe and awaited the evening's festivities. It wasn't quite what we had in mind, but

I think we were all just so pleased and satisfied to at last claim the European Cup – etching our name for ever in history as the first British club to do so. No-one will ever be able to take that honour or distinction away from Celtic Football Club.

Manchester United equalled the feat the following season, of course, when they defeated Benfica 4-1 in extra time at Wembley. I bet you they would dearly have loved to have been the first – my pal Paddy Crerand has admitted as much to me although, naturally enough, being a Celtic man he wasn't too distraught when we beat them to it. George Best caught up with Celtic a few times when we were in Ireland doing the rounds as part of our twenty-fifth anniversary celebrations of the Lisbon success. He surprised me one evening when he said, 'Celtic's feat was better than ours. You broke the barrier – you showed it could be done. Celtic opened the door for other British teams.' I hasten to add George was stone-cold sober at the time. His words were much appreciated. The Lions, it must be said, were a close-knit bunch of guys during our playing days and the same could be said today. We enjoy each other's company and there is a closeness among us I have never experienced with any other team. There is never a problem when someone gets in touch to say there is another Lions reunion coming up. It's no chore to spend time in their company, that's for sure.

I hope Celtic played a part in putting a smile back on the face of football that day in Lisbon. It was a triumph for football laced with flamboyance, flair and no little fire. It obliterated the negativity that teams such as Inter Milan had been relying upon to gain success. We demolished the notion you could only be triumphant if you concentrated mainly on defence.

It was a victory for the good guys.

10

OLÉ AND ADIOS

Big Jock took me aside and told me, 'Real Madrid are desperate to do us. We've just won the European Cup, but they still think they are the best team in Europe. Amancio is their best player – do your best to keep him quiet. Keep an eye on him. I want to win this one.'

It was only thirteen days after our victory over Inter Milan and we had been invited to play for the legendary Alfredo di Stefano in his Testimonial Game at the Bernabeu Stadium. Real Madrid had won the European Cup the previous year, beating Partizan Belgrade 2-1 in the final, and they were as determined as us to win this one. We had a player called John Cushley, a back-up central defender to Billy McNeill, and he spoke good Spanish. He read the newspapers and told us what they were saying about Celtic. Basically, they were informing everyone we had borrowed the European Cup from Real for a year. Oh, yeah? When we turned up at the Bernabeu that evening we knew we were not going to be involved in a friendly.

The great Alfredo, at the age of forty, graced the pitch for about fifteen minutes before taking his leave. Then we got down to the nitty gritty of seeing who was the best team in Europe. Wee Jinky was unbelievable that night against the

Spaniards. Di Stefano, along with Stanley Matthews, was the Wee Man's hero. He decided to put on a show for the Real legend – and what a show it was. The Real players did their best to get the ball off Jinky, but it was one of those nights when it was stuck to the toe of his boot. He would show them the ball, they would lunge in and Jinky would do one of his little serpentine-weaving manoeuvres and they would be left tackling fresh air while he took off on his merry way.

Even I felt like applauding every now and again as he displayed his awesome talent. Meanwhile, Amancio and I were getting acquainted in the middle of the park. He didn't like the attention I was paying him and we had a couple of kicks when no-one was looking. Nothing too serious, I hasten to add, but enough for him to realise I was there to do a job for Celtic that night. It may have been billed as a friendly, but, please believe me, this was no game where there was any pulling out of tackles. They were absolutely determined to hammer us and, equally, we were just as committed to the cause to show we were worthy European champions.

Jinky tore them apart in one of the most spellbinding one-man shows I have ever had the privilege to witness. He actually started to take the mickey at one point which was simply amazing. This wee guy from Uddingston playing in the most fabulous stadium on earth and giving their players a lesson in how to play football? It could only have been Jinky. Meanwhile, Amancio and I were still having an interesting evening. I don't know if I was marking him or he was marking me, but we weren't far from each other's side all night. Then things got a bit heated. There was a 50/50 ball and we both went for it. Crunch! There was a bit of a fracas. He threw a punch at me and I returned the compliment. The referee was far from amused.

He didn't hesitate as he pointed to the tunnel for both of us. To be honest, it was a fair decision. As I walked past Big Jock in the dug-out I looked over and said, 'Problem solved, boss.' He had the good grace to laugh.

But it was Jinky's night. It may have been Alfredo di Stefano's final farewell in a theatre of dreams, but I'm sure the name on everyone's lips that evening was Jimmy Johnstone. One of the Real Madrid defenders – I think it was a bloke called Grosso – must have had enough of our wee genius and tried to cement him. He came out of central defence and clattered into Jinky on the right wing. You could see that he thought he had sorted out the Wee Man. No chance! Grosso walked back to his usual post and must have been more than slightly alarmed when he looked over his shoulder and saw Jinky back on his feet and preparing to take the free-kick. Jinky, on that form, was irresistible. We played really well that night, despite my absence. Big TG was bombing up and down the left wing as only he could and he might have got a hat-trick. He had two superb efforts in the first half that brought out two excellent saves from their goalkeeper. He just kept going throughout the second half and it was easy to see why European coaches were acclaiming him as the best in the business.

We wanted to win this game and we duly did when Jinky – who else? – set up the only goal of a fiercely contested encounter in the second half. He had moved over to the left, in our own half, to take a pass from TG. He skipped past a couple of tackles in that effortless style of his and then planked the ball in front of Lemon, coming in from the right. Wee Bobby didn't even break stride as he hit the ball first time with his right foot and his effort flew low past the goalkeeper. Job done. Real Madrid knew then who were the true masters of European football. To be fair to their support, they started to applaud Celtic and especially Jinky. He would sweep past a defender and the fans would shout, '*Olé!*' It was a night for our wee magician to show everyone his tricks and flicks. I will never forget that performance. The Wee Man was unstoppable.

Jinky was going on holiday the following day with his wife Agnes. They left our hotel and the Wee Man jumped into a taxi and said, 'Take me to Benidorm, driver.' The cab driver asked, 'You want to go to the airport, señor?' Jinky replied, 'No, I want to go to Benidorm!' Geography might not have been Jinky's best subject at school because Benidorm is about 300 miles from Madrid as the crow flies. 'Are you sure, señor?' asked the driver who must have thought he had won the pools. 'Aye,' said Jinky and the driver pointed the taxi in the general direction of the holiday resort. Wee Jinky was a one-off, sure enough.

11

WAR GAMES

We were waiting to discover where our World Club Champion-ship play-off against Racing Club of Buenos Aires would be played. After two brutal confrontations with a bunch of Argentinian thugs who masqueraded as a football team, I thought I had a reasonable suggestion. I offered, 'Why not take it to Madison Square Garden?'

Back then, our 'reward' for winning the European Cup in 1967 would be a crack at the world title, playing the South American champions home and away. Unfortunately, those guys were a lot more interested in fisticuffs than football and I thought the mecca of world boxing in New York would have been an ideal location. We had just played two pulverising and punishing games against a vicious ensemble of assassins who had hacked, punched, kicked, pulled our hair, whacked us on the back of the head and generally violated us during the previous encounters.

I can take someone kicking me, but it is fairly hard to accept when someone comes up, with the ball about fifty yards away, and spits in your face. Then they would look at you and flash a wicked smile before running off. We had never encountered anything like this. Listen, when you can play in Scottish Junior football as a teenager, there is nothing left to frighten you on a football pitch. Junior football is full of big, burly blokes who would make all sorts of threats. They were clumsy to start with and you would have thought some of them were playing for massive bonuses the way they threw themselves into challenges. Maybe they were taking out a week's frustration in these games, but they went out of their way to intimidate you.

I wonder how many times some hulking brute sidled up to me during one these confrontations and whispered, 'Try that again, son, and I'll break your fucking leg.' Sometimes they varied it and promised to break your neck. I accepted all that from a very young age and I believed I could look after myself on a football pitch. Remember, too, I only played six games in Junior football! I was never frightened of the player who would tell me what he was going to do – it was the other guys you had to keep your eye on. I'm talking about those who never uttered a word and then suddenly, when you least expected it, would send you into orbit. I could take it and, when it was merited, I could dish it out, too.

But how do you react when you are left wiping spittle off your face for the umpteenth time? Where I came from in Maryhill there would be only one destination for a cretin who indulged in this disgusting behaviour – the Western Infirmary. Believe me, it's not easy to control your emotions at a time like that. However, I believe it is to my colleagues' enormous credit that we took all that from a bunch of cowards in two games in Glasgow and Buenos Aires and didn't allow it to interfere with our concentration levels. Everyone has a breaking point, though. And we were getting close to it as we prepared for that game in neutral Uruguay. We had been goaded beyond belief by these guys. Jock Stein beseeched us to be on our best behaviour when we travelled to Montevideo. Celtic could have packed up and gone home after the shambolic second game and our chairman, Sir Robert Kelly, didn't even want to travel to Argentina for that encounter after what he had witnessed in the first leg at Hampden. He said, 'If they want the trophy that badly, let's just let them have it.' He meant it, too. Actually, I have to admit I didn't always agree with our chairman, but I did on this occasion.

We were absolutely appalled at the misbehaviour and the indiscipline of the Argentines in Glasgow. They had no intention of playing football and that was a shame because these lads could play if they were allowed off the leash. They had conquered the best South America had to offer to reach this stage, just as we had seen off the cream of Europe. So, they had a certain pedigree, but, as Jinky said in his usual straightforward manner, 'Football went oot the windae that night at Hampden.'

Sadly, he was so accurate. Here was a platform for the two best clubs on the planet to put on a spectacle. We could have conjured up a genuine soccer showpiece, an extravaganza of spectacular skills to be applauded around the globe. We had an excellent opportunity to put on a football feast for everyone to enjoy. Unfortunately, it was more X-certificate than exhibition. Our ruthless opponents were determined to triumph at all costs and if that meant spitting on you, slyly nudging you in the ribs and bouncing Wee Jinky all over Hampden then that's the way they would perform. The ball was secondary to most of the action that night. Actually, it is a bit of an art form for a player to hammer you in the ribs from the side, slide his studs down the back of your ankle, pull your hair and control the ball in the same motion. If they had only concentrated on the skills of the game we would have had three wonderful encounters. Alas, that's not the way it turned out. These became spiteful, bad-tempered affairs.

The occasion at Hampden wasn't helped by an overly lenient Spanish referee in Juan Gardeazabal who, when you consider the circumstances, rather remarkably didn't book anyone on the night. A steward's inquiry might have been called. As anyone who knows me will tell you, I am not one for excuses. If I deserve it, I'll take my dumps. However, the fates were certainly conspiring to make sure that trophy – officially known as the Intercontinental Cup – didn't come back to Celtic Park. For a start, we would have preferred to have played the first leg away from home as there are obvious advantages in that situation. It means you know exactly what you have to do in the second leg in front of your own support. It also means that if there is a tie then the third match will be played on your continent.

Also, back then, Racing Club were given the opportunity to choose the match official from three referees who were put forward by the tournament organisers. To be fair, Celtic had the same option for the second game. Not surprisingly, however, Racing Club went for Señor Gardeazabal. For a start, he could converse with them in their native tongue given that Spanish is, of course, the first language of Argentina. During the game in Glasgow we could hear him talking to their players, but all we got were shrugs and gestures. How different would it have been if we had, say, a German or a ref from northern Europe in charge of the game? They knew what our football was all about; hard and fair challenges, high energy levels, physical commitment and so on. The Spaniard frowned on heavy tackles that were perfectly legal, something we did every matchday in

Scotland. We were annoyed that he favoured the 'style' – if that's the word – of our opponents. After all, that's what he was used to every week in Spain. So, it was advantage to Racing Club before a ball – or a Celtic player – had been kicked. You better believe me, though, we were still convinced we would win that trophy. Just so long as we were allowed to play football. But Racing Club had absolutely no intention of competing on a level playing field.

Racing Club were totally and ruthlessly dedicated to lifting the silverware. They were quite prepared to step over bodies on their way to picking up that trophy. That was their main goal for that campaign and that was obvious when you looked at their league form at the time. Our opponents had won only one game, had lost the previous three before they faced us and were sitting eleventh in a league of sixteen. Everything was aimed at beating Celtic and being crowned the best team in the world. They also had four players over the age of thirty in their line-up and they knew it was now or never for them at this level. We had Ronnie Simpson, who was thirty-seven, Stevie Chalmers was thirty and I was twenty-nine. The rest of the lads were a wee bit younger. Certainly, the Argentines had more experience, but we thought we had enough to beat them. We were afraid of no-one.

On 18 October 1967, a crowd of 83,437 turned up at Hampden Park to witness the biggest club game ever staged in Scotland. The Celtic team was: Simpson, Craig, Gemmell, Murdoch, McNeill, Clark, Johnstone, Lennox, Wallace, Auld and Hughes. Big Jock had left out Stevie Chalmers from our European Cup-winning team, this time preferring the unpredictability of John Hughes, known affectionately to everyone as Yogi after the TV cartoon character who was so popular at the time.

Our manager had put in overtime telling us what to expect. He urged us not to get rattled. He said, 'Don't let them put you off your natural game. Don't get drawn into any feuds. If you lose your discipline, you'll lose the game. Let the world see how to win the Celtic way. Remember who you are representing. Don't let anyone down. Fight for each other and we'll be OK.' He must have been exhausted after his team talk, but we all realised just how much these games meant to Big Jock. Everything. Just everything.

To be honest, we went into these contests without too much knowledge of our rivals. Remember, this was over four decades ago and technology was still in its infancy as far as television was concerned. DVDs and videos were a long way off, so we got precious little information on Racing Club. We had to rely on reports from South America, but, in reality, we went in blind. There was no chance of Celtic sending a scout to Argentina to spy on them. Back then, that would have been a twenty-hour trip each way. Of course, there would also have been the inevitable delays. It just wasn't feasible. The Argentines, however, saw Celtic in at least two games when they arrived early for the Hampden match. For instance, their manager Juan Jose Pizzuti saw us beat Partick Thistle 5-1 at Firhill and left with a bulging notebook. He did make these points: 'I agree with those who name Murdoch as the chief obstacle to Racing Club. He impressed me greatly. He studied his opponents for ten minutes, then began chipping beautiful passes to the left wing. I was also impressed by the generalship of Auld and the speed of Lennox, though not his football brain. But one player I liked very much was their goalkeeper, Simpson.' The Racing coach might have had his faults, but he certainly knew how to spot a player! By the way, thank goodness

Wee Lemon wasn't using his grey matter that day; he had to be content with only four goals. Thistle would have been in real trouble if he had engaged his brain.

Within minutes of the kick-off at Hampden, our opponents set out their stall. They weren't even going to camouflage the fact they were out to nail Jinky. He was clearly marked down as our main threat and we all took a sharp intake of breath when Juan Rulli sent the Wee Man flying with as crude a challenge as you would ever wish to see. Making it even worse, Oscar Martin came in from behind and looked as though he was attempting to volley our winger over the Hampden stand. Jinky rolled around in genuine agony after this double dunt and we looked at the referee wondering if he was going to offer our colleague any protection. We're still waiting. He didn't even admonish either of the Racing Club culprits and you could see them glancing at each other and their team-mates. They knew the referee was weak and, by God, did they abuse us for the rest of the evening. If the match official had taken strict action there and then, we might have had a football game. He failed lamentably and miserably in his duties and that was the signal for the Argentines to indulge in the dark arts of football. They knew that side of the business, all right.

However, there was nothing they could do to prevent Caesar, Billy McNeill, majestic in the air as usual, getting the only goal of an evening that was memorable mainly for all the wrong reasons. We thought our luck was out just beforehand when I slung over a free-kick in the fifty-fifth minute and our skipper thumped a header off the woodwork. Chances were few and far between against this side and we cursed our luck as that opportunity passed us by. However, all was right with the world again when Yogi swept over a corner-kick from the right. Caesar, who had been bumped, jostled, punched and blocked throughout at deadball situations, managed to get clear in a packed penalty box. His blond head met the ball perfectly and it seemed to take an age before it swept high into the net past their keeper, Agustin Cejas. Caesar leapt in delight and then had a few well-chosen words with Alfio Basile, who would later manage Argentina. Basile had tried to rough up our centre-half every time he ventured into their penalty area, but he was helpless as our impeccable captain got that so crucial goal. I asked Caesar afterwards what he had said to his opponent, but he feigned surprise and claimed he couldn't recall the incident. I got the drift that he wasn't inviting his opponent out for a drink afterwards.

A South American journalist asked their left-back Diaz what he thought about playing against Wee Jinky. At least the Argentine was honest. He said something along the lines of: 'I tried to tackle him fairly at the start, but I realised this would be impossible for the entire game. I elected to kick him when he came near me after that. He would have destroyed me.' And yet he wasn't booked by the referee. Racing's coach Pizzuti didn't take the risk of fielding him against Jinky in the second leg just in case a real match official turned up. He promptly dropped him and brought in another hatchet man called Nelson Chabay, who looked as though he was just another version of Diaz. Only harder and dirtier.

And so our great South American adventure was about to begin. We arrived in Buenos Aires after a tiring twenty-one-hour trip which saw us stop at Paris, Madrid and Rio before reaching our destination. We were met at the airport by the St Andrews Pipe Band and we were all handed flowers and garlands by a squad of local schoolchildren. We were all a wee bit surprised at this welcome. Each and every one of us was told it would be hostile. The Argentines still hadn't forgiven the British for their national team's failure to win the World Cup in England the previous year. They had come up against Sir Alf Ramsey's eventual winners in the quarter-final stage and, of course, had their influential skipper Antonio Rattin sent off in the first half. It didn't matter that we were Scottish. It was just unfortunate that we were the first club from the British Isles to land in the country since the World Cup. We didn't have time to give the Racing Club supporters refresher courses in history or geography. As far as they were concerned, we were as good – or as bad – as English. They hadn't forgotten that the England manager had attempted to prevent his players from swapping their shirts with their opponents after the game, won 1-0 by the host nation. They weren't impressed, either, that they had very publicly been branded by Ramsey as 'animals'. Thanks, Sir Alf, it was always going to be tough enough.

We arrived at our HQ, the Hindu Club which was situated about thirty miles or so from the Buenos Aires city centre. It wasn't quite Estoril, where we had enjoyed the countdown in Lisbon before the European Cup success over Inter Milan almost six months earlier. It was quite busy with local families using the facilities when our coach rolled in, but they dispersed as the day wore on. We had a wee walk around the place and saw that it had a pool, tennis courts, golf course and even a cricket pitch. Oh, did I mention the policemen with machine guns? There were at least four armed cops and another twenty involved in a round-the-clock watch in the grounds. That doubled on the day of the game, 1 November. What was this all about? We were there to play a football game, not start a revolution. There is something distinctly odd about having your breakfast and noticing a bloke with a machine gun walking past the dining room window. It's amazing what you can get used to, though. It was all very surreal, but we were there to do a job for Celtic Football Club and our supporters.

It was an interesting ride to the Avellaneda Stadium. The ground is actually on the outskirts of Buenos Aires, which gave you the impression it was a lot more affluent than its near neighbour Avellaneda, which is one of the poorer parts of the country, and the Racing Club fans, with little in life except their football, were determined to do everything to knock us out of our stride. I looked out the coach window as we weaved our way to our destination. Some parts made Maryhill look like Miami. There were beggars on the street, ramshackle dwellings and dogs everywhere. Some of them were even alive. I am a dog lover – I've got five at the moment – and it was distressing to see these impoverished animals roaming the streets searching for a morsel of food. However, I had to push all these disturbing images to the back of my mind. I continued to cajole my team-mates and help them to concentrate on the game ahead.

Unfortunately, I had injured an ankle in our 5-3 League Cup Final victory over Dundee the day before we flew out for Argentina. I was desperate to play, but I also knew Big Jock wouldn't take a risk on my fitness if I wasn't 100 per cent. There would have been no point in pleading with the manager; I can't recall too many occasions when he was swayed once he made up his mind. In any case, it wouldn't have been fair to my team-mates if I played and couldn't give my best. I looked at this monstrous oval-shaped grey-walled stadium as we got nearer and just wished I could be involved. This was a perfect setting for me. I also recall the supporters around the place seemed to have a death wish. They jumped in front of our coach and tried to get us to deviate from our route. The bus driver had obviously seen it all before. He simply steamed ahead and if a supporter was struck then that was his bad luck.

When we arrived I gasped – the riot police were out in force. They had cops on horses with massive sabres at the ready, armed policemen seemed to be swarming all over the place, they had cops with these leather lashes and they weren't slow to use them if they thought some fans were getting too excited. We were at the door of our destiny. The trip that had started back in Glasgow when we beat Zurich in the first leg of our first-ever European Cup tie had taken us through Switzerland, France, Yugoslavia, Czechoslovakia and Portugal before leading us to Argentina. My old mate Willie O'Neill, one of the most underrated players in the club's history, took my place in midfield as Big Jock selected this team: Simpson, Craig, Gemmell, Murdoch, McNeill, Clark, Johnstone, O'Neill, Wallace, Chalmers and Lennox.

The referee was a Uruguayan, Esteban Marino, who, we were told beforehand, was 'not strong'. Once again, the players realised they would be up against it. I took my seat in the stand beside the Celtic board and some of the other players who hadn't been selected. I was sitting beside Jose McBride and Yogi when we felt what we thought was a faint rain. It was a sunny afternoon and we believed it must just be a passing shower. Then we looked up at the tier on top of us and there was a group of disgusting lowlifes urinating on us. Spat on in Glasgow and peed on in Buenos Aires. I was beginning to agree with Sir Alf more and more.

The supporters were screaming at us constantly. It was utter bedlam as their contorted gargoyle-like faces directed outright hatred at us. I've been in more comfortable surroundings, but

I didn't realise just how close we were to a full-blown riot. You could only have guessed at the havoc this baying mob could have wreaked if the game hadn't got underway. And that situation wasn't unimaginable. Our keeper, Ronnie Simpson – Faither to his colleagues – was struck on the head as he checked his nets before kick-off. There were massive wire fences behind both goals, so some idiot either had an incredibly good aim or was extremely lucky, but Faither took a dull one and went down immediately holding his head. There were more sinister thoughts that our goalkeeper could have been hit by a photographer or someone else standing behind his goal. Security was remarkably relaxed as folk wandered around in areas where you would only expect people with official passes. Either way, Faither was down and Neilly Mochan raced on to administer treatment. From my place in the stand, with all the accompanying cacophony of noise battering my eardrums and deranged, fired-up supporters leaping about all over the place, I was desperately trying to see what was going on. Faither was no actor – if he was on the ground there was a good reason for it. To this day we still don't know what struck him. It could have been a metal bar, as was widely suggested, a bottle or a brick. The object mysteriously disappeared in the midst of all the pandemonium.

Now, as I said, Sir Robert Kelly wasn't too keen on even travelling to Argentina after Racing Club's unforgivable and unacceptable antics in Glasgow. Given half a chance at that particular moment he might just have ordered the Celtic players off the pitch and headed for the relative sanctuary of the dressing rooms. God only knows what would have happened if that had been the case. I shudder to even contemplate such an action. I doubt if we would have got out of the Avellaneda unscathed.

You don't know, either, how the powers-that-be would have judged such behaviour. A lengthy suspension from European tournaments could have followed for the club. FIFA probably wouldn't have been slow in slapping on a massive fine. Would you believe there was no UEFA representative at any of the three games in Scotland, Argentina and Uruguay? Yet we were representing Europe in these confrontations and I believe they weren't slow to take their cut of the gate at Hampden. Celtic were isolated and I have no doubt that officialdom would have come down heavily on us.

Anyway, the game eventually kicked off fifteen minutes late with reserve John Fallon in goal and, astoundingly, we were awarded a penalty-kick in the twentieth minute. As you might expect, it was an absolute stonewaller and the Uruguayan referee couldn't possibly ignore it. Jinky got past his markers, raced into the box and was clearly knocked to the ground by the outrushing Cejas. To be fair, ref Marino didn't hesitate as he pointed to the spot. Up stepped Big TG and, in his usual fashion, he clattered the ball beyond the keeper who was almost on the six-yard line when my mate struck his effort.

The lead, alas, was to last only thirteen minutes. Humberto Maschio, who had proved to be a tricky customer in their midfield at Hampden and was emulating that form in front of his own fans, picked out Norberto Raffo all on his own in our penalty area. Honestly, he looked miles offside and if you see pictures of that goal you will not spot a single Celtic defender anywhere near him. Our sweeper John Clark will forever be convinced that Raffo was in an illegal position. Anyway, he got his head to the ball and sent it looping over the exposed Fallon. I had hardly had time to settle into my seat after the interval when Racing Club scored a second through Juan Carlos Cardenas. He was a lively little raider and his well-struck effort found the corner of the net leaving the unfortunate Fallon helpless once again.

That's how it finished. There was the usual cynical, irritating pushing and shoving from the Argentines to kill the game once they had nudged ahead and they played it tight until the end to make certain there was a third game. Now, if goals away had counted double in those days, that trophy would have been heading back to Glasgow with us. However, the games were actually decided on points. That meant it was two points apiece and not 2-2 on aggregate as most people believed. Here's another thought. What would have happened if Fallon had been injured during the game and had to go off?

At that time teams could only name one substitute, a goal-keeper. So, Celtic could have been left with only ten men and with TG playing in goal in one of the most important games in the club's history. Remember, this was no bounce game in a public park. These were the organiser's most prestigious matches of the entire season, the blue riband of all tournaments. Needless to say, it was descending into farce and that should never have been allowed to happen. To say we were becoming just a bit disenchanted would be a massive understatement. And after a week or so in South America I guessed the mood of the camp was just to get things over and done with and return to Scotland.

The setting in Montevideo was hardly conducive to sport. For a start, we were told 2,000 plain-clothed riot police would mingle with the expected 60,000 crowd at the Stadio Centenario. They were anticipating trouble even before the kick-off and that got through to all the players. We knew how desperate Racing Club were to win this trophy and we also realised they would not be holding back at the third time of asking. Trouble was in the air and we all sensed it. But we didn't realise what a part we would play in the forthcoming mayhem.

Celtic asked for the Uruguayan referee Esteban Marino to again take charge of the third game in his native homeland. He wasn't the best match official we had ever witnessed, but we thought he was reasonably fair. However, our request was refused for whatever reason and, instead, it was announced a Paraguayan, Rodolfo Cordesal, would be the man in the middle. Let's cut to the chase here – the guy was hopeless. Utterly useless. I think he lost the plot at the toss-up. It was far too big an occasion for an inexperienced referee – I think he was only twenty-nine years old – and he hadn't a clue what was going on around him. I was back in the team after overcoming my ankle injury and Big Jock sent out this line-up: Fallon, Craig, Gemmell, Murdoch, McNeill, Clark, Johnstone, Wallace, Lennox, Auld and Hughes. Faither was still injured and had to sit it out again.

Strangely, the first twenty minutes or so passed relatively quietly. The referee blew for just about everything and I was told afterwards that he awarded twenty-four fouls against Celtic in the first half. That was about as many as we would expect to give away in an entire season at home! We kept possession and tried to play Jinky into the game as often as possible. Once again Chabay was marking the Wee Man and, as usual, wasn't slow to put the boot in. Jinky took a couple of sore ones in that opening period and the Argentines were clever in the sense it was almost a rotation system when it came to kicking Jinky. Chabay would foul him and, a couple of minutes later, another defender would hack him. Then another and another. The referee didn't twig what Racing Club were up to, but we did. Frankly, it was infuriating. We were getting close to breaking point, individually and collectively. We had had enough of being abused. This was no preconceived thought of retribution. No-one thought of bringing the good name of Celtic Football Club into disrepute. All you could see was a player smack in front of you who had spat on you constantly and thought he was going to get away with it. You can lose it in these exceptional circumstances.

The final straw came when Jinky was sent sprawling again and the weak match official awarded us a free-kick and didn't even admonish the offender. I admit we were wrong – so terribly, awfully wrong. However, we were so angry at everything we had been expected to endure against these guys. All these years later I can only apologise to that wonderful Celtic support. We were mere human beings and we just couldn't accept any more abuse. We had faced them three times in just over a fortnight and, I am sad to admit, we snapped. They pushed us over the edge. Amazingly, the first guy to be sent off was Lemon. This is the same Bobby Lennox who I don't think was ever even cautioned in his career before that. We were all astounded as Lemon made his way to the touchline and was then told to get back on by Big Jock who clearly thought there had been a mistake. The referee was told Lemon was the offender by Racing's own defender Basile, who was also dismissed. There had been a clash and the Argentinian hardman went down in a heap. Whoever hit him, it wasn't Lemon, that's for sure. Referee Cordesal ordered off Basile and then had a word with him. The Argentine pointed to Bobby as the man who had struck him and the dopey match official immediately pointed to the stand.

Lemon looked aghast. I can't recall him ever doing anything untoward on a football pitch. I really mean that. He was one of the fairest guys I can ever recall playing with or against. He hadn't a bad word to say about anyone and, certainly, no-one ever had a bad word to say about him. He took some woeful kickings, but, just like Jinky, he kept coming back for more. He had been a thorn in Racing's side ever since the first game and they were delighted to see him go off. Lemon was so bewildered that he came back on for a second time after having a word with Big Jock. No-one could believe he was being banished. However, he was finally persuaded to accept his removal when a riot cop with an enormous sabre came onto the pitch to act as his escort. My team-mate, as you might expect, thought better of pursuing the argument.

That was in the thirty-seventh minute and shortly after the interval he was joined in the dressing room by his best pal Jinky. He had been booted all over the place for two and a half games and their tough-guy defender Martin got a hold of his shirt yet again. Jinky tried to wrestle free and I think his elbow hit the Racing Club defender on the chest. He went down as though he had been shot. The referee couldn't get on the scene quickly enough to send off Jinky. No words were exchanged between the Celtic players. We just knew there was not going to be any justice in Montevideo that day. On a personal note, I was sick and fed up with players spitting on me. I wiped my hair at one stage and it was covered in spittle. You have to be an extraordinary individual blessed with remarkable patience if you can accept that sort of behaviour from an opponent.

The red mist came down and it didn't get any better when their player, Cardenas, rifled in a long-range effort for the only goal of the game in the fifty-sixth minute. Big Jock later blamed Fallon for not saving the thirty-five-yard effort, but, to be fair to our keeper, I don't think he had much of a chance. The ball swerved and dipped before it flew past him and thudded into the net. Believe me, like our manager, I was a serial critic of goalkeepers. I used to say that most of Celtic's keepers thought the net behind them was there to stop the ball. That was before Faither, of course. But I didn't believe Fallon was culpable on that occasion.

Racing had something to defend and they weren't about to give up anything without a fight. Literally. They continued to provoke us to the point where we couldn't take any more. The referee offered us no protection whatsoever and the game descended into anarchy. Yogi was next to be ordered off and I can smile now at his explanation of his dismissal. He followed a ball into the Racing Club penalty area and their theatrical goalkeeper Cejas came out to pick it up. To waste time, he collapsed on the ball. My colleague didn't stop in his pursuit of the backpass and, astonishingly, appeared to kick the ball while it was in the keeper's hands. Cejas deserved a Hollywood Oscar nomination for his acting ability as he rolled around. The referee didn't hesitate as he signalled it was the end of the game for Yogi. I asked him afterwards what he was thinking of. Yogi, as honest as ever, told me: 'I didn't think anyone was looking.' Only the rest of the world!

It was around about that time that Tommy Gemmell decided to take the law into his own hands after yet another melee had stopped the game. TG, still one of my best mates, had a kick at Raffo off the ball and the Argentine screamed in pain before hitting the deck. The referee didn't see it as our cavalier defender retreated to a neutral spot. Again, like the rest of us, he had had enough of our opponents dishing out abuse and decided to do something about it. There is no way you can condone such actions, of course, but if you had been out on that pitch you might have understood how an individual could have been driven to such retribution.

Rulli was next to go and his sending-off was long overdue. He had kicked us all over the place and the only remarkable thing was that it took him until five minutes from the end of the third game to be dismissed. A few minutes later the referee decided it would be a good idea to send yours truly packing. Naturally enough, I didn't agree. I clattered into one of their defenders and, as you would expect, he went down as though mortally wounded. The Paraguayan official raced over to me and pointed to the tunnel. I shrugged my shoulders and basic-ally told him I didn't speak Spanish so I hadn't a clue what he was indicating. I looked him straight in the eye and realised he was in a state of panic. He looked genuinely startled. I don't suppose too many players in his domestic league refused to be sent off when he was pointing to the dressing room. Well, there's a first time for everything and I simply refused to go off. What happened next even surprised me – he restarted the game with a free-kick to Celtic! That just about summed up all three games for the biggest and most glittering prize in club football. And I can also tell you that in the referee's official report afterwards he stated Bobby Murdoch had been sent off. There was no mention of John Hughes. The guy couldn't get anything right.

There was a picture of Bobby, nicknamed Chopper, looking as though he had a Racing Club player in some sort of wrestling hold. The guy was on the ground and Chopper had him by the legs. It looked like my midfield partner was trying to get his opponent in a Boston crab, I think it's called. The photo-graph did no-one any favours, but, in fact, my midfield partner was merely dragging the Argentine, clearly feigning injury, off the field in an effort to get on with the game. It was a bit drastic,

155

but, in the middle of all that was going on, it wasn't completely out of place. Like England a year before, there would be no swapping of shirts with our opponents. As I recall, there were no handshakes, either, between the players. It would have been pointless and we weren't going to be hypocritical. We hated the sight of these guys for what they had done and it was unforgivable. If we had had the opportunity to get out of that ground and immediately step onto a plane, still in our football strips and boots, and head back to Scotland, we would have taken it.

However, if we thought we had had a rough ride out on the pitch, it was a mere stroll in the park for what we were about to encounter in the dressing room. Big Jock was furious and laid into us in a way he had never done before. He looked as though he was about to explode. None of us escaped. 'You have all let down Celtic,' he bellowed. 'You have brought shame on this club. I told you not to lose your tempers. I warned you if you did that, you would lose the game. Yet you went out and fell for all their tricks.' Then he would point his finger at individuals and we couldn't muster an argument among us. We just sat there like errant schoolkids and took our punishment.

The Celtic hierarchy, led by Bob Kelly, were also raging at their own players and I, for one, couldn't blame them. We lost our discipline and our dignity in Montevideo. It was a dreadful outcome to what should have been one of the most momentous occasions in the club's history. Racing Club had got what they wanted and we were left sickened. To make matters even worse, the board of directors decided to fine every player once we got home. I believe we were due £250 each as our bonus for beating Dundee in the League Cup Final and the club decided to withdraw the cash and give it to charity. So, not only had we been kicked, hacked, punched and spat on, we were also fined for our troubles. Not every Celtic player was happy at that treatment from the board and Cairney, our right-back Jim Craig, spoke up to let his feelings be known. You had to feel for him as he had played in all three games and hadn't even been booked. It didn't seem fair, but, then, the entire South American adventure – or should that be misadventure? – was hardly fair to us as soon as that Spanish referee blew for the kick-off on the evening of 18 October at Hampden to set in motion three games we would all rather forget, but never will.

As a postscript, I was later told that Racing Club's captain Roberto Perfumo, not a bad right-back as I recall, asked his club not to display the cup in their trophy cabinet. Apparently, he had been upset at how his team had won the silverware. Their coach, Pizzuti, also left a week or so later to take over Boca Juniors. The words of Bob Kelly after the Hampden Park fiasco came back to me: 'If they want the trophy that badly, let's just let them have it.'

Unfortunately, the Celtic players had to endure another three hours of being booted around South America before our unworthy opponents did get their hands on the Intercontinental Cup. But, if they were being honest, I don't think one of their players genuinely believed they were the best club side in the world. We were. We just didn't have a trophy to prove it.

As we waited in the airport lounge to escape from South America at long last, Big Jock cut a forlorn figure as he sat at a table on his own. He looked inconsolable. There were occasions when it was best to leave our manager on his own and this was one of them. Like the rest of us, he found it difficult to comprehend what we had all been through in just a few days. We were all at our lowest ebb as we mingled around. There was very little dialogue among the players as there wasn't much to say. We were all hurting. We were sickened, battered, bruised and beaten. Our manager made no attempt to disguise his feelings as he sat looking at a cup of tea on the table in front of him.

We knew some of the board would have been happy to come home after the match in Buenos Aires. Jock, though, was determined to see it through. He had the utmost faith in us. He believed – and so, too, did the players – that Celtic could beat any team anywhere on the planet. That could only happen if we were allowed to play football. However, we had succumbed and taken the bait. We had descended to their level and, looking back, that should never have been allowed to happen. Perhaps we should have gone home early. Maybe we shouldn't have been there in the first place. But I repeat: How do you react when you are continually spat upon? Some of their players were more sleekit than the others; they never spat in your face. They would sneak up behind you and then you were aware of something landing in your hair. It was like a fly or a bee. When you put your hand up to your head you realised you had become yet another target for their reprehensible actions. It was a long journey home, believe me. The plane was transformed into a morgue. There was still no escaping the wrath of the manager as he took the opportunity to again give us a verbal hammering.

As we neared the final leg of our marathon and miserable journey home, Jock calmed down for a moment and said: 'We will never play an Argentinian team again if I've got anything to do with it.' No-one present in that Celtic party felt inclined to disagree.

12

THE ROAD TO SAN SIRO

Big Mick Jones wasn't happy with me the night we overwhelmed Leeds United 2-1 in the European Cup semi-final in 1970 at Hampden. I couldn't blame him – I had just 'done' the Elland Road striker minutes before half-time.

As we came out for the second half, the aggregate score was level at 1-1 after we had beaten them down on their own patch in the first leg. Jones was a giant of a man, a huge physical presence and, to be honest, I was getting more than a little fed up that he was getting away with all his barging and bumping of my team-mates. He was racing around like an angry bull elephant. That was his game, of course, and he was built for it. He liked to soften up opponents and I thought it would be a reasonable idea to give him some of his own medicine. I saw my chance as we neared the interval.

It was a 50/50 ball and Jock always insisted we should win these challenges. He never told us how he expected us to win them, we just had to make sure we got the ball. I flew into the challenge and I caught Jones. He squealed and went down in a heap. I didn't have much sympathy for him. If you dish it out, you have to anticipate that you might get some back in return.

So, Jones came over to me as we trooped onto the pitch for the second half. He sidled up to me and said, 'Hunter's going to get you. He'll sort you out, you little bastard.' I laughed in his face. I've knocked bigger men out of the way to get into a fight. 'I hope it's the White Hunter,' I said, making a reference to a television programme at the time about some bloke who wandered around jungles blowing away all sorts of wildlife with an enormous shotgun.

Jones, of course, was referring to his so-called hardman team-mate Norman Hunter, who rejoiced in the nickname of 'Bite Yer Legs' Hunter. Well, that terrified the hell out of me! Threats on a football field never bothered me. There was always some tough guy who was going to 'sort you out'. I don't know what the Leeds defender promised his team-mate at half-time about the retribution that was about to come my way, but I'm still waiting. Before the matches Leeds were already as good as European Cup winners, according to the English media. We were dismissed out of hand and that got right up my nose. Jackie Charlton should have known better, but he, too, was conned into believing it would be a walkover for his team. It rankled with me when I was watching television and the England international central defender announced, 'The next time we beat Celtic, I'm going to put them on my mantelpiece.' Wrong thing to say, Jackie.

Celtic and Leeds had played several friendlies around that period with respective managers, Big Jock and Don Revie, fairly pally. Now please note the word 'friendlies'. Jock would try new things in such games, move players around and so on. Leeds did OK in these encounters and maybe that lured them into a false sense of security. They hadn't realised that they hadn't witnessed the REAL Celtic on these occasions. That was all to change over the two legs of the European Cup semi-final. We won them both, home and away, and it was 'Goodnight, Leeds – thanks for the memories.'

Charlton was so incensed afterwards he admitted in a sports show that he had a little black book and there were two names in it. He vowed to get revenge on these characters – one was Peter Osgood, the former Chelsea striker, the other was me! At least I was in good company because Peter was some player. Ironically, I met him just before his death a few years ago and we had a wee chat about Charlton's Book of Bad Guys. It seemed to bother Peter as much as it bothered me.

We knew Leeds were a physical team. They bossed a lot of teams in England just by their sheer bullying presence. Revie had assembled an excellent outfit, but they could put it about, too. They had my wee pal Billy Bremner as skipper and he was afraid of nothing. They also contained players such as Paul Reeney, Johnny Giles, Paul Madeley, Charlton, Hunter and Jones. There wasn't a shrinking violet in sight, but if they thought they could intimidate us, they were terribly misinformed. How do you put the frighteners on guys such as Davie Hay, Tommy Gemmell, Bobby Murdoch, Billy McNeill, Jinky Johnstone and Willie Wallace? I was never going to be famous, either, for running for cover when the going got tough. Leeds were about to discover this to their cost.

They should have heeded the warning when George Connelly scored in the first minute in Leeds. He got a second, but it was ruled out for whatever reason. As I recall, George was well onside, but Jinky might have strayed offside. We contained them quite well and our goalkeeper, Evan Williams, wasn't exactly overworked. We came back up by train and even I was astounded at the reception committee that awaited us at

Glasgow's Central Station. Thousands of Celtic fans were there to welcome us home. I believe we all had to pile into a police van to escape to safety. If our wonderful support were happy then, it was going to get better in a fortnight.

Actually, we were stunned fairly early on at Hampden where the game had been switched to deal with the incredible demand for tickets. A crowd of 136,505 crammed into the stadium and that is still a record gate for a European Cup game. Bremner scored a screamer for them in only fourteen minutes and I have to accept the blame. I wasn't picking him up and considering he was on the right of their midfield and I was on the left of ours, I should have put in more of a challenge to prevent him from taking aim.

He was about thirty-five yards out when he looked up and walloped this effort at our goal. I can still see that shot flying in to this day. It seemed to pick up momentum as the ball hurtled towards Williams' top right-hand corner. It was in the back of his net before our keeper could move and I had to put my hands up and accept responsibility. Funnily enough, although that tied the score, I didn't think for one second we would lose and I am not saying that out of bravado now the result is in the history books. We knew there would be a winner that night and I just happened to believe it would be Celtic. My team-mates were in complete accordance.

We moved the ball around crisply and we could see Big Yogi, John Hughes, was giving Charlton problems with his powerful style. Jock had seen Yogi score two goals for the Scottish League against their English counterparts at St James's Park, Newcastle, one night and kept it in mind. The opposition centre-half on that occasion was the aforementioned Charlton. Yogi could play on the left wing or directly through the middle and our manager knew his presence in leading the attack would unsettle the man who put my name in his little black book all those years ago. Maybe he should have added Yogi's, too!

As I said earlier, Jones was rampaging around and getting away with it. I decided to let him know we would not accept his antics and, I readily admit, I did him. I still say, though, that it was a 50/50 ball and the challenge, fierce though it may have been, was not a foul. But I was determined to put down a marker to let him and his mates know that we would not tolerate such behaviour. I think I got the message across. So, I was hardly shaking in my boots when he made his threat at the start of the second period.

Actually, they had also tried to intimidate Jinky throughout the game with the same level of success. Our wee outside-right was absolutely immense that evening. He turned their English international left-back Cooper, rated one of the best in Europe, inside out as he darted around, weaving this way and that as only he could. Hunter was heard shouting at Cooper, 'Kick him!' Cooper roared back, 'You try and kick him!' Hunter tried and failed before retreating to his normal berth beside Charlton.

That second half was to become one of the most memorable of my entire career. Hampden was rocking to its foundations, the atmosphere was electric, the fans' ferocious vocal backing was inspiring and we couldn't possibly let them down. We didn't. I thought it was only a matter of time before we levelled and I'm glad to say I went at least a part of the way to atoning for allowing Bremner to score when I helped set up the equaliser. I worked a one-two with Davie Hay on the right, flicked over a neat cross and Yogi threw himself in front of the hesitating Charlton to bullet a header past the helpless Gary Sprake.

Leeds were on the ropes, to use a boxing term, and, in the same parlance, we were about to deliver the knock-out blow. Sprake went off with an ankle injury and Revie threw on substitute David Harvey, who was to become a mainstay in the Scottish international team a few years later and had happier times to come at Hampden. We put together a sweeping move down the right flank and Jinky passed the ball to the edge of the box, where my midfield mate Chopper Murdoch was arriving with his usual immaculate sense of timing to first-time an unstoppable right-foot shot low past the despairing Harvey. Game over. Where was Norman 'Bite Yer Legs' Hunter when you needed him!

I will always remember Chopper running away after scoring that goal. His chest seemed to be getting bigger and bigger as he took the salute of the delirious Celtic fans. It looked as though it was being pumped up and I thought it was going to burst through his shirt. I really liked Chopper – it would have been impossible not to – and I was so happy for him. He was always so proud to wear those Celtic colours and I realised just how much that strike meant to him. That enduring image of him at that particular moment in time will be with me for ever.

It says a helluva lot about their skipper Billy Bremner that he came into our dressing room at time-up to congratulate us on a 'phenomenal performance', as I recall. He must have been dreadfully disappointed and no-one would have blamed him for going away to hide in some dark corner of Hampden. But that wasn't his style. Actually, we all knew Billy was a massive Celtic fan and he was a fabulous talent. But where would we have fitted him into that side?

We had been promised a bonus by the Celtic directors if we reached the European Cup Final and a few days later we were all handed a cheque. Normally, the club would pay you in readies, but on this occasion they gave us cheques. Our reward for reaching Milan was £1,500 each – the same payment we had received for winning the European Cup three years previously. We weren't greedy, but none of us thought that was an adequate sum of money for what we achieved. The players met in the dressing room to discuss what we were going to do next. We decided to place our cheques on a table and tell Jock we weren't accepting them. We thought we deserved a little bit more.

The Big Man came in, looked at this pile of cheques and asked, 'What's this? Don't you want your bonus money?' One of the players told him we weren't too happy with the sum of money. Jock stared back at all of us and then glanced at his watch. 'Oh, well, do what you want – the cleaning lady will be arriving in a few minutes' time.' He then just walked out of the room. The players looked at each other. Quietly, we all moved to the table and picked up our respective cheques. That was the end of the matter.

Although it all went pear-shaped that ill-fated night in the San Siro Stadium, it must be said that the run to the final was nothing short of exhilarating. I will always remember our quarter-final tie against Fiorentina at Parkhead where, I believe, I had one of the best games of my career. It was one of those evenings when everything simply fell into place. We won 3-0, I scored one goal and set up the other two, one netted by Wispy and one put into his own net by the unfortunate Luigi Carpenetti. My goal was one of the sweetest strikes I have ever hit; a low left-foot drive from the edge of the box that swept past their keeper at his post. Big Yogi knocked it down, I controlled it in an instant and then hit it perfectly. A photographer, Eric Craig, of the *Daily Record*, came over to the park the following day to see if I could re-enact my effort. I was still on a high and there was no way I was going to miss the opportunity to show the thousands of readers of his newspaper how it was done. Eric got his snaps and I was plastered all over his paper the following day. We lost 1-0 in Florence in the second leg, but we were never in any danger of going out of the tournament.

Actually, our European Cup campaign got off to a blank start when we drew 0-0 with Basle in Switzerland and Harry Hood and TG got the goals in the second leg to give us a 2-0 victory. Next up was Benfica, Eusebio and all, and what amazing encounters they were, in Glasgow and Lisbon. TG and Big Jock had had a bit of a fall-out after our left-back was dropped for the League Cup Final against St Johnstone where I got the only goal of the game. TG had demanded a transfer the following day and it looked as though he was on his way out. But everyone knew he was a big game player; the more important the occasion, the better TG played. He was absolutely nerveless and a match against the Portuguese champions was one we all knew he would welcome. Jock realised that, too, so no-one was unduly surprised when TG took the field that night. And what an impact he made, too.

I think the game was barely two minutes old when we were awarded a free-kick about thirty-five yards out. There was only one man for the job – Tommy Gemmell. He raced up to the ball and gave it an almighty clatter. The thing just took off and the keeper hadn't an earthly as it rocketed into the roof of the net. TG was back – and how! Harry and Wispy got the others as we took a three-goal lead to Lisbon and we thought the job was done. Not quite!

With Eusebio in devastating form, the Portuguese gave us one hell of a fright. They were 2-0 up nearing the end of a fairly frantic encounter and searching for the equaliser that would take it into extra time. The minutes were ticking by agonisingly slowly as we tried desperately to keep them at bay. Eusebio had netted just before the interval and Garca piled on the pressure with a second after the turnaround. The game was deep in injury time when Diamentino got their equaliser. I have to admit it was deserved. They really put us through it in front of their own fans. There were no more goals in the extra half-hour and in those days the tie was decided on the toss of a coin. Caesar was called into referee Louis van Raavens' room and asked to make a call. Thankfully, our skipper got it right and, naturally enough, we were elated. I felt a bit for Benfica, too. They had put so much into the game and, in the end, got nothing because of the flip of a coin.

Fiorentina were duly despatched and then it was the turn of Leeds United. They were taken care of, home and away, of course, and we were racing certainties and massive favourites to lift our second European Cup in three years. What could go wrong? Well, just about everything!

13

MISERY IN MILAN

Jock Stein didn't often call it wrong. However, there is no getting away from the fact he made an error in judgement of epic proportions as we prepared for our second European Cup Final in three years against Feyenoord in the San Siro Stadium in Milan in 1970. We were always confident we could beat Europe's finest, but, sadly, on this occasion, I have to admit we were more than just a shade complacent. Remarkably, that emotion emanated directly from our normally-so-astute manager.

Jock had watched our Dutch opponents before we were due to play them on 6 May. He never hid the fact that he had been far from impressed by them. Of course, we had beaten the team already dubbed 'the best in the world' by the English media – Leeds United – in the semi-final. We had overwhelmed them home and away and were, rightly, installed as favourites to lift that glittering prize in Milan. Tony Queen, a bookmaker friend of Big Jock, had offered odds of 9/4 against our rivals with a goal of a start. We were rated 6/4 on.

Our boss, so immaculate and impeccable when talking about opponents, dissecting their strategies and exploring their strengths and weaknesses, didn't look overly concerned as he chatted about the calibre of our opponents. Feyenoord? We could have been talking about Forfar. Three years earlier in Lisbon, we could have told you what the Inter Milan players had for their breakfast we were so well prepared. This was different, though. Jock went as far as dismissing some of their team.

'The big guy on the left-hand side of their midfield won't last the pace,' he informed us. He was talking about Wim van Hanagem who would go on to play in over 100 internationals for Holland and also in the World Cup Final against West Germany four years later.

'The bloke who plays beside him is also one-paced. He won't give you too much trouble.' He was discussing Wim Jansen who, ironically, of course, would become Celtic manager one day. Jock told me, 'Don't worry about him – you won't see him after twenty minutes.' He was right – he kept running past me!

'Their main striker is not mobile enough. He doesn't work too hard.' This was the description of Ove Kindvall, who, as the history books now inform us, scored the winning goal as we collapsed to an abject and embarrassing 2-1 defeat in extra time.

I don't want to turn this into a litany of excuses, but there are some things that must be remembered. For a start, our season had finished on 15 April – three weeks before we took on Feyenoord while their league campaign was in full tilt. The only activity we saw during that period was a benefit match in Lossiemouth for the Fishing Boat Disaster Appeal around that time. Another squad of players went down to Gateshead for a match against the local side. Hardly ideal preparation, I hope you will agree. We also found we would be staying in Varese, close to Lake Como, as we prepared for the match in

Milan. We had been there the previous year when we had played AC Milan in the San Siro. I don't know if the Celtic hierarchy realised this, but the players hated the place. It was about an hour and a half's drive from the stadium and somewhere closer to the San Siro would have been far more beneficial.

When we walked onto the pitch that night we made the unforgivable blunder of believing we merely had to turn up to be given the trophy and then we could all go home. Undoubtedly, we underestimated the Dutch. We went from being overconfident at the start to being overwhelmed at the finish. There were 53,000 supporters in the San Siro and most, as you would expect, were bedecked in green and white. The best fans in the world who deserved an awful lot better that particular evening. Our somewhat nonchalant mood was further enhanced when we discovered Feyenoord would be fielding a goalkeeper who hadn't played for a year!

Their regular No.1 Eddie Treytel, we were assured, had been dropped after a bust-up with manager Ernst Happel. That meant veteran understudy Eddy Pieters Graafland coming out of moth-balls to face us. What could go wrong? It got even better when Graafland was picking the ball out of the net on the half-hour mark when we took the lead with a typical long-range effort from TG.

Bobby Murdoch neatly back-heeled a free-kick into the path of our marauding defender and he unleashed another of his explosive right-foot shots. We really thought it was our night when the referee, experienced Italian Concetto Lo Bello, appeared to distract the Dutch keeper. He might have been in Graafland's line of sight as the ball left TG's boot, but we weren't complaining as the ball whipped low into the net. One–nil up – we'll just take the silverware now, thank you very much.

Oops! In fact, we could have been two goals ahead at that point because Bobby Lennox, with that lightning pace of his, had got round the back of their defence and lashed a typical effort into the net. The referee ruled it out for offside, but TV pictures later on showed Wee Lemon had been played onside by THREE Dutch defenders.

But we were definitely out of sorts and, upon reflection, it would be difficult to pick out a Celtic player that night who would get pass marks. Goalkeeper Evan Williams would probably be the exception as he made several excellent saves. He had to be on his toes because he was getting precious little assistance or protection from the other ten guys out there in front of him. And, of course, I include yours truly. We couldn't get our passing game going and the Dutch were getting in about us. What about Hanagem, the bloke who supposedly invented slow motion? He was sauntering around spraying passes all over the place with devastating accuracy. Yes, he wasn't the quickest along the ground, but his brain was in overdrive and he could see team-mates in an instant. It didn't help our cause, either, that he had a left foot that reminded us all of Jim Baxter. I can pay him no higher compliment.

Meanwhile, Jansen was proving to be anything but slow in the middle of the park. In fact, he was a dynamo, a bundle of energy as he linked midfield with attack and also had time to have a couple of pops at Williams' goal. He also whacked me early on and I thought, 'We've got a game on tonight against these lads.' Kindvall? He was giving our central defence hardly any breathing space and was Mr Perpetual Motion. Davie Hay played right-back and I remember talking to him at one point as we prepared to defend a corner-kick. 'I thought that wee winger was supposed to be slow,' gasped Davie, looking more than just a little bit stunned at the quality of his opponent. 'I've hardly got close to him all night.' That was the story of the evening. We simply could not get our act together; we were struggling all over the park.

In normal circumstances, Chopper and me would link with the defence and feed the ball forward. Then we would join the attack and try to get ahead of the ball to ask some questions of our opponents' defence. They would be left wondering who to pick up. That just didn't happen that evening and I can only say once again that we underestimated Feyenoord who were ready to put themselves about for the cause.

Possibly, if we had held out until half-time, we might have had a chance. To go in at the interval 1-0 ahead would have afforded us the opportunity to redress where we were going so horribly wrong. Unfortunately, our advantage lasted all of three minutes before Feyenoord equalised with a looping header over Williams from their skipper Rinus Israel after we had failed to clear a free-kick from the right. What an adrenalin rush for Feyenoord. What a sickener for us. We continued to disappoint and there was to be no inspiration from the dug-out on this occasion and I hope that isn't being too unfair on Big Jock.

Jim Brogan took an injury early in the first half and, when it was obvious he was not 100 per cent, he should have been taken off. We had Cairney, Jim Craig, among the substitutes and he could have come in at right-back with Davie Hay moving into Brogan's defensive position alongside Caesar. That might have helped. But Jim, who had, of course, missed out on a medal in the 1967 European Cup triumph, was desperate to soldier on in the hope that he could be successful this time around. Jock allowed that to happen and that was just one more mistake in a night of many from us, on and off the pitch.

The half-time talk-in was strangely muted. Everyone – and I mean everyone – believed we couldn't be as bad in the second half.

Unfortunately, it didn't get any better after the interval. Feyenoord were really motoring. They smelled blood and they were going for the jugular. Astonishingly, we held out to take the game into extra time. There were no penalty-kicks in those days and there would have been a replay on the Friday and we all believed that was the best we could hope for. Feyenoord had caught us cold. They had surprised us with their ability, movement, stamina and strength. They would not have been able to emulate that in a replay, believe me. We would have been better prepared and they would have seen the real Celtic, the Celtic that dismissed Leeds United in two enthralling semi-finals.

If only we could keep the back door shut for another half-hour. Quite remarkably, we almost scored in the first minute of the extra period. We could hardly believe it as Big Yogi managed to battle his way into their box and find a direct route to their keeper. It looked as though he couldn't miss – we were going to win the European Cup again, after all. But Yogi, at the crucial moment, got into a bit of a fankle, the ball stuck under his boot and he just stabbed it forward, it hit Graafland and the opportunity was gone. We were to rue that miss.

The clock was ticking down and we were three minutes from that second chance when a strange thing happened, but it showed what a true sportsman Chopper Murdoch was. The Dutch were awarded a free-kick about fifteen yards into our half just inside the right touchline and our superb midfielder actually handed the ball to his opponent. Can you imagine that happening today? Looking back, Chopper should have feigned he didn't hear the official's whistle and booted it into the stand. Or just let it run on. That wouldn't have occurred to our man. As soon as he gave the ball to the Feyenoord player, he placed it on the ground and, in one movement, flighted over a cross towards the lurking Kindvall in our penalty box.

We didn't have the opportunity to regroup and pick up opposing players. Caesar was so startled that he stuck up his hand as he was falling backwards with Kindvall behind him. Normally, our skipper would have attacked the ball with his head, but he was taken completely off guard on this occasion. He actually did get a hand to the ball, but it dropped over his head into the path of their striker. Williams darted from his line, but Kindvall was too quick as he got a toe to the ball to lift it over our keeper where it nestled in the unprotected net. The klaxon horns screeched louder than ever at that moment and we knew we were beaten. What a way to lose. We would have beaten them two days later. I am not being churlish or unsporting in saying that. I really mean it.

Feyenoord were far superior to anything we expected and they thoroughly deserved to be crowned champions of Europe. They were worthy victors, but if only the groundwork had been done with its usual dexterity and thoroughness. Then it would have been an entirely different story. Jock, on this occasion, got it dramatically wrong. The players must take the blame, too. We had blown a marvellous opportunity to stage an action replay of that unforgettable day in Lisbon. Seven Lisbon Lions were on the pitch that miserable night in Milan – Gemmell, Murdoch, McNeill, Johnstone, Wallace, Lennox and yours truly. What a contrast from 1967.

I was substituted just before the end of the regulation ninety minutes. I had just gone down after a challenge from behind and a lot of people must have thought I was coming off because I was injured. But I was leaving the field to be replaced by George Connelly because I was having a stinker. There was no fluency about the Celtic midfield that evening as Chopper and I had difficulty imposing ourselves. I am not having a go at Jock just for the sake of it, but we wondered even before a ball had been kicked about his team formation. He had played three men in midfield – myself, Chopper and George – in the two games against Leeds United and it had worked a treat. Inexplicably, he went for two against Feyenoord, dropping George, and it simply didn't work. They swamped their midfield and we couldn't get a kick. We had most certainly under-estimated them and we paid a heavy price.

I can now admit I was physically sick when the European Cup was handed to Rinus Israel. Honestly, I went behind our dug-out and threw up. I was hurting and so, too, were my disconsolate team-mates. We simply hadn't turned up for the biggest game of the season and, to be absolutely fair, the better team won that night. We could have no complaints about the outcome.

Later, as we trooped out of the San Siro with our heads bowed, I looked up and spotted this big bloke wearing a Celtic tammy and smoking a huge cigar. It was Wim van Hanagem.

How I wish he had spent that evening sitting in the stand among all the other fans wearing green-and-white tammies.

14

BREAK-UP OF THE CHAMPIONS

I have often wondered what would have happened if Celtic had won a second European Cup in 1970. I ask because I believe Big Jock was just a bit too hasty in breaking up a team that had been good enough to reach soccer's summit, beating Leeds United along the way, but was dismantled just a year later.

I knew my time as a Celtic player was coming to an end when Jock took me aside and informed me, 'I think you should sign for Clyde.' Once I had gathered my wits, I replied, 'The only way I'm going to Clyde is if I have a turnstile at Shawfield on matchday! You're not on.' Absolutely no disrespect to Clyde or their excellent manager at the time, Archie Robertson, but I thought it was a bit of a quantum leap in the wrong direction to quit Parkhead for Shawfield. One year I was playing in a European Cup Final and the next I was being shipped off to Clyde. I wasn't having that. I would leave Celtic under my own terms.

Ironically, I thought one of my last games for Celtic might be a Glasgow Cup tie against the Shawfield outfit. There are always rumours flying around in football and Alex Wright, who was then the St Mirren manager, wanted to know if I might be interested in going to Love Street. I didn't rule that out altogether. I had just bought a bungalow in Newton Mearns and I had some of the mortgage to pay off – I think it was around the £5,000 mark. Alex asked me what it would take for me to go to Paisley and I named a figure which, I believe, would have taken care of what was left of the mortgage. I was told that wouldn't be a problem as there would be no transfer fee involved and I was about to become a free agent.

I trotted out to play against Clyde and it was one of those games where I could do no wrong. Even when I mishit a pass it would find a team-mate. The ball would bounce off the back of my head straight to a colleague. Sixty-yard passes were dropping right on the button. Even when I miscued the ball it still found a pal wearing green and white. This went on for the full ninety minutes and I was beginning to really enjoy myself. We won in a canter and I was more than just a little taken aback when Jock greeted me in the dressing room and hugged me. 'You're going nowhere,' he said. 'You'll finish your career here.' He still freed me a couple of months later, though!

Alex Wright was at the match, too, and he said, 'Bertie, there's no way Celtic will let you leave now. That was as fine a performance as I have seen all season. You could have done something about your timing!' St Mirren had appealed to me and I didn't want to be left on the scrapheap. What if no-one else wanted me? I used to worry over things like that. I had no trade to fall back on and I didn't see me setting up a carpentry business at that stage. And I still wanted to prove something on the field.

I did make my last outing for the club in yet another match against Clyde – we seemed to play them every second week – and it was an emotional occasion for all of us. It was the last day of the season and we realised Jock had changes in mind and a massive shake-up was coming. Ten of the eleven Lisbon Lions took the field that afternoon on 1 May 1971 – and I was on my way to Hibs five days later. Faither missed out as he had already retired with a troublesome shoulder injury and Evan Williams took his place in goal. But the other ten were the guys who had played so well almost four years earlier to entrance and entertain Europe.

I wasn't the only one who saw his Celtic playing days come to an end in a 6-1 triumph for us. John Clark and Stevie Chalmers were shipped out to Morton about four months after I left. Stevie was thirty-five years old, but Luggy had just turned thirty and, given his position where experience is crucial, I thought he would have got a bigger team. I heard some English outfits were sniffing around, but he, like Stevie, agreed to go to Morton. Why the Greenock club? It was no secret that Big Jock was very friendly with the Cappielow chairman Hal Stewart. Maybe he was doing him a favour.

A month after that Willie Wallace, along with John Hughes, moved to Crystal Palace. It wasn't long before Big TG was shifting, too, as he agreed to join Nottingham Forest. So, that was six seasoned first team pros all leaving within seven months of each other. Remember, too, that these individuals had all been good enough to help the club pick up their sixth successive title. Jim Craig would follow in May 1972 and it was all over for Bobby Murdoch a year later when he went to Middlesbrough. As I have already said in a previous chapter, it was simply marvellous to see him have such a good career in England.

Look, I know when the time is right to make way for new players and Jock had bought the likes of Harry Hood, Tommy Callaghan and Stevie Murray. There was also the emerging

Destiny awaits. Billy McNeill proudly leads the Celtic players onto the pitch at the Estádio Nacional on May 25, 1967 – an unforgettable day for the club. I'm fifth in the row between John Clark and Bobby Lennox. That was my favoured slot because of my superstitions.

Lisbon Lions. Here's the line-up that would make history. Back row (left to right): Jim Craig, Tommy Gemmell, Ronnie Simpson, Billy McNeill, Bobby Murdoch and John Clark. Front row (l to r): Stevie Chalmers, Willie Wallace, Jimmy Johnstone, Bobby Lennox and yours truly.

The European conquerors. Bobby Lennox, Willie Wallace and Jimmy Johnstone make me comfortable after the 2-1 victory over Inter Milan. The guy on the left? Never seen him before in my life!

Glasgow belongs to us. Willie Wallace, myself and Jimmy Johnstone hold aloft the European Cup as John Hughes, Bobby Lennox, John Clark and John Cushley look on. It was another wonderful day in Paradise.

We're the Bhoys. My good mate Joe McBride and I with the most glittering football prize Europe had to offer.

Spoilsport. Referee John Paterson gives me a telling off for booting the ball into the crowd after a Hampden victory.

The winner. Here's the goal that led to our celebrations that day – the League Cup clincher in a 1-0 triumph over St.Johnstone in 1969. The helpless defender on the goal-line is John Lambie, who later became my assistant boss on my managerial travels.

What a strike. This is one of my favourite goals as my left foot shot streaks low past the Fiorentina keeper. We beat the Italians 3-0 that night on our way to the 1970 European Cup Final against Feyenoord.

Another good day at the office. Billy McNeill, me, Tommy Gemmell and Bobby Murdoch are all smiles after a 3-0 triumph over Benfica in the 1970 European Cup run. We weren't smiling after the second leg! We needed a toss of the coin to go through.

CHEERS. I wave the Scottish Cup to fans after Celtic's emphatic 4-0 triumph over Rangers in 1969.

CHEERS. We've just beaten Leeds United 3-1 on aggregate to reach the 1970 European Cup Final. Goodness knows where the trilby came from!

TEARS. Billy McNeill holds me aloft after my last game for Celtic – a 6-1 league win over Clyde in May 1971. I joined Hibs a few days later.

Bertie the boss. The pre-season team photograph as I take over at Hibs from Partick Thistle in 1982. This was one of the happy occasions – there were others at Easter Road that didn't leave me with a smile on my face.

What a hat-trick. Burlington Bertie eat your heart out – this is the memorable Partick Thistle version!

Highland Fling. Here I am kitted out in the best of tartan gear that the great Harry Lauder would have been proud to wear.

Lone Ranger? No chance! I love horses and I'm taking this one for a wee stroll. Or is it the other way around?

Mine Host. I owned a few pubs in my day and became a dab hand at pouring a pint or two for thirsty customers.

What an honour. I was named in The Greatest-Ever Celtic team by the supporters. Left to right: Bobby Lennox, Henrik Larsson, Kenny Dalglish, Paul McStay, Jimmy Johnstone, yours truly, Billy McNeill, Tommy Gemmell, Danny McGrain and Ronnie Simpson. Sadly, Bobby Murdoch is missing from the picture.

Sinatra eat your heart out. Jimmy Johnstone and I blast out 'The Celtic Song' at a reunion of the Lisbon Lions. Stevie Chalmers, Jim Craig, Tommy Gemmell, Charlie Gallagher, John Clark, John Hughes and Billy McNeill add the backing vocals. I love these nights out with the lads – even if we can't hold a note!

A man and his medals. I won more than my fair share of the silverware during a glittering career in the Hoops. Marvellous times.

Back to where it all started. A recent photograph taken at 95 Panmure Street, Maryhill, where I was born and grew up.

Smiles better. This is one of my favourite photographs – an impromptu snap taken at Baird's Bar in Glasgow as Willie O'Neill, Bobby Murdoch, Jimmy Johnstone and I met before going to a supporters' function. I always get a warm feeling when I look at this picture as it's just so natural.

talent of Kenny Dalglish, Davie Hay, Danny McGrain, George Connelly and Lou Macari, among others, from the reserves. Time catches up with everyone, but I still find it difficult to get my head around the fact that so many left over such a short period of time. We hadn't all become duds in the space of twelve months or so.

Hibs manager Eddie Turnbull, thankfully, still had faith in my ability and, as they say in the *Godfather* movies, he made me an offer I couldn't refuse. It was sad to walk out of Celtic Park for the last time, but I had a new challenge to meet and I was going to give it my best shot. I didn't realise what a momentous move it would turn out to be as it completely reshaped and transformed my career.

15

WHAT A HAT-TRICK

I had what is euphemistically known as a 'memorable' international debut for Scotland. Well, who could forget it? I was sent off! What a baptism at that level.

It was against Holland in their Olympic Stadium on 24 May 1959, and we won 2-1. However, I was to hit the headlines for all the wrong reasons after I got involved in a bit of a brawl with one of their players, a bloke called Johan Motermann. Everything was going OK, Scotland were playing well enough when this guy decided to try and cut me in two. It was a crude challenge as he hammered into me from behind. I didn't see him coming and suddenly, without warning, I was left writhing in pain on the ground. There was a bit of a melee and, being no angel, I was involved. I saw Graham Leggat throw a punch, but the ref missed it. I was immediately singled out and, with their fans going crazy and throwing cushions onto the pitch, I was ordered off. As I trudged towards the tunnel, I was aware of two irate Dutch supporters racing onto the field in their efforts for a bit of retribution. Thankfully, two of Holland's finest stopped them in their tracks and ushered them away.

It was reported in one of the national newspapers as 'an over-hostile act by Auld'. Me? Hostile? They must have confused me with someone else. The referee, Miguel Campos, from Portugal, however, agreed with the reporter and unhesitatingly waved me off. As I made my way to the dressing room, I didn't realise my international career would be over after a further two games. Short and not-so-sweet. I won my three caps early in my playing days and, curiously, didn't even get a nod when I was in the form of my life for Celtic in the Sixties. Strange, that.

Actually, I played for my country before that match in Amsterdam, but it wasn't deemed as a full international as we drew 3-3 with a Jutland Select in Aarhus in Holland. However, I must have done well enough to keep my place a few days later for the game against the Dutch with a crowd of 55,000 watching the action. I felt quite at home and I was helped in the settling-in process by my old Celtic team-mates Dunky Mackay, Eric Smith, Bobby Evans and Bobby Collins who lined up alongside me. We had George Farm in goal with Rangers' Eric Caldow at left-back. Charlton's John Hewie and the afore-mentioned Graham Leggat, who would have such a good career with Aberdeen and Fulham, led the attack. Spurs' John White was in midfield. Denis Law, as ever, wore the No.10 and he was a fabulous performer – easily one of the greatest players in the world on his day. Collins and Leggat were our goalscorers that night.

The SFA appeared to back me after the fracas in Amsterdam when they selected me to play in the next game against Portugal in the Avalede Stadium in Lisbon a week later. They made one change and dropped Leggat with Rangers' Alex Scott taking his place in the frontline. That might have been the SFA taking their own action against the player. I played quite well, even if I do say so myself, and I was named Man of the Match by the reporter who covered the game for the *Evening Times*. I waited another five months before I donned the dark blue of my country again in a 1-1 draw with Wales at Hampden in front of 55,813 fans. Again, I thought I had a reasonable game and I set up our goal with a nice cross for my old chum Leggat to score. Our team on that occasion was: Bill Brown (Spurs); Eric Caldow (Rangers) and John Hewie (Charlton); Dave Mackay (Spurs), Bobby Evans (Celtic) and Bert McCann (Motherwell); Graham Leggat (Fulham), John White (Spurs), Ian St John (Liverpool), Denis Law (Manchester United) and yours truly. As I packed my bags and left the national stadium afterwards I wouldn't have believed I would never play for Scotland again.

I am as patriotic as the next Scot, but it didn't really bother me that I was continually overlooked for the international squads. The main thing for me was to play for Celtic. If Big Jock was happy enough to select me week after week then I knew I was doing something right. If the respective international gaffers chose not to include me, then fair enough. People have often said Scotland should just have played the Celtic first team en masse. We were all Scots, after all, and were the best team in Europe for several years in my view, not just in 1967 when we won the European Cup. I don't suppose too many Rangers fans would have turned out to see a Scotland line-up comprising eleven Celtic players! It was worth a thought, though. In fact, Bobby Brown selected nine of my team-mates for a friendly against Russia at Hampden in 1967. Denis Law and Jim McCalliog were the two guest stars. Unfortunately, it wasn't a particularly good evening for Scotland as we lost 2-0 and my big mate Tommy Gemmell scored an own goal with a lovely lob over Ronnie Simpson.

When you look at Celtic back then it is a bit of a mystery that Wee Jinky won only twenty-three caps. Bobby Murdoch picked up a mere twelve. TG, one of the best left-backs in the world, got eighteen. In fact, the entire Lisbon Lions team achieved a mere 114 caps in total – only twelve more than Kenny Dalglish managed on his own! Yes, I think there was a bit of bias against Celtic. If the SFA selectors had the opportunity of selecting Rangers centre-half Ronnie McKinnon instead of Billy McNeill I believe they would go for the Ibrox player. Absolutely no disrespect to Ronnie, a fine defender, but he wasn't in the same class as Caesar. The same went for Willie Henderson, too. Scotland invariably gave Willie the nod over Jinky at outside-right and, once again, I don't think the Rangers lad, good as he was, could touch my old colleague. Willie might even agree with that.

Scotland, back then, was supported mainly by Rangers fans for whatever reason. You would see them making their way to the game and they would be wearing Rangers colours. There was no such thing as the Tartan Army in those days. I know a few of my team-mates felt more than a little uncomfortable when playing for their country and that is pretty sad. The Ibrox support was never happy when, for instance, Davie Hay played at right-back instead of Sandy Jardine. I even heard Kenny Dalglish being booed by so-called Scottish fans. Mind you, that came to an abrupt halt when he left Celtic for Liverpool. I wonder why.

Yes, I would have loved to have played a few more games for my nation. It would have been brilliant to be involved in the day we beat them 3-2 at Wembley in 1967. Of course, they were world champions at the time and had been unbeaten since taking the trophy the previous year. Celtic had just overcome Dukla Prague the previous Wednesday and were only ninety minutes away from booking our place in the European Cup Final. Everyone was on a high at the time – except Wee Jinky. He took a sore one against the Czechs and had to pull out. That opened the way for Wispy, Willie Wallace, who had scored two excellent goals against Dukla. He was called in and helped Scotland get off to a flying start with a low shot which Gordon Banks spilled and that allowed Denis Law, the possessor of electric reflexes, to pounce and fire it into the welcoming net.

Bobby Lennox got our second goal with a typical flashing, low shot and Jim McCalliog got the third. Jackie Charlton and Geoff Hurst were England's scorers, but it was definitely Scotland's day. Slim Jim Baxter toyed with his opponents as only he could. He played keepy-uppy with wee Alan Ball snapping, unsuccessfully, at his heels. It was a marvellous afternoon and I was so happy for Faither, who was making his debut at thirty-six years of age. Big TG played right-back that afternoon to accommodate Eddie McCreadie on the left. Greigy, Ronnie and Slim Jim made up the impressive half-back line – as it was then – with Wispy, Billy Bremner, Jim McCalliog, Denis Law and Lemon making up the attack. That wasn't a bad side at all. Goodness knows where I would have fitted into that line-up, but I would have thoroughly enjoyed being on the Wembley pitch that day. Slim Jim and I would have needed a ball each!

My international career was complete as soon as English referee John Howley blew for time-up at Hampden on 4 November 1959 in the draw against the Welsh. I had played in three official games, won one, drawn one and lost one. And, of course, been sent off. All I needed was a goal and I suppose you could have said I had covered all bases.

16

SEEING RED

A fair percentage of the referees I have encountered in my many years in football would make a compelling argument for birth control. You know the ones I mean – those preening peacocks who labour under the mystifying notion that a game of football is solely taking place for their benefit. These guys, misguided souls that they are, appear to be under the illusion that they are there to take centre stage while the other twenty-two blokes invading their space are merely bit-part players in their own little theatre.

Bill Shankly, the former Liverpool manager, once said of referees, 'They may know the laws of football, but they don't know football.' Who am I to argue with a legend?

There are only seventeen laws in football and one that isn't there is common sense. But you know what they say about common sense, don't you? It's not that common and, you better believe it, I have seen match officials demonstrate that sad fact over and over again as a player, a manager and a spectator. These guys have the powers to spoil a spectacle. Unfortunately, they often do just that. The best referees are the ones you don't see. Unless you have been living on another planet, you will already know that Bertie Auld and match officials haven't always seen eye to eye. I admit there has been the odd confrontation with authority.

I seem to have gone down in Birmingham City folklore for an incident during a match against Fulham around Christmas 1963. I know there are a few websites that inform everyone of what is supposed to have happened that day. All highly amusing, I can assure you, but some of them aren't anywhere near as accurate as they might be. Here's what really happened when I was sent off for decking two of their players, one of them being England's international captain at the time, Johnny Haynes.

I was down in one of our corner areas when I was aware of Haynes at my back. He was trying to pressure me into giving them a corner-kick, but I was having none of that. I let him approach and then suddenly I whipped the ball through his legs and booted it upfield. 'Call yourself an international player?' I asked somewhat mischievously. Now Haynes was one of those immaculate guys – he was the David Beckham of his era. In fact, he was the first £100-per-week player in Britain. He was always elegant in the white shirts of Fulham and England and I had just made a fool of him. He wasn't best pleased. Back came the riposte, 'You lucky little Scottish so-and-so.'

I looked at him: 'Aye, and don't you forget it, Brylcreem boy!' That was the hair gel of the era and I think the Fulham player used to do a bit of modelling and endorsing of the product.

'What did you say?' he asked.

I said, 'You heard.' I realised I had hit a raw nerve, so I added, 'You Brylcreemed poof!' He didn't like it one little bit. We both trotted back to the halfway line, nattering away as we did so.

To be fair to Haynes, he gave as good as he got. 'I'll get you the next time, you little Scottish bastard,' he countered.

I snapped. As we got to the centre circle I thought it would be a good idea to give him a dull one. I whacked him. Our pitch was flint hard that night and Haynes' feet gave way beneath him. He went down like a sack of spuds. His head thudded off the surface and he just lay there. Unfortunately for me, the referee saw the entire incident. He came racing towards me shouting, 'Off! Off! Get off!' I answered, 'Ach, get lost – I'm going.' I started to walk towards the tunnel and I became aware of a shadow coming in my direction. The St Andrew's floodlights picked out this looming figure perfectly.

I looked around and there was their huge centre-forward, a bloke called Maurice Cooke. He was mouthing off, but I couldn't hear him properly with the place going wild. I don't think he was about to ask me for my autograph, so just as he came closer I hit him flush on the chin with a right hook any boxer would be proud to claim. He did exactly what Haynes had done seconds earlier – he lost his footing, crashed to the surface and clattered his head. Obviously, you cannot condone such actions, but the Birmingham support seemed to enjoy it. They were chanting, 'One! Two! Who's next?' As I reached the touch-line our physiotherapist came running towards me.

'I'm OK,' I told him.

'It's not you I'm worrying about, Bertie,' he replied. 'I'm just making sure the two Fulham guys are still alive!' I glanced backwards and both Haynes and Cooke were still flat out on the pitch. Thankfully, they were both fit to resume after treatment.

Naturally, I realised the English FA wouldn't be too enamoured with my behaviour and I wasn't surprised when I was summoned to Lancaster Gate in London for a special hearing. They actually called Haynes, too, because they wanted his version of events. Gil Merrick, the Birmingham manager, accompanied me to London on the train. He was backing me all the way and told me I had been provoked. I thought he was first class and I really appreciated the fact he took the time to travel with me to the English FA's rather imposing HQ. It was downright scary. There appeared to be about twenty guys behind this enormous desk that ran from one end of the room to the other. It looked like something out of the Nuremburg Trials! I was sitting at one end of this enormous place and Haynes was at the other corner. We nodded when we saw each other.

The chairman of the disciplinary committee listened to my pleas and then called upon Haynes to have his say. Remarkably, the English international captain actually agreed with everything I had said. He said, yes, there had been a bit of banter and it had, sadly, got a bit out of hand. I could hardly believe my ears. The great Johnny Haynes, whom I had flattened, was actually sticking up for me. Perry Mason couldn't have done a better job of acting as my defence lawyer. The FA chairman then produced a document that looked like it contained more that a hundred pages.

'Mr Auld,' he said solemnly, 'this is your disciplinary record. It's not too good, is it?' I didn't get the chance to answer. He started with, 'Sent off in your first game for Scotland.' He looked over at me and shook his head. Clearly, he wasn't impressed. He went through everything I had ever done. I think they had filed things like walking on cracks in the pavement and suchlike. Nothing was missed out. After what seemed like an eternity, he said, 'Twenty-eight days' suspension.' I sighed with relief – I thought they were going to bring back hanging! At the very least I thought I might have to serve my sentence in Barlinnie.

I thought that was the end of the matter but then they asked Haynes to stand up. They had a document on the English skipper that seemed to be a bit lighter than my own file – about ninety-nine pages lighter, in fact.

'Mr Haynes,' said the FA supremo. 'First offence. Seven days.' To be honest, I was surprised that they had suspended the Fulham player, but, to be absolutely fair to him, he had given a true version of events and must have realised that, in doing so, he might get himself in trouble. Actually, I well remember his words and he said, 'There was a lot of passion during that game and if you don't have that sort of passion then you shouldn't be in football.' It took a big man to say that and Johnny Haynes impressed me that day.

Much later in my career, when I was the Hibs manager, I was invited to a charity pool tournament in Edinburgh. I knew Haynes had settled in the capital, but our paths never crossed – I think he watched a lot more of Hearts than Hibs. However, I was about to take my shot when I heard this voice from behind declaring, 'I hope you don't hit the ball as hard as you hit me!' It was Johnny Haynes. We both fell about laughing and ended up shaking hands and apologising for the misunderstanding that eventful evening at St Andrew's. I was saddened when I heard of his death a few years ago when it looked as though he had a heart attack while driving his car. The world lost a fine man at that moment.

I was also ordered off in the strangest of circumstances when we were playing Liverpool in April 1964, around the time Liz had just given birth to our wonderful daughter Susan. The Anfield side was packed with so many good players and they had a solid Scottish backbone with the likes of centre-half Ron Yeats and Ian St John. They were battling for the old First Division title and, in fact, were crowned champions that year. But, on this occasion, we were giving them the runaround at St Andrew's and were 3-0 up at the time. That was most unusual because Birmingham City seemed to spend most of their time at the wrong end of the table. We were given a bonus of £200 per man if we beat relegation. I haven't a clue what we might have been offered for winning the championship because we were never in that position!

Yeats was a man-mountain. On the day Bill Shankly signed him from Dundee United, he called a press conference and said to the reporters, 'Does anyone want to go for a walk around my new centre-half?' Yeats had a mighty presence and he must have been more than just a little frustrated that evening as Birmingham absolutely outplayed the champions-elect. I was full of the joys and I couldn't resist the temptation to slip the ball through Yeats's legs at one stage. What happened next startled even me. As I made to run round the player he let out this bloodcurdling growl. Before I knew what I was doing, I jumped up and bit him on the nose! Goodness knows what possessed me. The referee, as you might imagine, was not best pleased with me and immediately pointed to the dressing room. You could say big Ron's nose was put out of joint twice that evening as we ended up beating them.

The following day, I turned up at the hospital where Liz had given birth to Susan. 'You'll never guess what happened last night, Liz,' I said. 'Yes I will – it's all over the newspapers, you silly beggar.'

Tiny Wharton was one of the most famous Scottish referees of my era. He was known as Tiny because he was about 6ft 4in and must have weighed about eighteen stone. If I am being truthful, I have to admit I didn't particularly like the man. I thought he was arrogant and there was no love lost between Tiny and me. I recall having a go at him after a game against Rangers at Ibrox. We were heading for the tunnel when I said to him, 'Well played, Tiny, you gave us nothing today.' He looked at me and said, 'I'm sure I awarded Celtic a shy at some point.' I didn't see the funny side.

I'm sure Jinky wasn't a fan, either. Tiny sent him off twice and I recall one came against Rangers in a New Year's Day game at Ibrox. Jinky had been fouled a few times, but completely lost the rag in the second half when he assaulted – there's no other word – Rangers' Icelandic midfield player Therolf Beck. I can't imagine what the Rangers lad had done to warrant such treatment from our little winger. Beck, as I recall, was a player of slight stature and was never going to be famous for throwing his weight around. Jinky just lunged at him, though, and, before Tiny got the opportunity to order him off, our winger just turned round and raced straight up the tunnel. He didn't need to be psychic to know what was coming next.

When I was at Birmingham City, Tiny refereed a Fairs Cup tie against Espanyol at St Andrew's in 1963. It was the second leg against the Spaniards and we had lost 3-1 in the first game. It had been a really bad-tempered affair and our opponents were into all sorts of dirty off-the-ball antics. The referee was weak and allowed them to get away with all sorts of stuff. However, we knew we still had to play them at our place, so we thought we would get our own back. First and foremost, obviously, we wanted to win the tie, but I know a few of my team-mates had earmarked a couple of our opponents for some 'special' treatment, if you catch my drift.

I had been walloped just before the full-time whistle in the first game. This bloke just charged into my back and sent me flying. I looked up and saw he was wearing the No.2 jersey. 'I'll remember that number,' I thought. Before the second leg, my colleagues were urging me to talk to Tiny and see if we could possibly get him leaning just a shade in our favour. Like that was going to happen! The Birmingham team back then consisted of mainly English players, as you might expect, but there were a couple of Welsh and Irish lads, too. I was the only Scot.

Tiny, as usual, came into our dressing room before kick-off to inspect our boots. I said, 'Well, how about that, you and me the only Scots on the pitch in a big European tie?' Tiny didn't respond. While he was looking at our studs I told my team-mates, 'Tiny is a great referee. He won't allow anything like we had to tolerate in Spain.' Tiny ignored my wise words to my colleagues. When he left the dressing room I warned them, 'Don't give him any backchat – he won't stand for that. His first warning is also his final warning. Watch yourselves.' I wish I had taken my own advice!

The game had barely started when I saw their No.2 going for a loose ball. It was either him or me as I went into the tackle. I caught him and he yelped in pain. Tiny knew me well enough, but never called me Bertie – it was always Mr Auld. He passed me and said, 'Don't think that tackle went un-noticed, Mr Auld.' Some time later I saw my opportunity for a bit more retribution. I nailed the guy again and once more he went down in a heap. Tiny came over to me and said, 'Remember when you said there would be two Scots on the pitch tonight, Mr Auld? Now there's only going to be one. Off you go!' And that was the end of the game for yours truly.

By the way, I later discovered that the Espanyol No.2 I hammered twice at St Andrew's was a replacement right-back for the guy who had played in the first game. The poor bloke must have wondered what he had done to incur my wrath that night.

I've often taken a bit of punishment on the park, but one incident I can still laugh about came in a game against Stirling Albion at their old Annfield ground. Unfortunately, the crowds could just about reach out and touch the players as I once found to my cost. They had a tough full-back by the name of George Pettigrew who always tried to intimidate opponents. He was a big bloke and thought nothing about giving you a whack if you came anywhere near him. It didn't matter that the ball was on the other half of the field, either. One day I had had enough of being walloped all over the place and he became the recipient of some retribution. The referee missed it, I'm glad to say, but someone in the crowd didn't.

I was running down the wing at one stage when I felt this almighty whack on the back of my head. I looked round and was sure it must have been Pettigrew, but he was nowhere to be seen. Then a voice came from the crowd. It was a woman and she yelled, 'Don't you dare hit my man again.' It was the Stirling Albion player's wife and she had just cracked me over the skull with a handbag! God knows what she had in there, but there must have been at least one half-brick!

I know I had the reputation for getting my retaliation in first. Let me say here and now that I hated cowards. Big defenders are always brave when you have your back to goal and they are coming in at speed from behind. But are they that courageous when it's face-to-face and it's a 50/50 ball? That's when some so-called hardmen backed down. I saw some of my teammates such as Jinky, Lemon or Stevie being booted around and I was never going to stand for that. If I had to remind some guys that they weren't playing a bunch of fairies, then so be it. I will state here and now that I never ever set out to deliberately injure an opponent, but I could be as tough as the next character if the ball was there to be won.

'Kick and be kicked,' said my dad all those years ago. And I remembered those words in every single game I played.

17

EDDIE TURNBULL AND ME

Eddie Turnbull – known to everyone as Ned – was a genius. Big Jock was the best manager I ever played with, but the Hibs boss was undoubtedly the best coach. There is the world of a difference between being a team boss and a coach, believe me.

Jock could spot a good player and buy him for Celtic. Ned could see potential and qualities in players no-one else would have detected. There was always intense rivalry when Jock and Ned were around – I don't think they actually liked each other too much. They had played against each other while Ned was at Hibs during their Famous Five era and Jock was captain of Celtic. I think they might have had a wee debate every now and again when they squared up on the football pitch.

They took that same desire into their jobs as managers where Ned started at Queen's Park, moved to Aberdeen and then returned to Easter Road. Ned was as hard as they come and I learned very swiftly that you had to match him when he was speaking to you. He was a bit of a gruff individual and wasn't much for making speeches. He was never in the running to take over from Michael Parkinson when the chat show host retired a year or so ago. It was football all the way for Ned and he continually came up with new routines for his players.

He once had us playing phantom football; no, I had never heard of it either. Shadow football, too, I believe it was called.

Basically, Ned took eleven players aside and informed them they would go out onto the pitch and play no-one. Sounds barmy, doesn't it? He warned us we had to play it like a real game. There would be no tippy-tappy stuff. He wanted us to do things at speed. We had to run into certain positions, fire the ball around as we would in an actual match and just go about our chores while imagining there were opponents trying to get the ball off us. OK, I accept someone might have been more than surprised if they had flown over Easter Road in a helicopter while all this was going on. Imagine it – eleven guys all running around, shouting for the ball with no visiting players in sight. But Ned was convinced it would help us during a game. He insisted it would help us all know exactly where we would be on the pitch at any given time.

Do you know something? It worked! It may have been a bit odd going through this routine, but I can assure you it was beneficial during a game. Ned was like that. He didn't give two hoots if critics thought it was bizarre – and, yes, it was highly unusual – but it was just another of the innovative things he would introduce to the players. He always kept us on our toes by coming up with fresh ideas. He would try anything to get a winning team on that field during matchday. He was ruthlessly determined to gain success. Ned could be aggressive, abrasive and even abrupt. You had to stand up to him, though. If you backed off then he would have you for breakfast. He wouldn't treat you as an equal.

I liked the fact he was willing to start at the bottom and fight his way to the top as a manager. Ned was a big-time player in one of Hibs' finest sides in their history back in the Fifties, but he didn't hesitate, when his football playing days were over, to take over Scotland's only amateur team in the top divisions, Queen's Park.

He was spotted by Aberdeen and he moved onto a bigger stage at Pittodrie. Actually, he almost joined Rangers at one stage, but turned them down when he discovered something and I think that was very much the manner of the man; it really does say a lot about his professionalism. He had been approached by the Ibrox side when they were parting company with Scot Symon, who had won fifteen trophies in his thirteen years in charge of the team. Rangers couldn't keep pace with events at Celtic after Jock Stein arrived. Symon was from the old school. He wore a suit, shirt and tie every day whereas Jock, like Ned, was seen as a tracksuit manager. He wasn't one for sitting at a desk all day – he wanted to get out there with his players. Rangers began looking for a more hands-on team boss.

Ned got in touch with Symon and asked, 'What's happening, Scot? Why are you leaving?' Symon told the truth, 'I've been sacked.' That was the first time Ned had realised Rangers were dispensing with their manager in such a desperately cold manner. It was no way to treat such a great servant of the club and Ned wasn't impressed. Rangers were told to look else-where for a successor to Symon – Ned might not have phrased it in such a manner – and the proposed move was very defi-nitely off.

I was signed in May 1971 at the age of thirty-three by chairman Tom Hart. Dave Ewing was the manager at the time, but he left in the summer to be replaced by Ned. I wondered what life in Edinburgh would hold in store for me. Quite a lot, really. As a senior professional I wanted to help out with the young lads in training. It wasn't any preconceived arrangement between Ned and me, it just happened. I recall one day talking to a young central defender called Derek Spalding. He was a novice, but I thought he had a chance. I was talking him through a few routines that I believed would sharpen his game. Ned must have been listening. Afterwards the management, staff and the players would sit down for a spot of lunch at Easter Road. The chairman, Tom Hart, had organised these meals and I think he was a bit ahead of his time. Everyone does it now, but it was a brand new concept back then. Anyway, Ned, trainer Tom McNiven and the other coaching staff used to sit at a separate table from the players. It wasn't a 'them-and-us' situation because they would be discussing things that were of little or no interest to players.

One day Ned came over to where I was sitting with the rest of the first team members and asked, 'Why don't you come and join us, Bertie?' I was elevated to a new status there and then. I was in with the big boys! Ned had liked what he had seen during the training sessions and, almost matter-of-factly, said, 'Why don't you become a trainer at the club?'

I looked at him, slightly puzzled and said, 'Me? A trainer? Why would I want to become a trainer?'

'Give it a try,' he urged. 'You might like it.'

So I got my little bucket which contained three things – water, a sponge and smelling salts – and my career was about to take another twist. I was sitting in the dug-out at Easter Road one day doing a stint with the reserves. We were playing Celtic and we were beating them 3-0 or 4-0. They had Denis Connaghan in goal and he was the busiest player on the park. I was minding my own business, thinking, 'There's nothing to this trainer's lark,' when I was rudely awakened from my reverie. Denis had raced from his goal and was in an accidental collision with one of our young forwards, a lad called Kenny Davidson.

'Right, you're on, Bertie,' I thought to myself as I raced onto the pitch. Raced? Well, I was quick for a trainer! What I saw next took my breath away. I looked at Kenny's leg and his foot seemed to be pointing in the opposite direction to where it should be. I knelt down beside him, took out the magic sponge and began splashing water on my own brow. I needed assistance – I almost fainted at the sight of his damaged leg!

Yes, it was difficult coming to terms with the fact that my footballing career was over. I made my debut for Hibs in a 1–1 League Cup draw with Motherwell at Fir Park. I played in another three games in the competition and also eight in the league. Injuries and Father Time were making themselves a bit of a nuisance. I scored three goals – the winner against Ayr United in a 1–0 triumph in September and another a month later in a 6–0 win over Falkirk.

Would you believe my last goal for the club was against Rangers at Ibrox on April 29? Yes, I netted the winner in a 1–0 triumph over my old rivals. Just as bizarrely, my last-ever appearance in the green-and-white jersey of Hibs was against Celtic in the 1972 Scottish Cup Final at Hampden. Normally a 6–1 scoreline for the Hoops would have me celebrating, but not that day. Hibs went into the game with a lot of promise and had guys such as Pat Stanton, John Blackley, Alex Edwards, Alan Gordon and Arthur Duncan in their line-up. It was 1–1 at one stage before the roof fell in on the men from Edinburgh. I didn't start the game, but came on as a second-half substitute for Duncan when Hibs were already 3–1 down and, to be honest, looking like a well-beaten side.

But I can never thank Ned enough for giving me the opportunity to take another step up the ladder. He had faith in me and I worked hard for him and the club. I didn't want to let him down and I hope I never did. As I said right at the start, Ned was a genius. Well, he spotted the managerial potential in me, didn't he?

18

GOOD BUYS AND GOODBYES

I was quite pleased with myself the day I managed to persuade Rangers into parting with £220,000 for our centre-half Craig Paterson. But that sterling piece of work in the transfer market was, ultimately, to go a long way to me losing my job as manager of Hibs!

Concentrating solely on the sale of our player for now, I have to admit it was a great bit of business when you consider the Ibrox side had offered only £80,000 to start with and I had no difficulty in informing them that a figure like that was just an insult. I insisted he was one of the best young players in Britain in that position and they would have to pay the going rate. I had to think fast, though, the day Rangers did get round to meeting my asking price because there was absolutely no way the player would have passed a fitness test!

I was aware that John Greig, my former Old Firm adversary, was taking the club to France for some pre-season training and was eager to have Craig Paterson in place to meet his new team-mates. I was happy enough with the offer of £220,000 – a lot of money for a defender in 1982 – but it was to lead to me having a remarkable and, it must be admitted, fairly heated row with the Easter Road chairman, Kenny Waugh. But, before that, I knew I would have to stall Rangers. Craig had a back injury and it would have shown up in any medical examination. The deal, I knew, would then be dead in the water and I wasn't going to allow that to happen.

Greigy had left the final negotiations to Tommy McLean, his assistant at the time. Most of the hard-nosed stuff had been done, anyway, so it was just a matter of getting Craig's signature on the transfer forms and registering him as a Rangers player. The quicker, the better, thought Rangers. Aye, right! Suddenly I became unavailable to calls from Ibrox. They wanted everything done and dusted by the early afternoon at the latest before they flew out. However, that would still give them plenty of time to put the player through all sorts of tests. I stalled, making excuses while my nose grew to Pinocchio proportions. That transfer cash was vital to me and I had already earmarked two players to come and join us. I hadn't received the money, but I had already spent it. I wasn't to realise then that Waugh, who was never a patch on Tom Hart as Hibs chairman, would, as far I was concerned, renege on what I considered a promise.

It was my belief that any money brought in from transfers would immediately be given back to me to strengthen the team. That sounded fair enough. I should have got it in writing. I played games with Rangers over Paterson. I knew just how much they wanted our player. They swiftly realised I wasn't bluffing; I wouldn't budge on the fee. There was a bit of to-ing and fro-ing as there always is with transfer deals. No-one wants to pay over the odds and no-one wants to undersell their assets. I thought £220,000 was only fair for Paterson, but, of course, he had his back problem and that would have scuppered everything. So, I was caught between a rock and the hard stuff as Rangers applied even more pressure to get the player on that flight to France.

'You said we had a deal, Bertie,' they said.

'Aye, and so we have,' I replied. 'He'll be a Rangers player soon enough.'

'When?'

'Once we are sure everything is in place.'

And so it continued as time marched on. Once I was absolutely certain Rangers no longer had a chance to put him through a rigorous examination I told them he was their player. We got the cash, they got Paterson. And, presumably some time the following day, they discovered he wasn't exactly 100 per cent fit! I think he even missed the start of the season.

I was stunned, though, when Waugh informed me he was putting the money straight into a high-interest account. I don't know the period of time it would have rested there, but that was no good to me. I believed the agreement was that I would get the cash there and then. I knew I could – and probably would – miss out on the two players I wanted in position at Hibs before the start of the new season. The grapevine is always buzzing with would-be transfer deals and even a week is a helluva long time if you are hanging around waiting for a player to come in. Other managers are alerted to the situation and have been known to intercept players en route to their new clubs. If you don't have that signature on the transfer forms, then you run the risk of losing a target. There's a lot of skulduggery goes on in that particular marketplace. Not that I ever indulged in these tactics myself, you understand!

Anyway, Waugh either didn't seem to realise this or didn't want to know. I was more than just a tad annoyed by his stance now the money was safely in the bank. But I'll talk more about this character in the following chapter at the point I was about to lose my job.

Undoubtedly, it is best to keep things strictly hush-hush when you are dabbling in the transfer market and I don't want to sound too dramatic. Jock Stein always insisted if two players of equal ability came up for sale and one was a Catholic and one was a Protestant, he would buy the latter. Why? He reasoned that with Rangers' archaic outlook back then they couldn't possibly sign the Catholic!

Transfers are a gamble, no doubt about it. Some you win, some you lose. One that definitely paid off more than handsomely when I was at Partick Thistle was the £50 I spent on bringing in a wee lad with red hair who would go on to become a somewhat controversial figure in Scottish football – Mo Johnston. A lot of the credit, though, must go to Pat Quinn who was working part-time at Thistle while full-time with Sighthill Community Centre. He spotted two youngsters he thought I should have a look at. One was a striker, Johnston, and the other was a left-sided midfielder, Graham Mitchell, and, of course, both were signed in due course.

I told Pat to get them down to Firhill and we would see how they shaped up. I was always interested in bringing through youth. I always remembered from my early days at Celtic being told, 'The reserves of today are the first team of tomorrow.' Obviously, we couldn't throw money around at Thistle, so we had to concentrate on bringing in the fifteen- and sixteen-year-olds to try to realise their potential. We had a reasonable youth team and I liked the look of one of our young strikers, a guy called Kenny McDowall, whom I had signed from Drumchapel Amateurs. Strangely, McDowall now has the same distinction as Johnston of having served both halves of the Old Firm. I couldn't have made that prediction.

Anyway, Johnston duly turned up and was ready and willing to impress me. Back then, I used to arrange a First Team v. The Youngsters game every now and again. I would join in and the only thing the players had to remember was the rule that I had to be on the winning team! We played the game and afterwards, after everyone had gone home, I was having a wee natter with Pat.

'That wee boy Johnston – how many goals did he score tonight?' I asked Pat.

'I lost count, but he certainly got a few,' answered my assistant.

'I think he's worth a chance. We'll have another look at him,' I added.

Mo trained hard and the one thing he wanted to do was score goals. He wasn't great on the ball, but, like all natural goalscorers, he came alive in the penalty box. He was electric in there. Any rebound or ricochet and you could be sure he would be in there snapping away. He was a natural. The only problem at Thistle, of course, was money. We could never lure youngsters the way the Old Firm could. They could take a chance on a kid's ability. Pat and I had to be sure about anyone we brought in. We didn't have too many S-Form signings, but I was determined to get Mo on the books in whatever capacity. I could offer him reasonable expenses, but the highest I could go to for a signing-on fee was £50. Thankfully, Mo accepted our terms and the rest, as they say, is history.

Wee Mo might have had his detractors and, naturally enough, his once-adoring legion of Celtic fans turned against him when he joined Rangers. It looked as though he would be returning to Parkhead after a deal with Nantes appeared to have been put in place. It transpired the official transfer papers hadn't been signed, so that left Mo to sign for someone else – and that, astonishingly, turned out to be Graeme Souness's Ibrox outfit. I'll tell you this, though. The player may have courted controversy off the field, but he was a guy who worked hard at his game and always gave 100 per cent during the match and in training. I liked his spirit and get-up-and-go attitude. He was a winner. I was sure of that when I signed him and he had the sort of career at club and country level he deserved.

One of the ones that did not work out for me was a transfer that should never have taken place – at the player's insistence. I watched Montrose while I was manager at Partick Thistle and I liked the look of one of their midfielders, Harry Johnston. I wanted him for Thistle, but he wasn't exactly keen on the move. Frankly, the boy wasn't convinced he could cut it in the top flight. I told him, 'Look, I have no doubt you can perform at that level. You're better than you think, trust me.'

Johnston still wasn't too enamoured about leaving homely Links Park for the hot-bed of Firhill! 'Honestly, Mr Auld, I don't think I have the ability to mix in that company. I'm not good enough.' I replied, 'Of course you are. I don't sign duds.' Johnston, albeit reluctantly, agreed to join Thistle. And do you know something – he was awful! He wasn't the most confident of characters in the first place and he simply shrunk into the shadows when he was away from Montrose. I tried everything I could to motivate him, to give him the opportunity to express himself. Nothing worked. I paid £15,000 for him and I got £7,000 when I sold him to Arbroath. I made a mental note – the next time a player tells me he is rotten, believe him!

You can get lucky sometimes, as I did when I went to see

Ayr United one day. Ally MacLeod, a marvellous man, was in charge of the Somerset Park side at the time and I just wanted to have a look at their reserves. I noticed their centre-forward looked more than just a little bit overweight. He looked as though he was about to explode out of that white shirt. I got the impression he might be fond of a pie or ten. But, the more I looked at him, the more I believed I could knock him into shape and get something out of him. It was Dougie Somner.

I casually mentioned him to Ally afterwards and I was quite happy to be informed he could go either for a small fee or a swap deal. Ally had been a more than decent winger in his days with Third Lanark, Hibs and Blackburn Rovers and he retained a fondness for guys who could get up and down the touchline. We had Johnny Gibson but, to be honest, he had a cartilage problem and I thought he was nearing the end of his career. He was never fully fit, but he had been a reasonable outside-right in his day. Ally remembered him. 'How about a swap with Johnny coming here and Dougie joining Thistle?' ventured the former Scotland international manager.

'Are you sure?' I asked.

Ally said, 'Aye, he's always been a good wee player. I think he could do a job for us. We'll take him and you can have Dougie.' It was as easy as that. Somner was willing to join us while Gibson had no qualms about moving to Somerset Park. Thistle also agreed to pay a nominal fee of around £1,500 for Dougie. I really worked him hard in training and, thankfully, he responded in kind. He started to put his back into his work and you could see the results almost immediately. He slimmed down, got quicker and started to put himself about.

The new, improved version of Somner quickly took the eye and the goals started to flow. St Mirren boss Jim Clunie was among those who took notice. He asked about our prolific frontman. 'Make me an offer over £100,000 and I'll think about it,' I said. A few minutes later the telephone rang again. 'How about £110,000?' It was the St Mirren manager once more. I took it. Not a bad return for a player who effectively only cost us £1,500.

I accepted £88,000 from Celtic for Ronnie Glavin and another £100,000 from Liverpool for Alan Hansen. Big Jock didn't want to go that high for our midfielder, but I was in a position where I was not under pressure from the Thistle board. There were wee stories circulating around at the time that there might be some English interest in Glavin. I wonder who put them around?

However, he was a rarity in that he was a goalscoring midfield man and I knew – and so, too, did Jock – that this was an extremely valuable commodity. Ronnie also wanted to join Celtic and, of course, I knew that feeling only too well. But I was Thistle manager, they were my priority and I wasn't in the business to do other teams favours. If Celtic wanted Ronnie, they, like Rangers with Paterson, would have to pay the price. They hummed and hawed, but eventually we got our cash. That allowed me to go to my chairman, Miller Reid, and his board of directors and exclaim, 'You'll never need money again!' What I meant was that they would not be scrambling around, bringing in a few quid here and a few quid there. I was confident I could bring through players the club could sell at a huge profit.

Celtic, by the way, could have had no complaints about the return they got from Ronnie. In season 1976/77 they won the title and my former midfielder netted twenty-six goals for them – making him joint top scorer with Kenny Dalglish. Another ex-Thistle player, Joe Craig, chipped in with twenty-two. Celtic won the league by nine points from Rangers. I would think Ronnie, at £88,000, was a good deal for everyone. We got £60,000 for Joe and that wasn't a bad bit of business, either.

And what about Hansen? I reckon he owes me a massive debt of gratitude. I got three identical offers of £100,000 for him. Bolton, Bristol City and Liverpool were the three clubs who met the asking price. I could have recommended Bolton whose manager, Ian Greaves, was pushing hard for the deal to go through. Or Bristol City, but I decided Liverpool were the club for Hansen. This may surprise you, but I never rated him too highly. I thought he ran as though he had ingrowing toenails. And, for a defender, he wasn't a great tackler. He was about 6ft 2in, but 5ft 4in when he jumped. He wasn't the most aggressive, either, and I saw that as a bit of a drawback for a guy who had to get in there and win the ball. He treated training with a rather leisurely outlook, too. But I knew Liverpool would protect him and, with their quality players around him, he could fit into their scheme of things. Hansen obviously agreed and was happy to go to Anfield on my recommendation. I think I did well in my selection process and, of course, he didn't do too badly down there, either, to be fair.

I recall another day when I was about to sign a big centre-half. I was chatting to him in my office at Firhill when I asked Pat Quinn to go and bring in this bloke who used to turn up for training sessions just to keep himself fit. I can't remember his name, but I know he had scored loads of goals in Junior football. Anyway, this chap arrived at the office and asked, 'Can I do anything for you, Mr Auld?' I said, 'Yes, can you tell this young lad how many goals you scored in your prime?' He thought for a moment and said, 'Over 200 for my three clubs.' The big centre-half must have wondered where I was going with this.

I asked him, 'Do you think you could stop him from scoring goals?'

He hesitated before replying, 'I think so.'

I snapped, 'You THINK so? Look at him. He's about three stones overweight, he's nearer forty than thirty and you only THINK you could stop him. I don't think you're the man we need!' With that, the place burst into laughter. We ended up signing him.

I signed another central defender, Frank Welsh from Kilmarnock, for all of £200 and the valuation must have come as a bit of a surprise to the player. I hope he doesn't mind me saying this, but I only had a few quid to spend at the time and I simply wanted to bolster my squad. We were a bit light in that department and I was looking for a big, honest centre-half and Welsh fitted the bill.

I telephoned Davie Sneddon, who was the Killie manager at the time, to enquire about Welsh's availability. Obviously, Davie wanted a lot more than £200 for his player, but, as ever, I pleaded poverty and, in the end, he agreed to the deal if it was OK with Welsh. The defender was in Glasgow on university studies when I tracked him down.

'Do you fancy a move to Partick Thistle?' I asked.

'I'm interested,' he admitted, so we arranged a date for him to come over to Firhill for a chat. Killie obviously didn't tell him the agreed fee because Frank must have had a high conceit of himself. We sat down for a natter and I asked him what he would be looking for as a signing-on fee. His response was just a wee bit staggering. 'If you've paid £150,000, then I want ten per cent – £15,000. If it's £100,000, I want £10,000.'

At this, my jaw must have dropped onto the floor. By the

time I recovered, I said, 'You're getting £150 – take it or leave it.' Thankfully, he accepted and became a good player for Thistle. He was certainly worth his £200 transfer fee!

I tried to persuade the Killie boss to sell me another of his players to whom I'd taken a shine. He was an emerging talent at outside-right and I believed he had the ability to go all the way in the game. He was clever, tricky, good on the ball and kept up a steady stream of crosses into the opponents' penalty area. I asked Davie to name his price. He answered, 'What can he get at Thistle that he can't get at Kilmarnock?' I knew what he meant. Both clubs were probably at a similar level and if Davie was going to sell his player it would be to the betterment of the individual concerned and I had to accept that. Celtic later bought Davie Provan for £125,000, but what a fabulous player he could have been for the Jags!

It was bad news for Thistle – and clubs of their stature – when freedom of contract came into being. It was more than just a little annoying to go out, spot a player, nurture him in the reserves, pick and choose the first team games where you knew he could prosper, see him becoming a regular in the side – and then see him walk off when his contract was complete and another club was waiting to take them on board for a fee that would be decided by the transfer tribunal. There were some notorious decisions from those sitting in judgement.

One of the decisions that went Thistle's way, I'm happy to say, was Colin McAdam's move to Rangers. His brother Tom, of course, already played for Celtic and Colin wanted to step up. Greigy targeted him and he took him to Ibrox when his contract expired. However, Colin, who could play in defence and attack, came to me one day and said, 'Boss, pay me £15,000 and I'll stay.' I looked at him, a big, burly guy, and said, 'Colin, son, if we get offered £15,000 for you, you will be out of here without your feet touching the floor!'

I was on holiday with the family in France that summer when the transfer tribunal agreed the fee. It was the days before mobile phones, so I had to scout around for a public telephone. I found one and got through to our general manager, Scot Symon, who, of course, had once been boss at Rangers. 'How much for McAdam?' I asked, fearing the worst. My holiday was complete when Scot replied – as if he was announcing a Lottery win – 'They have been told to pay us £175,000.'

I thought I had misheard him. 'Sorry, Scot, it's a bad line – how much?' In a firm voice he repeated, '£175,000, Bertie.' I had heard correctly. I have to admit the transfer tribunal had got it wrong – he wasn't worth that much! I wasn't complaining, though, as I returned to the bosom of my family and I would have needed plastic surgery to get the smile off my face for the rest of the holiday.

We lost out, though, when Ian Gibson dumped us to join Dundee United in extremely disappointing circumstances. It was a bit of a fluke that I signed him in the first place. I was going to a car auction to pick up a wee runaround for my wife Liz one quiet afternoon. After getting the business done, we were driving home when I noticed a few guys heading for a football game. Liz knew what was coming next. We had an hour or so to kill, so I stopped the car and followed these blokes to a ground where a game was taking place. I decided to have a look out of curiosity – you never know what you might spot.

Gibson was playing that day and I liked the look of him as he took charge of things in midfield. He had a nice touch and a lot of energy. He knew how to use the ball, too. I thought to myself, 'He's got a chance. Let's see what he can do at another level.' I got him over for training and, once again, I was impressed. We duly signed him and he came through the ranks quite swiftly to settle in the first team. His potential was there for all to see and, unfortunately, one who also spotted his emerging ability was Dundee United manager Jim McLean. I knew Ian was coming to the end of his contract with us, but I was confident he would be signing a new deal. There were no murmurs of discontent and I genuinely thought it would be a formality. I liked the lad and, as far as I was aware, he liked life at Partick Thistle. There were no indications otherwise.

Ian was a diligent lad, so I was a little surprised when he didn't turn up for training one Monday. There was no telephone call, no message. I thought he might be unwell and didn't think any more of it because he was not one for going missing. I knew he had a steady home life and wasn't one for disappearing off the radar. Anyway, I was a bit more perturbed when he didn't show up for training the following day. Once more, no-one had got in touch with us to explain his non-appearance.

On the Thursday, John Hansen, our right-back and brother of Alan, informed me he had bumped into a friend of Ian's wife and she revealed he had joined Dundee United. Upset? I can think of other words. The player I had found in a bounce game and had even made captain of the club had walked out without any warning. It was his right, of course, under freedom of contract, but I thought he could have handled it a lot better. A telephone call might have been welcome. I was also disappointed in McLean. The way everything was conducted was fairly unacceptable. About a year later I received a nice letter from the player. He outlined exactly what had happened and, basically, apologised for his part in joining United. That's football, I suppose. If you want loyalty, buy a dog!

It's unusual for a player to leave the Old Firm and join Thistle, but that's exactly what happened when Kenny Watson left Rangers to join us at Firhill. I paid £50,000 for him in 1980 and, obviously, that was a lot of money for us to spend. I had first noticed him when he was playing in midfield for Montrose. He was a big, powerful laddie with a nice touch and a good range of vision. He had fallen out of things at Ibrox, so I chanced my arm in asking them if they would consider selling him. I was delighted to hear that he was 'surplus to requirements', as they say, and I was happy enough to write a cheque for £50,000. I was even more elated when the boy accepted he would have to become part-time and he went back to his trade as a joiner. He was a good, solid performer for us and I think he proved to be great value for money.

We picked up Jamie Doyle for peanuts after my old pal John Colrain spotted him playing in a game at Roseberry Park in Glasgow where most of the schools' cup finals were played back then. As I have said elsewhere, Colly could spot a player and he took a shine to this wee bundle of energy in midfield. There wasn't much of Jamie – I think he was about 5ft 6in – but he could put himself about. Colly came to me and said, 'Bertie, I've seen this young lad who can play a bit, but he's a bit odd – he wears gloves!'

I said, 'I don't care if he wears ladies' underwear, just so long as he can play.'

Every team boss on the planet will tell you that they do not want to load up their squad with too many paperweights. It's just a fact of life – look at any pool of players. You will get a few wee guys in there, but, in the main, it will be tall blokes.

It doesn't mean they have got any more ability, but you will never see a team of guys around the 5ft 6in mark take the field on matchday. Believe me, it won't happen.

Anyway, I went to meet Jamie's dad and, not surprisingly, he was a bantam, too. There was another brother, Gerry, who was a bit younger and I had seen him play as well. I talked to the dad and at the end of the evening I had two Doyles on the payroll at Firhill. Again, I was delighted at how they performed for Thistle.

Jamie was a stand-out – what is it about Scotland that they can continually unearth these wonderful little dynamos? We have had guys such as Bobby Collins, Billy Bremner, Asa Hartford and Archie Gemmill, among many others in the past, who were never slow to shirk a challenge with guys who dwarfed them in the middle of the park. They played with a snarl and a snap. Jamie was in the same mould although, unfortunately, not at international level. But he wasn't slow to mix it and I wasn't surprised when Tony Dunne, the former Manchester United left-back who was then assistant manager at Bolton, came to me after a game at Firhill to have a word.

Thistle, at that time, had guys such as Rough, Hansen, McQuade, Lawrie and Rae around – a lot of the players who had been involved in that epic 4-1 League Cup win over Celtic in 1971. There was the inevitable talk about us losing our star men to bigger clubs and when Tony sought me out I wasn't surprised. However, I was a bit taken aback when he revealed who he wanted to sign. 'I fancy that young guy Doyle in your midfield,' he said. 'I'll give you a blank cheque here and now. Name a price, within reason, of course.' I thought for a moment and probably shocked the Bolton No.2 when I responded, 'He's not for sale.' I didn't think the time was right for the player to go anywhere and I added, 'He's still got a lot to do and, anyway, the Thistle fans have still to get a lot of enjoyment out of Jamie Doyle. Sorry, no deal.'

The only other transfers I have blocked concerned Alan Rough and Bobby Houston. Normally, I was happy enough to take the money to bolster the Firhill coffers and then go and search for cheaper replacements I believed I could coach into a similar standing as the departed players. The time just wasn't right for either of those deals to go through and I can tell you why. OK, I had a few run-ins with Roughie, but I was well aware of his worth to Thistle – at least seven or eight points a season. Remember, those were the days when you only got two points for a win. Roughie could be the difference between staying in the Premier League or getting relegated. I knew, too, how difficult it was to regain your top-flight status once you had slipped down the ladder.

Middlesbrough manager John Neal liked the look of our international goalkeeper and was prepared to pay £100,000 to get him on board at Boro. Now everyone knew Thistle were a selling club. That wasn't too difficult to fathom when you looked at our average gates of 4,000 or so. But, on this occasion, I wasn't about to be tempted. Again, the answer was, 'Sorry, no deal.' And that was the end of the matter. I found it a bit more tricky in knocking back the offer for Houstie. I got a call from Big Jock who had just joined Leeds United in the summer of 1978 after Caesar had taken over at Celtic. I knew he always liked Houstie, who was a massive Celtic fan. He used to turn ashen-faced when you told him he was going to play against his heroes. Naturally enough, he found it a daunting task to face his boyhood idols.

Jock telephoned to say, 'Bertie, I'm looking for someone who can get up and down the wing and I'm willing to pay £80,000 for Bobby Houston. What do you think?' I have heard and read that I used to give the player a right hard time and I admit I did sometimes go over the top in my criticism of him. It wasn't done with malice, believe me.

In the case of Roughie, I wanted him to push himself to the absolute limits to get the best out of his ability. Houstie was a good player rather than being a great one. But I can tell you this – he was a superb professional. He worked his socks off for the club. There was talk that Jock had tried to sign him for Celtic in a swap deal with Jackie McNamara, the father of the former Parkhead skipper. That deal fell through and McNamara went to Hibs with Pat Stanton travelling up the M8 to join Celtic.

Again, though, I had a decision to make. Thistle were actually at the top of the league at the time and I was eager to add to my squad rather than deplete it. I also knew the move would be a very good financial one for Houstie as well as us banking another £80,000. What to do? Reluctantly, I had to tell Jock, 'He's staying with us.' My old gaffer accepted there would be no transfer. Mind you, I don't know what would have happened to Houstie if the deal had gone through – Jock lasted only forty-four days at Elland Road before returning to Scotland where he would eventually take over from Ally MacLeod as Scotland manager.

By the way, I did get some of that £220,000 Craig Paterson transfer cash and I paid £80,000 of it to Middlesbrough for Bobby Thompson, who had also played for Morton. He was a big, powerful, muscular guy and I thought he would do a good job in the middle of the park for Hibs. Unfortunately, he spent most of the time sitting in the stand while serving suspensions.

I also paid a few quid for a tall central defender called Peter Welsh, from Leicester City, but, like Thompson, he never set the heather on fire, either. Maybe I should have left the money in the bank!

There was one young lad I fancied for Thistle, but there was a major obstacle in me attracting him to Maryhill and it had nothing to do with money. He was a lanky left-back – his surname was Greer – who had a lot of stamina, worked well in defence and attack and did it all with an effortless ease. I found out his name and duly turned up at his parents' house to talk about the possibility of their son coming down for trials. I discovered he was a player all right – the player of a piano! The boy was musically inclined and was only playing football for fun. He was quite honest. 'I would love to play for you at Thistle, Mr Auld,' he said, 'but it would interfere with my music. I don't think I can combine both.' That was a new one on me. Not that long afterwards I got a call from his parents to give me an update on their son. He was playing for one of the biggest bands in London and was regularly appearing at the Palladium and the other big shows. I don't suppose Liberace ever wanted to make a career out of football, either!

Some transfers can be tortuous and even tedious. You start the ball rolling and it seems to take for ever to reach its conclusion. Hitches can crop up all over the place before everything is agreed and put in place. Others are an absolute breeze. I recall talking about a young midfield player who was with that excellent Edinburgh nursery Salveson's Boys' Club. Goodness only knows how may top-class performers came off that particular conveyor belt of non-stop talent. I was with Hibs at the time and I was mentioning this youngster to Pat Quinn. A bloke who used to do a spot of scouting for the club overheard me and said, 'I might be helpful if you want to sign the lad.' I said, 'That's good to know, I wouldn't mind having a chat with the boy.'

'My car's outside if you want to pop in,' he added. 'I know where the boy stays. I'll take you there.' It sounded too good to be true. A signing minus the hassle? I took him up on his offer and, sure enough, he drove me straight to where the lad stayed. 'I'll come in with you if you want,' he offered. 'No problem,' I said and, as it turned out, there wasn't. I was a bit puzzled, though, when I saw the guy take the keys out of his pocket and insert them in the door. 'I told you I knew the boy well – he's my son.' He turned out to be Paul Kane's dad! It was a done deal before I had to make any sales pitch to the young midfielder who went on to have such a great career in football.

If only all transfers had been that simple.

19

BEING IN CHARGE

I was more than just a little excited back in 1978 when I heard a whisper that there was a chance that I could be appointed manager at Celtic. Me? Wee Bertie Auld from Maryhill? Manager of Celtic Football Club? The successor to the great Jock Stein? It seemed like a dream – and that's exactly what it was; just a dream.

Apparently, there were three names on the shortlist; myself, Billy McNeill and Paddy Crerand. I could hardly contain myself at the enthralling prospect. It didn't work out, of course, but I'll tell you this – they got the right man in Billy McNeill. Yes, I was disappointed, but how on earth could you disagree with the Celtic board's choice? Caesar, as we all know, is a Celtic man and he was emerging as an exceptional team boss at Aberdeen.

Paddy had left Manchester United and had a brief four-month managerial stint at Northampton. I had cut my teeth at Partick Thistle and, although I was perfectly happy there with a marvellous chairman in Miller Reid, I could never have knocked back Celtic. No chance. I knew there was much work to be done at my old club and I would have relished the challenge. They had finished fifth in the league – their worst position in years – and hadn't even qualified for Europe. That was unthinkable in my days as a player at the club.

Jock had been thirteen years in charge, but even he admitted it was time to move over and the story goes that he made the first contact with Caesar about returning to Celtic. I could believe that. Jock was always a huge admirer of our former captain and may even have seen himself as being his mentor. Billy, of course, had everything needed to be manager of Celtic. He had a presence, charisma and a genuine personality. It was a monumental job that had to be done by someone with real credentials. Caesar fitted that job description – no doubt about it. And look what he achieved in his first season. Celtic won the league title and the Scottish Cup, beating old foes Rangers 1-0 in extra time in the match at Hampden that ended in a riot with fans clashing on the pitch.

I would have loved that job, but I still insist it went to the man who deserved it most. Billy McNeill, I believe, was always destined to become boss of the club some day. It was just a matter of time. And when he got the nod, he didn't let anyone down. He came in with his own ideas, strengthened the side by bringing in the likes of Davie Provan, from Kilmarnock, and Murdo MacLeod, from Dumbarton, and generally just breathed new life into the team. That took some doing, believe me. The pressure on an Old Firm manager is total. Faint hearts weren't encouraged to apply for these jobs. Mind you, it could be quite intense across at Firhill, too.

I was privileged to manage Partick Thistle twice and I'll always remember how I got the job in the first place. I was player/coach at Hibs back in 1974 when I received a call from a newspaper pal of mine, Alex Cameron, of the *Daily Record*. He was known as Ace and he was the top man.

'How do you fancy becoming boss of Partick Thistle?' he enquired one day.

'You're kidding me on, aren't you, Ace?'

He replied, 'No, I'm perfectly serious. I've had a chat with Miller Reid and I know he is looking for an ideal candidate to take over from Davie McParland. I think you are that man.'

As simple as that.

I agreed to leave Hibs, who, thankfully, didn't put too many obstacles in my way, and that was me, at the age of thirty-six, on a journey through the crazy world of management. They say you have to be a bit daft to be a goalkeeper. I think you have to be off your head to be a manager. Having said that, I enjoyed most of my time in the dug-out and I relished the opportunity of taking over Thistle. Being a Maryhill boy, I always had a soft spot for the club and here I was now embarking on a new venture in football. Yes, it was difficult, extremely difficult, to accept that my playing days were over. Like every other foot-baller in the world, you are never really prepared for that day. However, at my age and given that I had won a stack of medals, I knew it was time to give the management side of it a bash.

I went to the 1974 World Cup Finals in West Germany as part of the Hibs entourage which I thought was an excellent gesture by our chairman Tom Hart and his directors. They knew I was on my way to Partick Thistle, but they still treated me so well. When I was in West Germany I met up with Jock who was holding court with a few reporters. He had been told I was becoming manager of Partick Thistle and he said to me, 'So, what do I call you now, Bertie?' I answered, 'Just give me the respect I gave you, boss.' And that was that.

But there were problems right at the beginning at Firhill – Davie McParland had taken just about every member of his backroom staff with him when he left. I had to start from zilch. There were guys such as Eddie McCulloch, Donnie McKinnon, Jackie Husband, Willie Ross and Jimmy Dickie around, but I realised I needed to get my own men in and that is no disrespect to those blokes. Pat Quinn became a trusted right-hand man and he had a fabulous knowledge of the game. As I said before, Miller Reid was a great bloke to work with. He was more of a friend than a chairman and he let me get on with the job without any interference. That was appreciated because the last thing you need as a manager is a meddling chairman. And there are more than a few around, too.

One of the first things I wanted to do at Thistle was sack Scot Symon! The former Rangers manager was in a backroom capacity and I didn't want him looking over my shoulder. He had blanked me one day and I kept that in mind. I didn't think we would get on, but I am glad he stayed around. He became invaluable to me and was a superb confidant. Shortly after I had taken over, he pulled me aside and gave me a great bit of advice. He said, 'Always tell the players what you think of them – no matter how harsh. Be truthful because these guys can get you the sack. They'll knife you in the back without any hesitation.' I knew what he was saying after the awful way he had been treated by Rangers. I enjoyed my talks with Scot in the manager's office at Firhill. He would tell me things about Rangers and I would exchange stories about Celtic.

I had my eyes opened at Thistle. It was only recently that I discovered I had prevented Alan Rough from going with Scotland to the 1974 World Cup Finals. Roughie has stated that he could have made the squad as back-up goalkeeper to David Harvey, of Leeds United, and Kilmarnock's Jim Stewart, but Willie Ormond, the international boss at the time, finally chose

Dundee's Thompson Allan. I don't know how my old keeper has worked that one out – I became manager of Thistle AFTER those World Cup Finals. Maybe I psyched out Roughie with telepathy. I don't mind standing up to be counted when I have done something wrong, but the only thing I ever did to upset Roughie was stick the ball past him a few times during my playing days!

In fact, when I come to think about it, he should be thanking me for making sure he was Scotland's goalkeeper in Argentina in 1978 and in Spain four years later. I admit I worked him hard and I don't apologise for that. Yes, I called him a big girl's blouse on more than one occasion! Look at Roughie. He was well built, stood about 6ft 2in tall, weighed in at around four-teen stones and I wanted him to clear that penalty area when the ball dropped into the vicinity. Roughie, though, preferred to stay on his line and let his defenders clear the ball. I urged him to take more responsibility because I realised he had the ability to do so.

I liked Roughie and that admission will probably surprise him considering what I put him through. Simply put, I wanted him to maximise his potential. On his day, there was no-one to touch him. Old Firm fans might talk about the merits of Artur Boruc or Andy Goram, but, take it from me, big Roughie was every bit as good. He was a great shot-stopper and he had to be because he got plenty of practice at Thistle! He was one of the rare full-timers at the club and I made sure he trained well. Thursday was one of our biggest nights when we tried out so many things. We were largely part-time, of course, so we majored on deadball efforts. We would need every advantage when it came to playing full-time clubs on matchday.

However, there was one Thursday when Roughie would have been better not turning up. He had been at some sort of awards ceremony in the afternoon and let's just say he might have had a little bit too much to drink. If he had thought about it, he should have phoned in and made some sort of excuse. I would have accepted that. I would have had my suspicions, naturally, but I would have looked the other way. Roughie, though, must have thought he could disguise the fact he had chucked a few behind his necktie that afternoon. He must have used his cufflinks as kerb-feelers on his way to the ground that night!

I was in the manager's office at the ground when Donnie McKinnon, one of our trainers, popped his head around the door and said, 'Boss, come and have a look at this.' Now Donnie was no clipe. If he had merely smelled alcohol on Roughie's breath he wouldn't have mentioned it to me. Roughie, though, had one too many and it was obvious. Looking back, I can laugh at it. He was going through these routines and he was utterly hopeless. The big man had put me on the spot and I realised I would have to take some sort of action. Remember, Tommy Gemmell and I had once been sent home from a tour of the States by Sean Fallon after we had had a few at a night out. Actually, I thought that was grossly unfair at the time and I still do.

What did we do wrong? I admit we had a few bevvies after being at some function where a lot of kids were being awarded certificates for whatever reasons. We were stuck there for hours when TG and I decided to repair to the bar. It was a good idea at the time. Sean didn't agree, telephoned Big Jock, who was back in Scotland, and that was that. We were on the plane home the following day and, as you might expect, there were all sorts of daft stories doing the rounds. We were supposed to have insulted a waitress. I can tell you, there were only waiters around at that particular ceremony and neither TG nor I upset anyone. Big Jock accepted our version by the time we turned up at Parkhead and that was an end to it. But we had been punished somewhat harshly. I don't think any of the Celtic players wanted to be on that trip, anyway, because we had just lost the 1970 European Cup to Feyenoord.

The fans, as ever, were great. They did their absolute best to console us and we were invited along to so many functions. But, truth be told, we would all have preferred to be back home. That defeat took an awful lot out of all of us as I have already described fully in another chapter. Maybe TG and I got lucky by getting home early!

So, anyway, there I was, manager of Partick Thistle, taking training before a big game on the Saturday and there was my goalkeeper making a bit of a fool of himself. It wasn't a big decision for me – Roughie was dropped and John Arrol, solid and dependable, played a couple of days later.

As I recall, John performed exceptionally well in a few games in succession in the first team and he would have remained there but for a leg break that sidelined him. I think he clashed with Motherwell forward Willie Pettigrew in a match at Fir Park and I had no option but to put Roughie back in the first team. I think I got the message across to our goalkeeper. Behaviour like that was not going to be tolerated. We had to be a bit more professional than that and Roughie must have known he had let everyone down. It was unusual for him because, believe me, he really put his back into training. He worked hard to reach his targets and I respect him for that. Yes, we argued a lot and I don't suppose he relished being called a big lassie in front of his team-mates. But I had to push him all the way to get the best out of him. Which Partick Thistle player has won most caps for Scotland? Alan Rough. Who has played in most games for Partick Thistle? Alan Rough. Who made him the goalkeeper he was? I'll let you decide!

I enjoyed my two spells at Firhill and there was a lot of laughter around the place on occasions. I recall I was sitting in my office with two journalist pals – Jim Blair, of the *Daily Record*, and Alan Davidson, of the *Evening Times*. There had been a midweek game at the park and we were unwinding afterwards. Yes, we had a couple of drinks as we shot the breeze. I liked their company and we always got on well. I trusted them and I thought they were knowledgeable about the game. Anyway, time marched on as we chatted about a whole range of subjects. I think it was beyond midnight when I received a telephone call from Maryhill police station.

I picked up the receiver. 'Mr Auld,' came the voice of the desk sergeant. 'Is there any chance you could get someone to switch off your floodlights? We've had a few complaints from the residents!' The groundsman had locked up after everyone had left, but had forgotten to turn off the lights which were still burning brightly and obviously keeping some of the neighbours awake. It could only happen at Thistle!

A few bizarre things could happen at that club, believe me. I once purposely left Thistle with ten men when I wasn't happy with one of my players, Jim Melrose. As I recall we were playing Hearts and I had already put on our two substitutes, the permitted amount back then. I was shouting instructions to our frontman, but I was getting the notion that nothing was getting through. Basically, he was ignoring me and, given that we had committed our subs, he must have thought he was bombproof.

I leapt out of the dug-out and gestured for him to come off. Pat Quinn must have thought I had forgotten I had no players left to put on the pitch. I heard this voice behind me, 'Bertie, what the hell are you doing? You'll leave us with ten men.' I wasn't listening and I wasn't going to be rubber-eared by any of my players. Melrose's face was a picture as he realised I wasn't joking. I wanted him off and he trudged towards the tunnel looking fairly mystified. It worked as we won 2-0.

At the after-match press conference, I knew what to expect. Someone asked fairly logically, 'Why did you take off Melrose? He didn't look injured.' I looked at my inquisitor and replied, 'You've got it in one. He wasn't hurt, but you never know when you might be left a man short, someone sent off or injured, and you have to be prepared for these sort of things. It was just a wee test of our team in a game where I thought we were in control.' I don't know if any of the press corps swallowed that explanation, but they duly jotted it down in their note-books and there was no more mention of the incident.

As I said earlier, I was left without much of a backroom at Firhill when I first arrived. I telephoned my old Celtic mate John Colrain to see if he was interested in doing some scouting work for us. Colly was in Ireland at the time, but he agreed to return to help us out. He could spot a player all right. I told him we couldn't spend too much. I think we agreed £10 per week with some expenses thrown in. Now I know they were legitimate expenses. Colly could take in three games in one day, watching schoolboys, amateurs and Juniors. I remember he submitted some receipts one day to our treasurer John Moynihan. He was from the old school with one of those amazing moustaches that defy gravity. Biggles would have been envious of that effort as it curled up at both ends. He would twiddle with the edges of this thing when he was checking expenses. One day he called me over. He was frowning at Colly's receipts. 'Look at this, Bertie,' he said. 'He's charged us for a fish supper!' That's how tight things were at Thistle. Miller Reid paid for Colly's lunch, I seem to recall, taking the money out of his own pocket.

I also had a silly bust-up with Sir Alex Ferguson – who was just plain Alex back then – when a Thistle v. Aberdeen game was called off on a Saturday morning. Brian McGinlay was the referee and he wasn't happy with the condition of the pitch one winter's day. There was fog threatening, too, and he decided there would be no football that afternoon. I knew Fergie and the Dons players were staying at the Excelsior Hotel near Glasgow Airport and I thought it was only right and proper that we should tell them they had made a wasted journey. I asked Donnie McKinnon to telephone the Aberdeen gaffer to relay the news. Donnie came back, slightly agitated, and told me, 'Fergie's calling you all the names under the sun. He thinks you wanted the game to be called off.' I wasn't going to have any of that.

As we all know, Fergie has a slight speech impediment. He seems to have a difficulty pronouncing the letter 'r'. When he says 'true' it comes out 'twoo'. Proud becomes pwoud. It's just as well he was born in Govan and not Genoa – can you imagine his pronunciation of arrivederci! Only joking, Fergie – keep up the good work! Anyway, I wasn't going to have him calling me names to a member of my staff and I angrily put a call through to him at his hotel. He came on the line and I gave him both barrels. 'If you've got something to say to me, say it to my face,' I said and added, rather needlessly, 'you stuttering buffoon!' I realise neither the adjective nor the noun is correct, but I couldn't prevent myself. Before Fergie could say anything I slammed down the receiver. About half an hour later Donnie received a call from one of the Aberdeen contingent. 'What on earth did Bertie say to our gaffer?' he was asked. 'Fergie's going off his head – he's kicking chairs and tables all over the place!' I loved winding up Fergie and Jim McLean at Dundee United. I used to say to them. 'Who cares about what you do away up there in the frozen north? Glasgow's the place to be!' Ironically, both got the chance to manage Rangers and both turned down the opportunity.

This will surprise you, but one of the managers I really got on well with was Jock Wallace. I know he came across as a big, gruff guy and I believe he liked that image. However, I think he was a real gentleman. He would always make a point of coming into the Thistle dressing room to shake hands with me after a game. We had a few good results against Rangers back then, but he still went out of his way to congratulate me. I really appreciated that.

Managing Thistle was tough, though. Money was tight and that led to a pay revolt at the club that I have never spoken about until now. We had agreed wages, bonuses and appearance money at the start of the season. We had posted the bonuses on a board on the wall and everyone seemed satisfied. Well, that was until we won promotion, as early as January, I believe. Some of the senior players, captain Jackie Campbell among them, came to me and I was informed they weren't happy with what was on offer. Considering they had accepted the deal at the start of the season, I couldn't quite see their argument. What was the point of accepting it in August and knocking it back in January? They threatened to go on strike nearing the end of the campaign when we were due to play Forfar in the now-defunct Summer Cup. I was told they wouldn't play in this game unless the club coughed up extra dosh. I was far from impressed, as you might imagine.

I told Pat, 'Right, let's get the reserves and youngsters in – they'll be playing in this match.' It wasn't a bluff. I would have dropped my entire first team to face Forfar. I wasn't happy, either, when the first team players tried to persuade their stand-ins that it would be a bad idea to perform in their absence. They even tried to prevent them getting on the coach for the game. Eventually, everything was sorted out, the players got more cash and played against Forfar. I would have thought more of them if they had stuck to their guns. If they believed they had a genuine grievance, they should have shown a bit more profes-sionalism. When we negotiated wages and bonuses after that I made absolutely certain that there was no room for manoeuvre afterwards. I wasn't going to stand for any more of that kind of nonsense.

I knew it was time to leave Thistle, though, when I took my seat in the dug-out at Firhill one day. I looked across the pitch and there was this enormous banner that proclaimed, 'We want the old Thistle – not the Auld Thistle.' That hurt. The old adage, of course, was Firhill For Thrills and, believe me, I desperately wanted to entertain those fans just as much as I had done at Celtic in my playing days. However, my priority was to keep Partick Thistle in the top division. That was my remit and I had to play to my players' strengths. I didn't set out to be delib-erately defensive, but there were better teams than us in the Premier League back then and a draw was a point gained and not one dropped. I had been there six years and, as Miller Reid continually told me, I had a job for life. However, after a while, you wonder if you have taken the club as far as you possibly can. I knew they were OK financially although, of course, Thistle would never compete at the top table as far as transfers went. So, I had a decision to make. Do I stay? Or do I go? The more I looked across at the banner being held by a few fans – I think they were students – I knew instinctively that it was time to move on. Enter Hibs in 1980.

I was fortunate enough to meet another top-class chairman in Tom Hart. I had a lot of time for him and I was shattered when he died on our way to a game against Aberdeen at Pittodrie. What a tragedy and it hurt the entire club. Kenny Waugh took over and I might as well have handed in my resignation there and then. We would never be seeking out each other's company away from the park, that's for sure.

Maybe I had been spoiled at Thistle and Hibs with two forthright individuals who were gems to work with. Waugh had other ideas about what a stewardship of a football club is all about. When I realised I would have to fight to get cash to spend on new players after selling Craig Paterson to Rangers for £220,000, it was the beginning of the end for me at Easter Road. I couldn't contain my anger. I told Waugh, 'Listen, I am an employee of Hibs between 8am and 5pm. I'll talk to you in between those times. But after 5pm, I don't want to know you. I am no friend of yours.' I suppose I broke it to him gently! As you might expect, my words of wisdom did not go down too well with Waugh. Possibly, upon reflection, I could have handled it differently. But I was angry and I have always spoken my mind. I never saw the point of slating someone behind their back. If it was worth saying, it was worth saying to their face.

I'll never forgive him for the way he treated Willie Hunter. He was chief scout at the club and was a smashing lad to have around. He did so much hard work for the club that largely went unnoticed. When I took over from Willie Ormond I swiftly realised we were not getting the best of the young players in Edinburgh. The scouting system at this level had been allowed to slip a bit. I knew Hunter had connections in the city and I persuaded him to leave a good job at Portsmouth to come and rejoin Hibs where he had been a fine midfield player. He went about his new job with loads of enthusiasm and we started to attract a lot of the young talent on offer in the capital. A lot of that was down to Willie.

There was a day, though, when he returned home from training to find out he had been fired with someone delivering a letter to his house. John Smart, a guy who did so much behind the scenes for the club, was similarly dismissed. No-one said a word to Hunter all day; no-one had thought to take him aside and have a quiet word. I was manager and I hadn't a clue what was about to happen to Willie. That was awful, a cowardly act, but typical, in my opinion, of how the club was being run at the time.

Pat Stanton has admitted he was shocked to be offered the manager's job at Hibs. I wasn't. I had been told the night before Stanton's appointment that I was going to be sacked. I can't reveal the identity of the caller because it would embarrass him. Suffice to say, though, that it was someone with inside knowledge of what was going on at the club. Waugh wasn't a member of the Bertie Auld Fan Club, so I wasn't too taken aback that I was about to be removed from my position although it was a sore one to accept at the time. No-one likes to lose their job and it's even worse when it is done in the full glare of the public spotlight.

Anyway, I took the call one eventful evening – I think I had just got back after a game against Airdrie at Broomfield – and I realised it was time-up in Edinburgh. My informant could even tell me that Stanton would be bringing in another two ex-Hibs players, George Stewart and Jimmy O'Rourke, with him. I wonder if they were surprised, too! I duly got another telephone message the following day to have a meeting with Waugh. I knew what was coming, of course, but I had to feign some sort of shock. I'm certain I could detect a smile on Waugh's face as he broke the news. I didn't bother shaking his hand. He wanted my keys to the company car. I had left it at home in Strathaven because I knew what was coming. I threw them onto his desk, saying, 'There you are – you'll need someone to go and collect it. It's parked in my driveway at home.' I just wanted out of there. By the way, Stewart and O'Rourke quit at the end of the season and Stanton wasn't too far behind them. Waugh had made all sorts of promises to the Hibs fans about this being the start of a new era. Easy to say – not so easy to put into action.

I had been two years at the club and was instrumental in getting a team of youngsters in place in the professional youth league. I would like to think I had left behind a reasonable legacy. Stanton, though, was to discover the hard way that his new chairman wasn't a big spender and may not have been as ambitious as he wished to be portrayed. Stanton actually signed a youngster from Ormiston Primrose, Graham Harvey, I think, and he went straight into the first team the following week. Another signing was Malcolm Robertson who, I believe, met Stanton quite by chance in Waverley Station. He had been released by Hearts and Stanton took him to Hibs. New era? Don't think so.

Hamilton's multi-millionaire chairman Jan Stepek, a Polish immigrant who made his fortune out of travel and electrical goods, bombarded my lawyer with telephone calls in his bid to lure me to Douglas Park. To be honest, I wasn't really interested in taking over Accies. I knew I would be back in football some day, but I didn't envisage it at Hamilton. Stepek, though, was a persistent character. After the umpteenth call, my lawyer said, 'For God's sake, Bertie, talk to this guy. He's not going to go away.' I thought long and hard about it. I relented and decided to meet Stepek. He was a very persuasive gentleman and, eventually, I decided to give it a go. After all that, he ended up sacking me! John Blackley, the former Scotland international, had quit the post to join up again with Stanton at Hibs. I thought I would give it a go.

There were some good players at the club such as Ally MacLeod, namesake of the former Scotland boss and a player I had at Easter Road, and Brian McLaughlin. I felt heartsick for Brian. What potential he had when he was emerging at Celtic. He oozed class, could play in midfield and attack and really looked the part. I knew Big Jock rated him every bit as good a youngster as Kenny Dalglish and that tells you all you need to know. Football can be cruel, though, and Brian was on the receiving end of a terrible challenge by Clyde's Willie McVie one day. He never fully recovered and his career went into a bit of a decline. What a shame – he could have gone all the way to the very top at Celtic.

Once again, there wasn't a lot of money in the kitty at Hamilton, so I had to dabble in free transfers and the Junior market. I thought I would make a move for another of my former Partick Thistle players, Bobby Houston. I liked him and I thought he could do something at Hamilton. I phoned him. 'How do you fancy joining up with me again at Hamilton?' I asked. Houstie wasn't too sure. 'Give me a bit of time and I'll get back to you,' he said. Around about this time Houstie, I was told, had found religion. I think he had become a Jehovah's Witness or a Baptist – something like that. He duly did get back to me and informed me, 'I'm not joining Hamilton – I don't think I could take your swearing.' Quick as a flash, I answered, 'Fuck off then!' I hope the irony wasn't lost on him!

Houstie might have had a point, though. I recall a game when Thistle were playing Kilmarnock and, by that time, he was a player with the Ayrshire club. I noted that he was getting ready to come on as a substitute and I decided to wind him up a little. 'That's it, they've chucked in the towel,' I shouted, well within my old player's earshot. 'They're putting on Houstie they are that desperate.' And so it went on as Houstie ran up and down the touchline. I must have hit a raw nerve – he was sent off about two minutes later for kicking one of my players. That wasn't his style, so I must have got through. Sorry, Houstie!

I wasn't too downhearted when I became the first managerial casualty of 1984 when I was told Hamilton were dispensing with my services on 10 January. Folk have said I was stabbed in the back by John Lambie but I don't believe that for a minute. He got my job and, along with Gerry Collins, did very well. However, I don't bear any grudges and that's just the way it is in this game. If you want a manager's job, you have to wait until some unfortunate guy either moves on or is sacked.

I got a call from Partick Thistle secretary Peter Shand to see if I would be interested in rejoining my old club on 30 March 1986. I had taken a two-year sabbatical just to recharge my batteries. Benny Rooney had been in charge, but the club was anchored at the foot of the Premier League and looked favourites to go down. Benny, one of my former players first time around at Firhill, was under pressure and, truth be told, was suffering a bit. I think he actually provided a doctor's line to emphasise the strain he was under. Pressure at Partick Thistle? Listen, I knew all those fans by their first name. I knew the chippy they used to go to after the game and it was never too busy! I agreed to take the job until the end of the season. Benny, who was later relieved of his managerial duties, had left behind Mike Jackson, my old mate Dino from Celtic days, and Billy McLaren, who was in charge of the reserves.

I had a chat with both of them and I told them the club was in dire straits. I looked at the first team squad and told Dino and Billy, 'We've got to play to our strengths. We are going to have to grind out results to stay in this division. The hard work starts now.' Thankfully, the players rallied round and we did escape relegation. It wasn't pretty, but we did what we had to do. The support probably didn't appreciate how we lined up, but it was either that or slipping out of the top flight and that could have been Thistle out of the spotlight for some considerable time.

As far as I was concerned, I had done the job I was asked to do. I thought I would be leaving the club again at the end of the season, but once more I received a call from Peter Shand. It was a Sunday afternoon and I had been out playing golf with my mates. Peter wanted me to come to the club immediately and meet its new owner, Ken Bates. 'Peter,' I said, 'I haven't even had time to shave.' He was persistent. Bates, who was also chairman of Chelsea at the time, was heading back to London that evening and wanted to have a word with me. Against my better judgement, I agreed to meet him. Deep down, I knew it was a waste of time.

It would be fair to say I wasn't greatly impressed by Bates and certainly not after he had told me he had bought me a player. I said, 'If I stay here, I'll buy and sell my own players. I don't want anyone else throwing players at me.' Bates said, 'He's a great player and I'm bringing him up from Chelsea – it's Derek Johnstone.' I didn't care if it was Pele – transfers were my business and no-one else's. Bates persisted, 'I would keep him at Chelsea, but we've got Kerry Dixon and Derek can't get a game.' It just got better.

I replied, 'If he's not good enough for Chelsea, then he's not good enough for Partick Thistle!' The more we debated the move, the more I realised I would not be in charge of Partick Thistle in the new season. I also had a fair idea that Bates wanted me to groom Johnstone to one day take my job at Firhill. Did he think I had straw hanging out my ears? 'Good luck,' I said and left the building. That was the end of my career at Thistle. I didn't announce my decision until I had spoken to Dino and Billy – that, I think, was the proper thing to do. I didn't want them losing their jobs, either.

I thought Johnstone might also bring resentment in the Firhill dressing room through absolutely no fault of his own. I was pretty sure he would have been earning a lot more at Chelsea than any player was getting at Thistle. Of course, Johnstone did get the manager's job at Thistle, but that only lasted a few months before Billy Lamont was brought in.

Dumbarton must have been impressed by the way I had led Thistle away from the relegation trapdoor and they got in touch through their managing director, Alex Wright, who had once tried to sign me as a player when he was boss of St Mirren. They were scrapping away at the wrong end of the old First Division and had a young management team in John Arrol, my former Thistle goalkeeper, and Mark Clougherty. I agreed to take over just so long as John and Mark were kept on, but I believe they resigned a couple of days later. I had three months in which to turn things around at Boghead, but, unfortunately, time was against us on this occasion. We went down and I left shortly afterwards.

To be honest, I had had enough. I was sickened by some of the individuals I had come across. Promises meant nothing to some of these characters and there is just so much double-talk you can take. There were disappointments, betrayals and back-stabbings. Some directors I have met appeared to be more concerned about losing their appetite than losing a football game. Sometimes you wondered if you were on the same frequency when you were attempting to have a conversation. It was not a nice environment in which to work. After a while, playing golf at the weekend becomes a very tempting proposition.

The management game ended for me in 1988 – Celtic's centenary year. I was fifty years old and had enjoyed a career that had spanned thirty-three years. I got out at the right time, but if I had ever received a call from Celtic I would have been back in the game like a shot. Sadly, that call never came.

20

LET THE GOOD TIMES ROLL?

If my son Robert intended to send a jolt through my system he certainly achieved his goal. He looked me straight in the eye and asked, 'How long did it take for you to get a reputation in football? Why give it up so lightly?' Nineteen words and two simple questions. That conversation took place a year or so before we moved into a new millennium. I have never touched spirits since.

Robert wasn't preaching, but, in an instant, he got through to me and those words changed my life. They will live with me for ever and I am so grateful that he was concerned enough about his dad to pose those questions. Listen, I never saw myself as an alcoholic, but I could have given Jim Baxter and George Best a run for their money when it came to knocking back the booze. And, by that, I don't mean to be disrespectful to two of the finest footballers I have had the great pleasure to watch. Sadly, as we all know, these two colourful characters found it easier to get past an opponent than to beat the bottle. I would have done my darnedest to keep pace with these guys, you better believe it.

I always thought I could rein in the bevvy when I thought it was necessary although I admit I could be a binge drinker. One was never enough and that's not a good sign. When there was work to be done, I was okay. However, even when you are not involved in mainstream football, you will always find people to drink with. You never have to look too far for someone to accompany to you to the pub or befriend you in a hostelry. There are football fans everywhere. It could be New York or Newtongrange, Dubai or Dublin, Melbourne or Millport. They are there and they want to talk to you. I don't mind that one bit. I've often said that the time to worry is when you are ignored. However, if you are in a pub then these guys, complete strangers, will come over, introduce themselves and you know what happens next. Drinks are bought and, before you know it, you are in the middle of a session.

When I left Dumbarton in 1988 it gave me a lot more time to play golf with my pals at Strathaven Golf Club. I don't know if I improved my golf, but I certainly improved my drinking. I was never out of control, but it would be fair to say that spirits never brought out the best in Bertie Auld. I could be as cantankerous as the next guy with a few brandy and ports in me. I hate to admit it, but it is true. Something had to give and when Robert uttered those nineteen simple words that did it for me. He couldn't have made more of an impact if he had hit me over the head with a sledgehammer. There and then, I vowed, 'That's the end of the spirits.' I've kept my word and, my God, do I feel better for it. I might have an odd shandy or a cider these days, but that's the end of it. Binge drinking and me are now distant strangers, I'm delighted to inform you.

There were occasions in the past when I could be abrasive. I've told more than a few football fans to go forth and multiply when they have intruded into what I believed was my own time. Take, for instance, when I have been out with my wife

Liz and a couple of friends for a drink and a bite to eat after a game. The supporters can shout and bawl all they like during the match, but not during our private time. That was sacrosanct. I rarely welcomed guys coming up to our table uninvited and trying to get their points across only hours after the final whistle while the adrenalin is still pumping. Some of the time I would listen to their comments, daft or otherwise, and say something like, 'Aye, we'll do better next week.'

At other times, I would snap and tell them, 'Get lost – I'm having dinner with my wife.' That happened quite a lot, as I recall. Now we all know how these things can grow arms and legs. The bloke would go away, tell his pals about our confrontation and they would pass it on to someone else. Chinese whispers, I believe it's called. By the time the story gets back to the original guy it has been bent completely out of shape. Liz used to say to me, 'Bertie, why do you treat them like that? Just be polite.' That's my wife, though. There were occasions when I couldn't be bothered doing 'polite' or trying to explain myself.

Put yourself in my position. You could put in a lot of hard graft all week preparing your team for the match. You would be working on tactics and suchlike. You would be looking at your opposition's strengths and weaknesses and trying to gee up your own players. You could delve into little things like the ball going out for a shy on the halfway line. Which of your players takes the throw-in? If it's on the left, does the left-winger come back for the shy? Or does the left-back race forward to accept responsibility? Same over on the right. The players have got to be primed properly. They shouldn't be in situations where they hesitate and don't know exactly who should be doing what. Who is picking up which player and so on?

Free-kicks – do we bend them in or swerve them out? Does their goalkeeper come for crossballs? All that is swirling around in your head as you do your level best to put out a winning side.

Then what happens? The referee makes a dreadful decision that turns the game. A defender loses concentration at a fatal moment. Your keeper throws one over his shoulder. And the game is lost and it's back to the drawing board. After moments like that, the last thing you need is some fan invading your privacy to inform you that your team is a pile of crap. Sometimes I reacted and sometimes I didn't. I will always listen to what sensible, reasonable football fans have to say, but it has to be in the right place at the right time and just when you are about to have your main course is not one of those circumstances.

Spirits could certainly fuel my vehemence when I thought someone was taking a liberty. So, when my son asked me those two questions all those years ago, he did me a massive favour. He could have asked me to stop drinking and I wouldn't have. He just framed the words in such a simple manner that they hit their target. No more spirits for me. I'll give you a couple of wee instances.

I had been meeting Alex Gordon as we sifted through material for the book and he helped me get some thoughts down in print. We normally met about once or twice a week at the Georgics Bar and Restaurant, part of the Millennium Hotel, at George Square in Glasgow. One day we decided to try the haggis and neeps – normally we had been tucking into their excellent fish suppers. On this occasion, we fancied a change. The waiter might have been a little startled when I asked if there were any spirits in the sauce. Sometimes they put brandy into the mix and, of course, it's an old Scottish tradition to put a wee dash of whisky in the haggis. It was only when I was assured by our ever-helpful waiter that the sauce contained no alcohol whatsoever that I went ahead and placed my order. Now I know that is only a small point, but I hope it underlines what it means to me to ignore spirits.

Another time I was on a jaunt with TG, Tommy Gemmell, and a few football friends in Benidorm when we were in the pub and I decided to get a pint of cider and told everyone, 'That will do me for the rest of the night.' I didn't mind one little bit how much alcohol they shifted between them, I was going to sip quietly at my drink and that would more than satisfy me. Anyway, at one stage I went to the loo and then returned to pick up my cider. TG asked, 'How long have you been off the spirits now, Bertie?'

'Oh, about nine or ten years,' I replied.

As I went to lift the glass to my lips, TG asked again, 'Are you sure?' The penny dropped instantly. While I was away from the bar some would-be prankster had dumped a large brandy into my cider. I didn't see the funny side of that and I told the culprit in no uncertain terms. I ordered a fresh half-pint of cider and that was me for the duration.

There have been some funny incidents concerning booze, of course. I recall Robert and my daughter Susan coming back from holiday and phoning me to ask if I would pick them up at the airport. 'Sure, no problem,' I responded. They forgot to tell me it was MANCHESTER Airport they were flying into. Thanks, my precious offspring! Anyway, I thought I would drive down with a friend and possibly pop into my old mate Paddy Crerand's pub, the Park in nearby Altrincham, to see how things were with him and his wife Noreen. We duly arrived and the place was closed. I knocked on the window and could see Noreen busy behind the bar. She didn't even turn round as she yelled, 'We're shut – come back later.' I rattled on the glass again and she looked over her shoulder. Noreen looked visibly relieved to see me standing outside her husband's pub.

She opened the door. 'Come in, Bertie, we're going to be really busy in about thirty minutes or so,' she informed me. 'Paddy has arranged for an Irish band to come in this afternoon and we are going to be packed.'

'And where's Paddy?' I enquired.

'He's not here – he's only gone to Ireland with some friends, that's all.'

'How many bar staff have you got on with you today?' I asked.

'Just me,' answered an obviously anxious Mrs Crerand. 'And you, if you want to help out!'

What's a guy to do? I couldn't possibly leave her there on her own, so there was nothing else for it – I was Paddy Crerand's unpaid and overworked barman for the day. Noreen was absolutely right, unfortunately. It was a full house and I was pouring pints as quickly as I could. There was a major problem, though. Someone in their wisdom had laid a thick carpet behind the bar. Now I've owned hotels and bars and I can inform everyone that the one place you don't ever want to see a carpet is behind the bar. Obviously, there's all sorts of spillage and the carpet just soaks it up. It's difficult to lift your feet in these circumstances. It's like walking on quicksand. So, if a guy at the end of the bar asked for a pint, he would have to wait about two minutes until I poured it and another half-hour for me to deliver it!

I had to laugh when three huge, hulking Irish navvies came in. They had obviously just come off a building site. They were covered in concrete. It was in their hair, on their faces, on their clothes, on their boots and, I'll swear, one had it in his teeth! Anyway, they made their way to the bar. 'Three pints of lager, sir,' ordered one. 'I'm not a sir, I'm a count,' I replied. They got the joke. I did as I was asked and passed over their glasses. One just about demolished the drink in one go. They downed another couple when one of them said, 'Hey, you, count, I think this beer is off.'

I managed to fight my way to where they were standing. I must have looked like Frankenstein's monster as I tried to extricate my feet from the now well-soaked carpet. I looked down at his glass that was only about a quarter full – or three-quarters empty, if you're a pessimist. I picked it up and drank the remains. 'There's nothing wrong with it,' I informed him. He just laughed and said, 'Aye, you're right, count – another three pints please!'

And, yes, I poured more than a few halves that day in Paddy's pub and, no, I wasn't tempted once to partake. I like the new, improved Bertie Auld. So, too, does my son Robert. And everyone else who knows me, I suppose.

21

MURDOCH THE MAESTRO

Bobby Murdoch was one of the quietest guys I have ever come across in the dressing room. Others, with only a fraction of his ability and the merest hint of his talent, would be shouting the odds and talking a good game. Bobby, without fuss, simply put on his gear, tied his bootlaces and went out onto the park and took centre stage. He wasn't interested in getting involved in all the brash ballyhoo before the game; it was the actual 90 minutes that meant something to him. That's where he did his work.

As you will have gathered by now, I have been extremely fortunate to have played alongside team-mates gifted with so many different qualities. Wee Jinky, quite rightly, was voted by the supporters at the turn of the century as the greatest ever Celtic player. An accolade he so richly deserved. But, for me, Bobby was the guy I rated the highest among them all and, believe me, that is praise indeed.

Sir Alex Ferguson said around about the time of Aberdeen's 25th anniversary of their 1983 European Cup Winners' Cup triumph over Real Madrid that the Lisbon Lions were the finest club side ever produced in Scotland. No argument here, Alex.

He also stated we had two genuine world-class performers – Jinky and Bobby. Actually, I think he might have added a third, Tommy Gemmell. I have stated in various chapters throughout the book that I thought TG was the finest left-back in the world in his heyday. He revolutionised that No.3 position and was simply awesome when he charged forward into attack.

Bobby, though, was the man I always looked up to. He was my midfield partner in a system that was mainly 4–2–4 back then. Four at the back, Bobby and me in the middle, two wide players up front and two strikers in the middle. You would be lucky to find teams playing those tactics week in, week out these days as they are far too adventurous. The onus was on the two guys in the middle of the pitch to do a lot of fetching, carrying, passing and running. So, I was ideally placed to see how my mate was dealing with the pressure. I didn't see him even come close to buckling. The man was everything you could possibly look for in a colleague. He put himself about for the team.

He was Jinky's unofficial onfield minder, too. If Bobby – who answered to either Chopper or Murdy – thought his little pal was getting roughed up and getting a kicking, he would saunter over and let the offender know he was keeping an eye on him. Jinky, it must be said, could look after himself, but Bobby wasn't a bad back-up, that's for sure.

I really liked Bobby on and off the pitch. He was such an unassuming character. Fame meant nothing to him. He arrived at the club in 1959 and departed in 1973. In between, he picked up eighteen winners' medals in a glittering career and his head was never swollen by all the applause and plaudits that came his way. He would often say, 'All that cuddling and embracing stuff, that's not for me. It's appreciated when the fans want to be close, but I'm just not that type of guy.' Don't take that the wrong way. Bobby loved mingling with the supporters, but he was basically a shy guy and never wanted to step into the spotlight. Apart from, of course, when he was on the pitch and that's where he expressed himself best.

I nominated Jinky as my Man of the Match against Inter Milan in Lisbon, but it could so easily have gone to Bobby. What a performance he put in that day. I can tell you for certain that he wasn't even fit against the Italians. He took a sore one on his right ankle early in the game and that severely hampered the use of that foot for the rest of the ninety minutes. Luckily, being such an accomplished player, he could use both feet, but his right was definitely the stronger. I noticed he was using his left almost exclusively and at one point in the first-half when there was a lull in the play, I sauntered over to him and asked if he was OK.

'Take a look at this, Bertie,' he said. I looked at his right ankle and it was beginning to balloon. If he had taken off his right boot at the interval I don't think there was any way he would have been able to get it on again. He didn't even complain, though. He was quite content to play through the pain barrier and if you ever get to a chance to see a rerun of the entire European Cup Final I bet you won't even notice that Bobby was performing with such a disadvantage. Believe it or not, a lot of his team-mates that day didn't have a clue about his injury. It was only after we had all come out of the bath that someone looked at his right ankle and exclaimed,'Christ! What's happened here?' Bobby, in that wonderfully understated way of his, waved his hand and said, 'Och, it's just a scratch!'

I love the story, which just happens to be true, by the way, of how Bobby came to make his debut for Celtic as a mere seventeen-year-old on the opening day of the 1961/62 league season. He had just returned to the club after being farmed out to Cambuslang Rangers in the Juniors, as was so often the case in those days to toughen up youngsters. Bobby turned up at Parkhead that afternoon believing he would take his place in the stand with a few of the other youngsters to witness the visit of a strong Hearts team. He was astonished, though, when he had to answer an SOS from manager Jimmy McGrory.

Would you believe one of the Celtic first team had forgotten to bring his boots! Honestly, I don't know the name of the individual, but we should find out and erect a statue to him outside the ground – we owe so much to his absentmindedness. Bobby, as you might expect even as an untested teenager, went out, scored the opening goal and Celtic won 3–1. It was the start of something good. I caught up with him four-and-a-half years later and, by God, did we have some enjoyable games together. I never heard anyone say a bad word about him and, in football, that is some testimony.

Billy McNeill was, of course, our captain, but Bobby was never slow to accept responsibility on the field. In fact, he thrived on it. I don't think he ever particularly wanted to be skipper, but if Jock had ever given him the nod in the absence of Billy I can assure everyone he wouldn't have let anyone down. He never did. I have said often enough about his having the ability to fill that Celtic jersey. Bobby loved those hoops. I swear his chest got bigger and bigger as he pulled that shirt over his head.

He was a generous guy, too. He was the sort who would give you his last. I'll tell you a wee story that underlines the warmth of the character. After Bobby returned following his successful stint as player, coach and manager at Middlesbrough, he ran a pub in Rutherglen called, appropriately enough, the Sportsman. I know Bobby had had his eye on this property for some time. He had a team picture taken with his Boys' Club outfit when he was just a kid in a field and the Sportsman pub was in the background. He was tickled at the thought of growing up, achieving everything he could in football with his beloved Celtic and then settling down to play host at this pub.

Anyway, he was putting together the Sportsman when he asked a photographer friend to see if he could dig out any pictures of himself in action. The photographer explained he would have to get the printers in his newspaper's dark room to enlarge the images to make them presentable for framing and putting them on the walls of the pub. They normally asked for a fee because they did it in their own time and it required a fair bit of work to get the job done properly. 'Nae problem,' said Bobby and forked over the readies. The photographer duly turned up one Saturday evening with piles of action shots of Bobby. He delivered them to the bar where my old mate was working. Bobby opened the parcel and began leafing through the pictures. Needless to say, the locals wanted a wee look, too.

'Bobby, can I have this photo, please?' one would ask. 'Can you autograph it for me?' The rest would join in. Aye, you've guessed it. Within about ten minutes Bobby had signed all the photographs and was left with none. He had to get in touch with his photographer pal again, shell out once more and get another set of the same prints. Knowing Bobby, he would have to go through the process time and again, continually paying out of his own pocket to present images of himself for the punters. I wonder if a single print ever got onto a wall in the Sportsman!

Unfortunately, I never got the chance to play alongside George Best, but I rated him an absolute genius. He played for Manchester United against Celtic in a few friendlies over the years and I thought he was unbelievable. He had everything. Name it, he had it in abundance. He had all the skills and the tricks, but I can tell you he was also an exceptionally brave player. Like Jinky, there wasn't an awful lot of him, but he was afraid of nothing. People mention Bestie these days and they talk about this goal or that goal, his performance in Lisbon against Benfica when United won 5–1 and he was christened El Beatle, the start of the showbiz lifestyle that was to ultimately rob him of his hunger and desire to perform at the highest level. They will go on about his excellent solo goal against the same Portuguese opposition when United triumphed in the European Cup Final a year after us. No-one talks about his courage, though. Sometimes you can spot a player who finds a welcoming little air pocket to disappear into when the going gets tough. Not Bestie. He simply rolled up his sleeves and went for it.

I have been privileged to have played with and against some first-class exponents of this wonderful game. Bobby and Bestie have a place of honour among the pantheon of greats. Right at the top – where they undoubtedly belong.

22

CELTIC IN ENGLAND

I have no doubt Celtic would be the biggest team in Britain if they joined the English League. Yes, I genuinely believe they would dwarf the likes of Manchester United, Chelsea, Arsenal and Liverpool.

For a start, I think Celtic would have to restructure Parkhead to accommodate 100,000 fans every matchday. They can attract 60,000 supporters at the moment for games against the likes of St Mirren, Kilmarnock, Hibs and Hearts. What could they expect against teams such as Fergie's lot? They would have to build a new stand at the park to meet the demand from the punters. I'm convinced they could attract at least 90,000 season ticket holders. Hopefully I'm not overstating the case – I genuinely believe it.

It's ridiculous to think that clubs being relegated from the English Premier League get a parachute payment of around £30 million each. That's an astonishing sum for failure. What could Celtic – or Rangers, for that matter – do with that sort of cash? And I don't think for a moment that either would be relegated if they got in about the money that is on offer down there. The £60 million clubs can expect from Sky, Setanta and suchlike is fantastic and is way above anything the Old Firm can expect in Scotland.

I believe English fans might like to see Celtic in action in their league. After all, which is the most sought-after club when it comes to testimonials across the border? Over the years, my old club have played sell-out matches at Manchester United for Bobby Charlton, Bryan Robson, Ryan Giggs and Roy Keane. They've also figured in games at Arsenal, Liverpool, West Ham, Leeds United and Spurs among others.

I recall a Testimonial Match Celtic played at Upton Park against the Hammers. Bobby Moore, of course, was the golden boy of English football after captaining his country to their 1966 World Cup success. He could have chosen any team in Europe – probably the world – to provide opposition for his big night, but he didn't hesitate in making his selection: Celtic. The game ended 3-3, as I recall, and was everything that is good about football. West Ham, as well as ourselves, loved to play in an attacking manner and I'm sure the crowd that crammed into their tight ground that evening thoroughly enjoyed every minute of it.

While the fans might welcome Celtic, I'm fairly certain the clubs wouldn't. I can see their argument, selfish though it may be. If the top teams voted to accept the Old Firm into their top flight, it would mean two of them dropping out because neither Celtic nor Rangers would ever be relegated. Logistically, then, there would be two fewer places for English clubs for ever. Could you imagine the sort of players Glasgow's Big Two could attract to Parkhead and Ibrox if they could match the cash that is splashed by the likes of Manchester United and Chelsea? They could compete at the top table and that is a mouth-watering prospect.

It would also prevent English clubs from cherry-picking the best on offer at Celtic. Looking back to the Seventies, Celtic sold Lou Macari to Manchester United, Davie Hay to Chelsea and Kenny Dalglish to Liverpool. Later on, it would be the turn of Charlie Nicholas to be lured from Parkhead to Arsenal and the club couldn't match the wages being paid by Alex Ferguson when he whisked Brian McClair to Old Trafford. As far as I am aware, not one of those five players wanted to leave Celtic, but they were getting better offers elsewhere. If those deals had been matched I am sure they would have stayed.

How galling, too, that Stilian Petrov and Shaun Maloney elected to quit the club to join Aston Villa. I've nothing against Martin O'Neill or the Midlands outfit, but they aren't at the races when it comes to the appeal of Celtic and Martin will surely know that after his years in Glasgow. It's all down to cash. I was particularly annoyed to hear that young Shaun had gone south. He had been brought through the ranks at Parkhead, the club invested a lot of time and energy in him and, as soon as he looks like he's going to make the grade, he's up and off. You can't tell me he believed Villa were a better option than Celtic. That move wouldn't have taken place if Celtic had the pots of gold the English clubs possess. He's back now, of course, and he's already stated he should never have left. I know the feeling!

As I've already said in another chapter, Celtic could have possibly picked up another European Cup or two if they had held on to Macari, Hay and Dalglish. Money talked, they walked and Celtic proved they were a selling club and that's a shame when you think about how enormous they are with such a worldwide fan base. They should never have been put in a position of being forced to offload their best players. I know I was annoyed when I was boss at Partick Thistle and I had to sell my top talent. How must Jock Stein and Billy McNeill have felt at Celtic in having to allow such wonderful players to move on?

It's not all about cash, though. Celtic would enhance the English Premier League, I'm sure of that. Forget the Testimonial Matches and the friendlies. Look at what my old club achieved on their run to the UEFA Cup Final in Seville in 2003, for instance. They played Blackburn Rovers twice and Liverpool twice in the earlier rounds. Need I remind anyone of the outcome? Two wins over the Ewood Park side, 1-0 in Glasgow and 2-0 down there, and a 1-1 draw with the Merseyside outfit at Parkhead and, against all the odds, a 2-0 triumph at Anfield. Those were competitive matches and a good barometer for what Celtic can achieve.

They were hardly disgraced when they lost 3-2 to Manchester United at Old Trafford, but reversed that with a 1-0 triumph at Parkhead with that unstoppable Shunsuke Nakamura free-kick in the Champions League qualifiers in 2005. If you took all six games and awarded points Celtic would have amassed thirteen out of a possible eighteen. Not bad going, if you ask me.

Celtic have been asked to punch above their weight in the European arena simply because of the money that is thrown at the richest clubs in the land. When Manchester United beat Chelsea on penalty-kicks to lift the Champions League in season 2007/08, it was the eleventh time an English club had conquered Europe. That levelled them with Italy and Spain. How can Scotland compete with these nations? It's a question that has been asked over and over again and I think Scottish clubs are like a boxer going into the ring with one arm tied behind his back. He might get lucky every now and again, but he won't do it on a consistent basis. If only someone would allow him to use both hands!

Neutral supporters may say Scottish football might suffer if the Old Firm ever abandoned Scotland. Once more, I can see their point, but there are a few ways of looking at it. Without Celtic or Rangers other clubs will collect a lot more silverware. Fans will come out of the woodwork if they see their sides being successful, playing in Cup Finals and getting regular runs in Europe. They may even see their teams performing on an even playing field because no-one will ever be bigger than the Old Firm in this country. You will always get clubs who will put in a challenge such as Aberdeen, Dundee United, Hibs and Hearts have done over the years, but none of these teams has been able to sustain it. Celtic and Rangers will have their lapses, of course, but expectation levels at these clubs are so high that second is failure.

It's all a fantasy, of course. There are many strictures that would prevent the Old Firm from heading south quite apart from the cash-conscious clubs wanting to make sure no-one dips into their reservoir. It's an interesting thought, though. Around 100,000 fans at Celtic Park every matchday? Will it ever be allowed to happen? Time will tell!

23

FOREIGNERS IN SCOTLAND

I used to stand up and applaud that little magician Lubomir Moravcik – and that was just when he was warming up to come on as a substitute!

What a player. The midfielder may have been virtually unknown when he was brought to Celtic for a modest £250,000 by Jozef Venglos in 1998 from his German club MSV Duisburg. He was also thirty-three years old, but I had a sneaky feeling we were about to see something special. For a start, he had won around sixty or seventy caps for Slovakia and had also captained his nation. You don't earn that amount of international honours without being a class act.

Of course, it didn't take him long to make an impact – his third game, in fact. Suddenly the Celtic support realised their club might just have picked up the bargain of the century. Moravcik netted twice in a one-sided 5-1 triumph over Rangers at Parkhead on 21 November. A crowd of 59,783 witnessed a flawless display from a player who was supposed to be on his last legs. Too often players past the age of thirty are written off as being over the hill, but I don't subscribe to that theory, that's for sure. I was the same age as Lubo when I left Celtic for Hibs and, believe me, I was not going to Edinburgh to merely go through the motions. I still had a lot to prove.

Lubo combined everything I love in a player. First up, he oozed class and had more than his fair share of talent. Make the ball talk? He could get it to recite poetry. His first touch, even in the most awkward and tricky of conditions, was simply sublime. And he possessed a lot of self-assured cheek. What about that time the ball dropped out of the sky – against Hearts at Parkhead, I believe – and he trapped it with his backside? Even I might not have attempted that.

I mention the Slovakian because I am often asked about foreigners in our football – are they a good influence or do they stifle young Scottish talent? Let me say straight away that a player of Moravcik's calibre would be welcome in any country. Football may be big business, but I don't think we should lose sight of it still being an entertainment. And that wee guy knew how to play to the gallery, that's for sure. He was anonymous when he arrived, but he had the Celtic fans eating out of his hands when he left.

Youngsters would surely learn a thing or two mixing with a player such as Moravcik – just as I had done all those years ago when I was around the likes of Charles Patrick Tully, Bertie Peacock, Bobby Collins and so on. These guys are inspirational; you desperately want to get to their level of excellence. If they can do it then so, too, could you.

But for every Lubomir Moravcik there are more than a few who come and don't do football in our country any favours. How much did Celtic pay for that Brazilian Rafael Scheidt? Something like £3 million, I believe. Now that, quite plainly, is money flushed down the drain that could have been put to good use elsewhere. I don't think he even played ten games for the first team. He was bought by John Barnes in 1999 and booted out by Martin O'Neill a year later. I know Barnes bought him, but who sanctioned such a big-money move in the first place? Did anyone actually see him play – or was it all done by video tape? Even at my age, I could put together a tape of me in action that would make me look good!

I've already stated in the previous chapter that Celtic would be flooded by cash if they ever got to play in England. If that ever happened, I hope they would still encourage youth as they have always done. Yes, it's nice to write an astronomical cheque for a big-name glamour player, but youngsters should never be ignored. In an ideal world, you could mix the Moravciks with the home-bred McDonalds, Murrays and McCanns. That would be perfect because youth must be encouraged to come through. It's not fair to continually frustrate a player who has come through the ranks, knocks on the first team door and then sees the club go out and splash a lot of dosh on someone else who plays in the same position. That, clearly, does not send out positive vibes to any kid. A lot of them could be lost to the game before they even get started and that could deprive supporters of home-grown talent. It wouldn't do the Scottish international team any good, either.

So, I think foreigners are good for our football, but only if they have something to offer. The ones who have reached the veteran stage and are just topping up their bank accounts won't do much for our game. What on earth was Fabrizio Ravenelli doing at Dundee? The Italian had been there, seen it and done it, but he still came to Scotland in the twilight of his career. You must wonder why. I am not inferring he didn't give it his best shot at Dens Park – I am sure he is too much of a professional not to give 100 per cent – but it is just another transfer into this country that leaves you a little bewildered. Agents, of course, have got to make a living and they will always talk up their clients. That's their job, after all, but after that it is down to the manager to discover the player's potential and make the right decision. Of course, transfers can be a gamble, but there are some that just don't stack up. Don't get me started on Hearts' transfer policy! Have they really introduced better players than we already have here? I'll let you decide.

Have you noticed I haven't mentioned Henrik Larsson yet? Like Moravcik, he was another who was good for our game and brought attention to Scotland with his dashing skills. He was a fabulous talent and it used to annoy me when I read articles by certain journalists insisting he should quit our game to go elsewhere and prove himself. Why? Wasn't he doing that very thing in our country? And he was doing it on the inter-national stage for Sweden, too. So he was mixing with the best in the world and underlining his devastating ability. He scored 173 goals for Celtic in 221 games over seven years and, remember, he missed the chunk of one season after breaking a leg in that horrendous accident against Lyon in 1999. Cynics said he could score goals in Scotland, but could he do it else-where? The answer is yes as his international record shows – 36 goals in 93 games for his country. Case closed!

Again, like Moravcik, Larsson was a snip, bought for only £650,000 from Feyenoord by Wim Jansen in 1997. It's hard to believe that the transfer output for the Swede and the Slovakian didn't even come to £1 million. Rafael Schiedt cost more than three times as much. Go figure.

24

AWAY FROM IT ALL

I have lost count of the number of times Frank Sinatra has soothed my furrowed brow. Not Ol' Blue Eyes in person, you understand, but some of the finest lyrics, arrangements and tunes you could ever wish to experience. Francis Albert, with that unmistakably smooth voice of his, was something else altogether.

The Auld household has gently swayed over the years to truly wonderful songs such as 'My Way', 'New York, New York', 'Witchcraft' and 'Me and My Shadow'. All done in his inimitable style that will never be copied or replicated perfectly by anyone else, no matter how hard they try or how much they practice. You could have had a bad day at the office, but everything seemed so much calmer, life appeared that much better while he was crooning merrily away on the turntable. To me, he was The Man. Other people had their favourites, Bing Crosby, Louis Armstrong, Nat King Cole, Perry Como, Tony Bennett, Matt Monro and even Elvis among others. Brilliant artists each and every one of them, but it was Sinatra for me. I've got a bit more time on my hands these days, of course, and I must be driving Liz crazy when she sees me going through our record and CD collection. She's got a fair idea of what is coming next.

Actually, you would think turning seventy years old I might have TOO much leisure time, but that's not the case. And I'm quite happy about that. The last twenty or so years seem to have flown by. Yes, there have been occasions when I have missed being involved in mainstream football. But there always seems to be something to do, somewhere to be or someone to meet.

For a start, the family home in Strathaven also possesses stables. My granddaughter Tina loves horses – maybe that's something she picked up from my mum all those years ago in Girvan. So, there is always something going on there. Liz loves animals and there are always dogs about the place. As I said, I love music and, naturally enough, I am a great lover of sport, with football being right up there at the top. I don't miss too many Celtic home games and that keeps me happy. It's been interesting watching from the sidelines as managers such as Wim Jansen, Jozef Venglos, John Barnes, Kenny Dalglish, Martin O'Neill and Gordon Strachan have come in and gone about the job. It's intriguing to see the likes of Chris Sutton, Neil Lennon, John Hartson, Stilian Petrov, Eyal Berkovic, Henrik Larsson, Lubomir Moravcik, Artur Boruc and Shunsuke Nakamura, among others, being bought and then witnessing them attempt to fit into the Celtic system.

Luckily enough, I have been a regular guest on Celtic Television and that's another way of getting your point across. I would like to believe that I can give my views without fear or favour. I always try to be constructive. There is no use simply shredding an individual's display if it doesn't warrant it. You've got to look deeper to try to fathom why someone hasn't performed in the manner expected. There are so many 'experts' out there who appear to like the sound of their own voice.

Others try to be controversial just for the sake of it. Hopefully, I don't come into either category. I've been around a bit and would like to think my experience helps me in these situations. I'll tell it like it is because old habits die hard. I watch a fair amount of football on television when I've got the time or when I'm allowed! Being associated with Celtic is an amazing experience and it means you are being constantly invited to functions all over the globe. I'm still regularly invited to parts of the States, Canada, Australia, Dubai – oh, just about everywhere. If I took them up on all their kind offers I would never be home again. Mind you, Liz might not complain too much about that! Being a Lisbon Lion is a bit special and we seem to have transcended the age barrier. I am as likely to be asked for an autograph by a six-year-old as a sixty-year-old. It's always a pleasure to accommodate and still nice to be recognised.

I am glad to have Willie Haughey, a well-known Glasgow businessman, as a friend. He is a huge Celtic fan and has done so much behind the scenes to benefit the club and the players. His wife Susan is a bit special, too – they really are a smashing couple. Willie was also very friendly with Wee Jinky and Bobby Murdoch. I know they thought the world of him. Nothing is ever too much trouble for Willie and he is one of those guys who will go out of his way to do someone a good turn. It's always appreciated, believe me. Another pal is a bloke called Pat Knott. Like Willie and Susan, he and his wife Linda are a wonderful double-act and they do so much to benefit others. They do it without craving publicity and I can only thank my lucky stars that I can consider them very welcome chums.

The Lions, away from the glare of publicity, do a fair bit for charity and, believe me, we are always happy to play our part. It can be a bit harrowing at times when you are asked to do a hospital visit, but I would never shirk these duties. These are unfortunate guys who want to spend time with some of the Lions and if we can't go out of our way to make these visits then I don't think we would be much in the way of human beings. You can see some desperately ill person smile genuinely when you turn up at their bedside. That means so much to us all. It makes you feel humble.

Golf, of course, is another leisure pursuit and I probably play more rounds in a year than Tiger Woods! Again, the likes of Tommy Gemmell, Billy McNeill, Stevie Chalmers, Bobby Lennox and so on will get invitations to take part in all sorts of tournaments. By the way, don't believe a thing Big TG tells you – I am not a bandit! Billy and I play regular games against Stevie and Bobby, who was a late starter, but now loves the game and, in fact, is a member of the Largs Golf Club near his home in Saltcoats. Believe me, they are always fairly competitive because none of us has learned to be a loser yet. Stevie is a great player – he could have been a pro – and if Billy and I win we know we have deserved our prize. I've been known to hit the ball around the Strathaven Golf Club. It's so relaxing to get out there and face all sorts of elements in the pursuit of putting a wee white sphere in a hole in the ground. Who invented this crazy game?

I keep up to speed with world events in the newspapers every morning and you won't be surprised that, yes, I do turn to the back pages first! I enjoy my relaxation time when it's just Liz, granddaughter Tina and myself having a day off. I'm also so proud of my other grandkids, Lisa and Jordan. My son Robert's wife Susan is a horse-riding instructress and she has been showing Lisa and Tina the ropes. Lisa is displaying great promise on that front and is already at a good level in show jumping. My mum would be proud.

Jordan could make it as a sportsman, but not as a footballer. I believe he is more likely to be a golfer. He is already looking quite comfortable with the sticks. I wonder if he'll need a caddie at The Open in a few years' time! My leisure time is more than welcome, but it's also nice to feel wanted, so when that telephone rings I can see Liz's eyes mist over and she knows something is looming on the horizon that will have me on the move again. I wouldn't have it any other way.

I've owned hotels and bars since quitting. One of the most pleasurable experiences was working every Friday, Saturday and Sunday night in that well-known watering hole Baird's Bar in Glasgow's Gallowgate. There was no pressure on me and I was happy enough pulling pints for the punters. My old Celtic mate Willie O'Neill looked after the bar and I took charge of the lounge. People may have been more than a little surprised to see me behind the bar, but I enjoyed the craic. I love the Glasgow sense of humour and I didn't tell the owner, Tommy Carberry, this, but I would have done it for free.

Big TG, of course, is a hunting and fishing man and we've gone walkabout on several occasions. Something always seems to happen on these trips. I recall once we were up in Perth and there were about six or seven of us. If you've never been out shooting, I'll give you a tip – always point the gun forward when it is loaded and ready to go. As I recall, my good pal Phil McAulay was with us and a bloke called Frankie who was a massive Celtic fan from the Gorbals. It was getting dark as we made our way through the dense forest. We all walked in a line about twenty yards or so apart. When you heard a bang you had to shout out to make sure we hadn't accidently shot one another. BOOM! 'You there, TG?' He would shout back, 'Safe and sound.' 'Phil?' 'OK.' And so it went on as we made our way through the woods.

This went on for the best part of an hour when it suddenly dawned on us that we hadn't heard from Frankie for a while. 'Frankie, you there?' Silence. 'Oh, God – we've shot him!' said someone as we frantically searched for our partner. We retraced our steps, but there was no sign of Frankie. Night fell as we clambered around looking for our friend. Needless to say, we were all getting a bit anxious at the non-appearance of our chum. Eventually, we made our way back to the bothy, thinking we would have to get the gamekeeper to call in the search parties. But, sitting at the fire, large as life, was the good Frankie. He had been enjoying a large half or two. 'Och, I couldn't be bothered with all that shooting,' he said by way of explanation. 'I was just letting you guys get on with it.'

Frank had a fairly formidable wife called Kathie and he had promised her some pheasant from the shoot. We split up the kill and Frankie claimed a brace of pheasants. Unbeknown to him, however, Phil switched bags and replaced the pheasant with two wood pigeons. Frankie eventually got home and proudly presented his 'trophies' to Kathie. She took one look at the pigeons and exclaimed, 'Where were you shooting – George Square?'

The best thing about being out of football is the time you can spend with your family. As a player, a coach and a manager, you could be away for hours and it was all down to Liz that son Robert, daughter Susan and granddaughter Tina have turned out the way they are. They are an absolute credit to her. I missed them growing up because of the demands of football and it's wonderful to spend time with them these days.

25

THE LAST WORD

At one stage in my career I was earning £18 per week as a young player with Celtic while my dad Joe was on £13. That didn't seem fair because he grafted a lot harder more days of the week than I did, but that was the going rate for a footballer back then. I wasn't picking up exorbitant amounts and we weren't really that far removed from each other on the cash register.

It's changed a bit these days, hasn't it? I am not being envious, but I believe what the players are earning at the moment is nothing short of obscene. How can an individual justify £200,000 per week for kicking a ball about? That works out at something in the region of £10.4 million a year. Wages haven't just gone sky-high, but are now in a different stratosphere. Please don't tell me about the pressures of the game because they are no different than from when I played.

Satellite television has poured millions of pounds into clubs' coffers and it's entirely up to them how they dispose of the cash, but today's players appear to be preoccupied with money. To some, it seems an obsession. There are all those ostentatious demonstrations of their new-found wealth when they get married – buy a castle, ocean-going liner or the latest sports car. I wonder what Jock Stein would have made of Bertie Auld modelling the latest line in gents' underpants or endorsing perfume? I've a fair idea.

I realise it can come across as sour grapes from someone who missed out on the gravy train, but that's not the case. Yes, as I have already said, I believe a successful Celtic side should have looked after their players a bit better on the financial front. However, we were paid what was commensurate at the time, so why moan now?

What I am trying to say is that these so-called soccer super-stars – or is it megastars? – are losing touch with the people who matter most. I'm talking about the man in the crowd who has possibly saved all week to go and see his heroes on matchday. Do these players go to supporters' functions up and down the country? I recall at Celtic when Big Jock ordered players to go to functions all over the place. You could be leaving after a game on Saturday only to be told you were expected in Banff the following day. There were no arguments. Do they even make themselves available to sign autographs for fans after the game? Or do these pampered prima donnas just take off in their Bentleys and Ferraris and get as far away from the ground as fast as they can? I think we know the answers.

It's a shame because football, to me, is for the working man. That's his relaxation at the weekend; that's his main form of entertainment. Or, at least, it used to be.

I played football in an era where players and fans alike could drink in the same bar afterwards. We could share a joke and a laugh, go through the ins and outs of the game. We got to know each other by our first names. We could stop and have a chat in the street.

Football opened so many doors for me. The friends I have today are my real friends and I am privileged to have them.

Today's players may have mountains of money in the bank, but I've got my own treasure chest – memories. All those unforgettable moments, the rollercoaster of emotions, the people, the good times and the bad – they all reached their right and proper place in my own memory bank. There are some things that money cannot buy and no amount of pictures of the Queen's face on a sheet of paper could replace what I have experienced. I am rich beyond belief on that front.

Lisbon 1967, scoring two goals in the breakthrough Scottish Cup Final against Dunfermline two years earlier, watching Jinky skim past defenders, Bobby Murdoch, chest puffed out, after scoring a marvellous goal against Leeds United in the European Cup semi-final in 1970, Tommy Gemmell thundering up and down that left wing, Billy McNeill soaring majestically to get his head to the ball, unbelievable European nights at Parkhead. Medals? One European Cup, six league championships, three Scottish Cups and four League Cups. I've made 279 appearances for the club I love and scored 85 goals in the process.

I was voted into Celtic's Greatest Ever team by the supporters in an official millennium poll. What an honour when you consider how many talented individuals had played in my position in over 100 years of Celtic history. Six of my Lisbon Lions team-mates joined me in this finest of accolades by the people who really know the game: Ronnie Simpson, Tommy Gemmell, Bobby Murdoch, Billy McNeill, Jimmy Johnstone and Bobby Lennox. We had to make space for Danny McGrain, Paul McStay, Kenny Dalglish and Henrik Larsson. Where do you want me to stop?

THE LAST WORD

It's been a wonderful experience looking back over the years and, at last, getting it all down in print. Right at the start, I said that my dad Joe told me in 1955, 'Give your best for this team, son, and the Celtic fans will never forget you.'

I've got a message for the Celtic supporters. I'll never forget you.